Perspectives and Points
of View

LIESELOTTE E. KURTH-VOIGT

Perspectives and Points of View: The Early Works of Wieland and Their Background

THE JOHNS HOPKINS UNIVERSITY PRESS
BALTIMORE AND LONDON

This book has been brought to publication with the
generous assistance of the Andrew W. Mellon Foundation.

Manufactured in the United States of America

The Johns Hopkins University Press, Baltimore, Maryland 21218
The Johns Hopkins University Press Ltd., London

Library of Congress Catalog Card Number 74-6829
ISBN 0-8018-1617-3

Library of Congress Cataloging in Publication data
will be found on the last printed page of this book.

FOR MY MOTHER
AND IN MEMORY OF MY FATHER

‖ Contents

‖ Prefatory Note

Throughout this study continual reference has been made to important works on Wieland, in part as an acknowledgment of the debt I owe to others who have furthered my understanding of the writings of Wieland and informed me on particular aspects or more general matters. My personal obligations are many. I am exceptionally grateful to Harold Jantz for his unceasing encouragement from the inception of this work, his constructively critical readings of the entire manuscript, his suggestions for its improvement, and the generous trust with which he placed his library of rare books at my disposal. I am also most grateful to Maurice Mandelbaum who read the chapter on philosophical background with great care and penetration and who has given me valuable advice on scholarly questions connected with his field.

Through the past years I have talked about this study with other colleagues and friends. William H. McClain, in particular, has often patiently listened to my ideas and has in stimulating conversations helped me to find solutions to puzzling problems. It is with sadness that only here and now, too late for him to know, can I express my gratitude to Earl Wasserman for the time and trouble he took to discuss with me aspects of the English background, often suggesting useful possibilities and important connections. Another debt I owe is to the librarians of the Johns Hopkins University, in particular the staff of the rare book room and the interlibrary loan office, whose cheerful assistance has often turned a tiresome task into a pleasant and successful enterprise. My most personal gratitude must be reserved for two people here at home, Friedel and Otto Eberspacher, who graciously permitted me to verbalize first notions and thoughts, and who helped me to overcome the inevitable uncertainties and doubts. Their assistance in altogether practical matters made much of the writing an undisturbed and enjoyable experience.

‖ Introduction

In Germany, as in England and France, the prose narrative now commonly known as the novel underwent subtle mutations during the early decades of the eighteenth century and was marked by far-reaching innovations from about the mid-century onward. One of the German writers who contributed most significantly to the development of the genre in its modern form was Christoph Martin Wieland. His early works appeared at a time when critics were engaged in lively controversies about the aesthetic merits of the "prose epic" and its place in the hierarchy of letters, when they debated with unprecedented intensity the diverse possibilities of the depiction of reality and the portrayal of man in fiction and discussed the various narrative techniques of a genre habitually neglected in traditional poetics and contemporary theories of literature.

Wieland stood in the midst of these controversies. His early works were measured by the differing standards of conservative and progressive critics, and they were often praised and condemned for the very same artistic features. The contradictory evaluations of his works undoubtedly influenced the maturing writer, and his changing attitude toward literary principles and poetic values reflects the transitional nature of contemporary standards. At the same time, however, the modification of his position manifests the relatively independent development of a perceptive young man who was to become one of the masters of eighteenth-century verse and prose narrative.

For the past two centuries Wieland has generally been regarded as a writer of true stature, and no historian of literature has ever relegated him to oblivion. But critics and scholars have varied greatly in their judgment of his works, and virtually every generation has shaped its own image of the writer and the man. One of the first eminent critics of the young poet during his initial idealistic stage was Gotthold Ephraim Lessing. Like others before him he disapproved of the seemingly affected piety in Wieland's religious poetry and censured apparent flaws in his dramatic works. Although overly harsh and ruthless, Lessing's objections were partly justified and probably had a decisive influence on Wieland, who was unusually receptive to valid criticism. The early novels were more favorably evaluated; their artistic accomplishment was readily recognized, and they have received considerable attention ever since the publication of the first in 1764. Again acting as the spokesman for many, Lessing called the *Geschichte des Agathon* (1766) "one of the most excellent works of the century" and, clearly reiterating the admiration of others for the work, described it as "the first and only novel for the thinking man, of classical taste."[1] From this time on many of Wieland's works were translated into major European languages almost immediately after their appearance in German, and they were approvingly reviewed in distinguished periodicals, among them important English, French, and American magazines.

Although fairly widespread, the reverential regard for Wieland was not universal, and during the last quarter of the century he was again subjected to angry assaults, this time by two factions of the younger generation, the idealistic poets of the *Göttinger Hain* and the defiant writers of the *Sturm und Drang*. Wieland's satirical censure of their literary activities was not well received; the young men resented his criticism, especially—as Goethe stated it—"the fatherly tone" in which it was expressed. They also opposed the premises of his judgment and did not sanction the artistic and philosophical principles underlying his own writings. The distorted image they derisively fashioned was that of a hedonist, a skeptic without any true convictions, an incompetent critic, and the unpatriotic admirer of foreign literatures.[2]

This opposition of the younger generation to a major representative of an earlier period transcended the limits of rational dispute and is symbolic of the constant strife of youth against age. With passing time relations became less strained, the mutual criticism grew more

---

[1]*Sämtliche Schriften*, ed. Karl Lachmann, 3rd ed. Franz Muncker (Stuttgart, 1894), x, 80.

[2]A dissertation by Käthe Kluth, *Wieland im Urteil der vorklassischen Zeit* (Greifswald, 1927), is a well-documented study that treats specifically the criticism of Wieland by Lessing, Gerstenberg, Herder, the young Goethe, Wagner, and Lenz.

objective, and almost every one of the temperamental rebels arrived at a truce with the venerable gentleman in Weimar.

At the turn of the century another generation, the Romantics, felt the need to assert themselves against their predecessors, and Wieland was again singled out as a representative target. The strangely ambivalent attitude of the Schlegel brothers was no doubt symptomatic; it was initially marked by congeniality and a spirit of cooperation, indeed even by affectionate admiration for one of the "great masters" of literature. Apparently, however, their personal and artistic ideals did not allow them to maintain an unqualified approval of the traditional moral and poetic values typified by Wieland. Open hostilities were possibly sparked by Wieland himself; an incautious reference to his own time as the dawn of literature and to the modern period as an age of decline may well have been the provocation. Furthermore, his failure to interest one of his publishers in August Wilhelm Schlegel's Shakespeare translation was perhaps, though without justification, misconstrued as the malevolence of an established author toward a struggling member of the younger generation.

The periodical of the Romantics, the *Athenaeum*—clearly modeled after Wieland's earlier *Attisches Museum*—was in part intended as an organ of harsh polemics. For their first volume the Schlegels planned to include something especially "piquant," perhaps an article on Lessing or a note on Klopstock, evidently a persiflage of either one, or an even more destructive contribution, the auto-dafé of Wieland.[3] In contrast to these ambitious plans, the actually published invectives were of a milder nature. Alongside a few disapproving allusions, the first volume contained only one derogatory piece, a *Fragment* in which Friedrich Schlegel ridiculed Wieland's comment on the contemporary decline of literature as an "optical illusion."[4] More serious insults appeared in the second volume of the *Athenaeum*: Wieland was censured for planning to include worthless literary products in the definitive edition of his works, and in a parodistic advertisement he was accused of what the author of the article deemed plagiarism: a *citatio edictales* invited all of his literary creditors to file their claims against him for the illegitimate use of their property.[5]

---

[3]Friedrich Schlegel in a letter to his brother of December 18, 1797; see Oskar F. Walzel, *Friedrich Schlegels Briefe an seinen Bruder August Wilhelm* (Berlin, 1890), p. 333. Two studies of Wieland's relation to the Romantics are particularly informative: Ludwig Hirzel, *Wielands Beziehungen zu den deutschen Romantikern* (Bern, 1904), and Albert R. Schmitt, "Wielands Urteil über die Brüder Schlegel," *JEGP*, LXV, No. 4 (1966), 637–661.

[4]*Athenaeum*, I, 2 (Berlin, 1798), 72.

[5]*Athenaeum*, II, 2 (Berlin, 1799), 340.

Although this condemnation, in effect a rejection of the adaptive method, was primarily intended as a specific disapproval, it implies a broader renunciation of traditional principles and values. The criticism is essentially directed against eighteenth-century theories of poetic imagination and the corresponding practice of poets of borrowing subject matter, motifs, or configurations from literature and mythology. The concern of the Romantics with originality apparently induced them to reject works that seemed even slightly derivative. From their superficial accusation one might even be tempted to infer that the young Schlegels lacked the necessary sensitivity to appreciate Wieland's subtly significant adaptations of subject matter, his meaningful modification of older motifs, and his creative use of literary artifacts for the purpose of symbolic extension.

Wieland himself naturally advocated a distinctly different attitude toward the artistic use of traditional motifs and inherited materials. He was convinced that many literary features could be traced back into the remote past, and he knew that the greatest of poets, among them Shakespeare and Milton, had borrowed freely for their own purpose from literary sources. The procedure, he believed, should not be uncritically rejected, for the adaptation of subject matter did indeed constitute genuine invention: "Die Bearbeitung des Stoffs ist die wahre Erfindung."[6] A similar conviction was, incidentally, shared by Goethe, who also approved of the adaptation of older motifs, provided, of course, the poet was judicious in his selection and an artist in carrying out his intention.

In later years the Schlegels judged Wieland more objectively, Friedrich in his Vienna lectures of 1812, and August Wilhelm in the "Vorrede zu den kritischen Schriften" (1828).[7] His own commentaries on the writings of previous generations had unfortunately been misunderstood, A. W. Schlegel explained, and he felt unjustifiably censured when a reviewer accused him of an "artificial petulance" in his criticism of Wieland. At this time Schlegel even encouraged an unbiased study of Wieland's writings, which was still lacking but seemed urgently needed, for it would undoubtedly disclose the true significance of this "charming author" to the development of letters and would demonstrate the real extent of his influence on the language and form of German literature.

The changing attitude of the Romantics toward Wieland reveals a pattern that was not uncommon; it was, for example, prefigured in Goethe's life. As a young student in Leipzig he had admired the poet, but during the *Sturm und Drang* period he joined the antagonists of

---

[6]*Literarische Zustände und Zeitgenossen. In Schilderungen aus Karl Aug. Böttiger's handschriftlichem Nachlasse*, ed. K. W. Böttiger (Leipzig, 1838), i, 255.

[7]*Sämmtliche Werke*, ed. Eduard Böcking (Leipzig, 1846), vii, xxix.

Wieland and participated in their criticism of his works. Within a few years, however, Goethe's judgment grew less biased, and the two men established a lasting friendship that was characterized by cordiality and mutual respect. At the death of Wieland in 1813 it was Goethe who offered an eloquent and gracious tribute in a eulogy delivered before the Freemasons of Weimar. With understanding and empathy he traced the extraordinary development of the man and the poet, identified his beneficial influence on contemporary society, and commended the excellence of his contributions to literature.[8]

The tradition of diverse critical verdicts was perpetuated for decades to come. The introduction to this study is naturally not the proper place for an extensive treatment of the controversial reception of Wieland in the nineteenth and twentieth centuries.[9] To be sure, it might be a rather intriguing enterprise to analyze contrasting critical evaluations, particularly since such an investigation would not only enhance our understanding of Wieland but offer significant insights into the different schools of literary criticism and aesthetic theory. A casual glance at the relevant writings reveals a dual image. Whenever literature was viewed as a German national product, whenever the presentation of ethical values in literature was expected and originality was accentuated, Wieland was rejected as un-German, immoral, and imitative. Less biased historians of literature, however, stressed the cosmopolitan qualities of his work and called attention to his prominent role as mediator; they acknowledged his artistic achievements and recognized his genuine contributions to the development of poetic form and literary language.

The adverse criticism by influential nineteenth-century historians, their emphasis on content and subject matter, and the prevalence of positivistic and biographical approaches may have been some of the reasons for the late beginning and hesitant continuation of Wieland scholarship. The application of modern critical methods, however, is presently providing a fresh impetus to scholars, and their mediation on his behalf may well help to recapture the interest of Wieland's favorite audience, the intellectual and creative reader of all times.

In recent years numerous important studies of Wieland have appeared; although they approach his writings from various points of view, they most often concentrate on the works that were published after his return from Switzerland in 1760, or on the novels, begin-

---

[8]Goethe's *Werke*, xxxvi (Weimar, 1893), 313–346.

[9]The reception of Wieland in the nineteenth century still requires a thorough, well-balanced study. Allan M. Cress has explored part of the territory in his richly documented dissertation "The Decline of a Classic" (University of Illinois, 1952), but he has placed the main emphasis on the adverse verdicts and at the same time overlooked some of the more important favorable ones.

ning with the first, *Der Sieg der Natur über die Schwärmerei oder die Abenteuer des Don Sylvio von Rosalva*, of 1764. Whenever in these studies Wieland's artistic techniques are discussed, the term "perspective narration" is not far behind. Most critics consider this literary method a striking innovation that suddenly emerges in *Don Sylvio* without having any antecedents in the German novel or in Wieland's earlier writings.[10] Actually, however, the perspective portrayal of men and events in literature is not really as surprising an occurrence as it may seem at first glance, for the *Don Sylvio* is neither the first German novel that is significantly characterized by the extensive use of perspective narration[11] nor is it the very first work of Wieland in which the observance of point of view is important. Comparable artistic techniques are to be found in most of Wieland's numerous works that precede his first novel, and they abundantly demonstrate his effective early experiments with the literary method of perspectivism.

More generally, the profound concern of artists and critics with point of view in literature is not as uniquely modern as contemporary studies of fiction tend to intimate. Perspectivism and considerations of points of view are actually aspects of a complex of problems, and individual elements have their roots in the most diverse writings of the past. Philosophers searching for a viable theory of knowledge and attempting to explain the phenomenon of cognition have discussed the complicated role the sense organs play in the process of perception and have centrally or incidentally touched upon questions of perspective and point of view. Since the inception of their field, psychologists seeking to understand the nature of personality and trying to elucidate the concept of identity have observed man's struggle for self-knowledge and have probingly analyzed the tendencies of

---

[10]These critics accept, implicitly or even explicitly, the statement of Wolfgang Kayser that in Wieland's first novel a "new narrative prose," characterized by the appearance of a personal narrator and the skillful manipulation of perspectives, is "suddenly present," and they tend to agree with him that these apparently original techniques cannot be explained as a development: "Die so beliebte Kategorie der Entwicklung scheint hier zu versagen—ob wir von der Geschichte des deutschen Romans oder der des Autors her schauen." Wolfgang Kayser, "Die Anfänge des modernen Romans im 18. Jahrhundert und seine heutige Krise," *Deutsche Vierteljahrsschrift für Literaturwissenschaft und Geistesgeschichte*, 28 (1954), 417-446, particularly, p. 427. See also Steven R. Miller, *Die Figur des Erzählers in Wielands Romanen* (Göppingen, 1970), p. 13.

[11]At an earlier date I introduced an important predecessor of Wieland whose narrative techniques clearly anticipate Wieland's supposed innovations in the matter of "perspective narration." See "W. E. N.—*Der teutsche Don Quichotte* . . . Ein Beitrag zur Geschichte des deutschen Romans im 18. Jahrhundert," *Jahrbuch der deutschen Schillergesellschaft*, ix (1965), 106-130. The novel itself recently appeared in a new critical edition: Wilhelm Ehrenfried Neugebauer, *Der teutsche Don Quichotte, Oder die Begebenheiten des Marggraf von Bellamonte* [1753], ed. Lieselotte E. Kurth and Harold Jantz (Berlin, 1972).

individuals to view themselves and others from subjective, often strangely biased points of view. Rhetoricians, fully aware of the histrionic games orators are inclined to play, have acknowledged the point-of-view presentation of ideas and arguments as an effective device and have consequently recommended it as a successful oratorical technique. Authors of poetics have recognized the problems of identity that face the creative writer; they have, in fact, not infrequently advocated the poet's enactment of different roles and his experimentation with various personalities so that he can portray men and events from a favorable point of view and act as a spokesman with an unusually broad perspective, or perhaps even an intentionally limited view. These theoretical considerations have contributed importantly to the evolution of literature; the writings of all ages have increasingly reflected the varied interests in such matters, and the development did attain, as I shall show in greater detail, a culmination during the first half of the eighteenth century.

The intellectual and literary writings of the past, in part reflecting this evolution, form part of the frame of reference for many of Wieland's works. The many overt and covert allusions to other writers and poets, to characters and episodes in literature, to figures and events in history, ancient and modern, require a creative reader who is willing to investigate the territories of allusion and inform himself of contextually meaningful relations. Scholars have, of course, called attention to the connections of individual works of Wieland—their specific themes and motifs, particular figures and artistic techniques—with the writings of his predecessors. The broader context of his early and persistent interest in matters of perspective and point of view and the use of corresponding methods in his earliest important works have, however, not yet been sufficiently recognized or extensively treated.

To map part of this area is the aim of the present study. Its specific intention is threefold: the first three chapters delineate relevant tendencies of writers before Wieland and trace the perspective techniques that went into the making of literature in eighteenth-century Germany; the following chapters examine the earliest works of Wieland to discover the extent and manner in which they foreshadow his later mastery of the point-of-view technique; and the final chapters analyze or identify characteristic aspects of his early verse and prose fiction that are important here, but have not yet received the close attention they deserve.

The chapters on background are by no means intended as a complete survey of every mention of the topic or each occurrence of the technique in literature; they are, rather, meant as an anthology of important and typical examples with which Wieland became acquainted in the course of his formative years. The sketch of background should not be understood as an attempt to demonstrate the poet's dependence on other writers. The parallels cited here are not to be considered as direct sources, and the indication of analogues does not mean that my purpose is the study of influences on Wieland's writings. What is often designated as "influence" may, for the truly creative artist, be no more than a stimulus that induces the discovery of affinities. But this does not mean that sources are unimportant; the very act of stimulation may well lead to contemplation which brings about the development of weak and vague notions into strong and clear convictions that ultimately find their expression in a work of art.

Wieland himself acknowledged the importance of many writers whose works he read with great care; others are only briefly mentioned, but it is safe to assume that unconsciously his mind was colored by their style and thought as—to borrow a phrase from Leibniz—"men walking in the sun have their faces browned without knowing it."[12] Quite clearly several forces had a stimulating effect on Wieland's early works: the echoes of Greek and Roman literature are easily discernible, and the reverberations of contemporary thought are evident. Although he adapted existing materials and used previously employed techniques, Wieland was not simply a borrower, but rather an imaginative artist who intentionally combined traditional values with distinctly personal qualities in his efforts to create unique works of literary art, an undertaking in which he was eminently successful.

[12]Gottfried Wilhelm Leibniz, *The Monadology*, ed. Robert Latta (Oxford, 1898), p. 2.

1 ‖ Philosophical Background

Point of view in fiction and perspective in literature are often assumed to be uniquely modern concerns of literary critics.[1] But at the beginning of the eighteenth century poets and critics were already expressing a more than casual interest in these and related matters. Characteristically, the man of the Enlightenment was fascinated by the science of perspective and the art of seeing. One of his favorite positions was that of an observer who sometimes viewed objects from an intentionally fixed standpoint and on other occasions analyzed man and ideas from multiple points of view. Guided by his insights he recognized the relativity of judgment resulting from the bounds of his perspective, frankly admitted the limitations of his knowledge, and viewed the concept of absolute truth with considerable skepticism. New words and formulations added to contemporary vocabulary reflected a growing awareness of the importance of the complex phenomena. Significantly, the terms *"Standpunkt"* and *"Gesichtspunkt"* became firmly established and entered the dictionaries;[2] they were not only employed in art criticism but were with increasing frequency used as metaphors in poetics and literature.

[1]Percy Lubbock's *Craft of Fiction* (London, 1921) is one of the earliest in a long line of relevant studies. The introductory sentence of his seventeenth chapter serves as the starting point for many an investigation: "The whole intricate question of method, in the craft of fiction, I take to be governed by the question of point of view—the question of the relation in which the narrator stands to the story." An earlier German study treating a similar aspect, with emphasis on nineteenth-century literature, is Käte Friedemann's *Die Rolle des Erzählers in der Epik* (Leipzig, 1910).

[2]The *Grosses vollständiges Universal-Lexicon Aller Wissenschaften und Künste,* ed. Johann Heinrich Zedler (1732-), does not contain an entry under *"Gesichtspunkt."*

Early in his life Wieland began to share the interest of his contemporaries in questions of perspective and point of view. He recognized their significance for the creative writer, their far-reaching
implications for the critical evaluation of literature, and their specific
importance for the artistic portrayal of man and events in fiction. His
lasting concern for these matters was unquestionably stimulated by
extensive readings in philosophy, the classics, and modern European
literature. It is well known that Wieland was an avid reader.[3] His
father's library and many others to which he had access in his youth
contained a large number of books from which he could have derived
theoretical insights and representative models for the perspective
method in the verbal arts.

The philosophical views of the young Wieland have previously
received scholarly attention.[4] Attempts have been made to construct
a unified *Weltanschauung* of the many, certainly varied, if not contradictory, statements extracted from his personal correspondence and
from the literary works of the early period.[5] Such efforts are destined
to fail, for Wieland was unsystematically eclectic in his selection of
intellectual thoughts and uniquely imaginative in the adaptation of
philosophical ideas, some of which he did not fully understand and
others which he whimsically misinterpreted. The diverse views of
seemingly authoritative thinkers were bound to confuse the impressionable youth. He soon realized that he was singularly unsuccessful

---

Other terms, "*Augen-Punckt,*" "*Haupt-Punct,*" and "*Standpunkt,*" are defined in connection with perspective in art and geometry; their figurative meaning was not yet
given. The later dictionary of J. C. Adelung, the *Versuch eines vollständigen
grammatisch-kritischen Wörterbuches der Hochdeutschen Mundart* lists "*Gesichtspunct*" (II, 623) and "*Standpunct*" (IV, 669) and gives the figurative meaning for
both words. The *Deutsches Wörterbuch* by Jacob and Wilhelm Grimm only refers to
Leibniz, Gellert, Lessing, and Möser as the users of the term "*Gesichtspunkt*" during
the seventeenth and the early eighteenth century; see Vol. 4, 1st section, 2nd part
(Leipzig, 1897), cols. 4103–4104. An excellent study treating related aspects particularly in the later decades of the eighteenth century is Albert Langen's *Anschauungs-
formen in der deutschen Dichtung des 18. Jahrhunderts, Rahmenschau und
Rationalismus* (Jena, 1934).

[3]The chronological bibliography which accompanies the first volume of Wieland's
correspondence from 1750 to 1760, when he was twenty-seven years old, contains more
than four hundred works mentioned in his letters. Of course it is not possible to affirm
that he read all of these in their entirety, nor could one say that other works, not
mentioned, were not known to him. See *Wielands Briefwechsel, Anmerkungen zu
Band 1*, ed. Hans Werner Seiffert (Berlin, 1968), pp. 461–470, henceforth identified as
Wielands Briefwechsel.

[4]Emil Ermatinger, *Die Weltanschauung des jungen Wieland* (Winterthur, 1907);
Karl Hoppe, *Der junge Wieland, Wesensbestimmung seines Geistes* (Leipzig, 1930).
See also Victor Michel, *C.-M. Wieland, la formation et l'évolution de son esprit
jusqu'en 1772* (Paris, 1938).

[5]The complete correspondence of the young Wieland was not available until quite
recently, and earlier conclusions drawn from incomplete evidence are in need of
reevaluation.

in trying to construct his own philosophical system and predicted, not without a sense of irony, that in retrospect he would most certainly consider these attempts a rather ludicrous undertaking.[6]

Almost every one of his early "philosophical" works was in a later, generally revised edition accompanied by an apologetic preface and often identified as the product of an immature idealist with a tendency to view the world through the falsifying mirror of an ardent imagination.[7] Wieland admitted that these works were characterized by a peculiar mixture of philosophy and enthusiasm, "arbitrary principles, questionable opinions, incorrect observations, and dubitable sentiments" which would not stand the test of a rigorous philosophical analysis.

Nevertheless, in his search for a viable *Weltanschauung* Wieland acquired an extensive knowledge of the major writings in Western philosophy, its many controversies and contrasting views. One of the main sources of his information was the well-known *Historia critica philosophiae a mundi incunabulis ad nostram aetatem deducta* (1742-1744) by Johann Jakob Brucker.[8] Through this work and a more formal study of individual philosophers undertaken during his student years in Klosterberge and Tübingen, he became acquainted with the theories by which Greek thinkers endeavored to explain the phenomenon of cognition, with their attempts to establish acceptable theories of knowledge, and with their speculations on the nature of truth. The order in which Wieland acquired his knowledge must, perhaps, remain a matter of speculation. The esteem he expressed for Brucker's history may indicate that through a systematic reading of the work he traced the development of philosophical thought in chronological order. Conclusions drawn from his writings and correspondence would suggest a more sporadic reading, however, or a rather casual consultation of philosophical writings with emphasis on those works that particularly appealed to him at a given time. And the evolution of his own subjective philosophical principles, expressed or implied, indicates a growing interest in modern concepts and contemporary schools of thought.

---

[6] *Wielands Briefwechsel*, I, 80.

[7] Christoph Martin Wieland, *Gesammelte Schriften*, ed. Deutsche Kommission der Königlich Preußischen Akademie der Wissenschaften. Erste Abteilung: *Werke*, II (Berlin, 1909), 297. This edition will henceforth be identified as *Werke* (Akademieausgabe).

[8] The work contains six volumes and was published in Leipzig. In a letter written between the 6th and 26th of March 1752, Wieland mentions his reading of Brucker's *Historia*; in September of 1758 he offered to lend parts of the work to Johann Georg Zimmermann. See *Wielands Briefwechsel*, p. 51 and p. 361; a note to a later edition of *Die Natur der Dinge* (1798) refers the reader for more extensive information concerning the "erhabenen Träumen der Jüdischen Theosofen" to Brucker's "Historie der Filosofie"; *Sämmtliche Werke, Supplemente*, I (Leipzig, 1798), p. 94.

Of the many early Greek and Roman philosophers mentioned by Wieland,[9] several were of particular importance for the young poet. From Democritus he learned that there are two kinds of knowledge; one, obscure; the other, genuine; the former is derived from the senses; the latter from the exercise of thought upon the nature of things. This exercise of reason to produce certain knowledge Democritus confessed to be exceedingly difficult; truth, he stated, "lay in a deep well, from which it is the office of reason to draw it up."[10]

Protagoras, another philosopher mentioned in Wieland's *Geschichte der Abderiten*, adopted Democritus' doctrine that the atoms of which bodies are composed are in perpetual motion. Yet he believed that objects are liable to such continual fluctuation that nothing can be certainly known. Contradictory arguments may be advanced upon every subject, and all natural objects are perpetually varying. The senses convey different reports to different persons, and even to the same person at different times. Although the Sophist insisted that two mutually contradictory statements might be equally true, he conceded that one might be "better" than another.[11] The relativistic doctrine of Protagoras, "man is the measure of all things," and his assertion that there is no objective truth but only subjective opinion may well have appealed to the maturing Wieland. These philosophic principles foreshadow his perspective presentation of ideas, which are often discussed by the characters of his works from multiple points of view and without the author's attempting to support or invalidate the subjective opinion of any one of his fictive figures.

The critical discussion of Protagoras' views and the inquiry into the nature of knowledge in Plato's dialogues, particularly the *Theaetetus*, probably did not escape the attention of Wieland.[12] In his early youth he greatly admired Plato and presented several of his ideas, subjectively selected and imaginatively interpreted, in his philosophical poem *Die Natur der Dinge* (1751). In the "Vorläufige Anmerkungen" preceding the poem he specifically mentioned another of Plato's dialogues, the *Timaeus*, as containing thoughts that

---

[9]Ermatinger's study, pp. 160–161, contains a useful list of philosophers and writers mentioned in Wieland's *Die Natur der Dinge*.

[10]The *Historia* of Brucker appeared 1791 in an English adaptation: William Enfield, *The History of Philosophy from the Earliest Periods: Drawn up from Brucker's Historia Critica Philosophiae*. I am quoting from the edition of 1840, p. 248. Cf. Brucker, *Historia Critica Philosophiae*, 2nd ed. (Leipzig, 1767), Part I, p. 1186.

[11]See John Burnet, *Greek Philosophy*, Part I, *Thales to Plato* (London, 1928), p. 116.

[12]This dialogue was translated by Leibniz. It contains the idea, of great interest to Wieland, that thinking and contemplating may be considered a kind of interior dialogue.

had served as a stimulus in the formation of his own ideas. Through these dialogues, perhaps even the sixth Book of the *Republic*, and most certainly through Brucker's analysis and evaluation, Wieland became acquainted with essential aspects of Plato's theory of knowledge. Although Brucker, allegedly in agreement with other critics of Plato, felt that the *Timaeus* particularly was a "chaotic mass of opinion, which no commentators have yet been able to reconcile, or to explain," he attempted to summarize Plato's doctrines "as collected from his dialogues."[13] In his *Erste Anfangsgründe der Philosophischen Geschichte* Brucker introduced his readers in a simplified manner to important details of Plato's complex theories, and the fourth *Lehrsatz* of his work is the doctrine that implies clear and distinct knowledge of "ideas" in a previous state: "Die Seele ist eine wächserne Tafel, und hat schon Erkanntnis, ehe sie in den Leib kommt, deren sie sich hernach wiederum erinnert,"[14] a principle much debated by Brucker's and Wieland's contemporaries.

Wieland himself was soon to become highly critical of Plato. In a letter of May 25, 1752, he wrote to Johann Heinrich Schinz in Zurich: "Plato ist ohnstreitig ein übertriebner Philosoph den es zuweilen zu verdriessen scheint, daß wir Menschen sind. Seine Betrachtungen werden sehr oft zu Phantomen u: Hirngespinstern."[15] Later he began to question Plato's method and criticized the dialogues. They lacked, he felt, a fair balance of viewpoints, and the portrayal of the individual interlocutors was objectionable; for the Sophists, very much in contrast with their true intellect, frequently replied like immature boys, whereas the representatives of Socratic philosophy were, quite unrealistically, always portrayed as eloquent and invincible debaters.[16]

Far better dialogues, more carefully balanced in form and content, were presented by Cicero—a critical mediator of Greek thought—whom Wieland read throughout his life with constant interest and affection. Like Plato's dialogues, they are not predominantly of the dramatic type with relatively brief questions and answers, but contain much continuous exposition. Unlike Plato's speakers, however, the leading interlocutors are more fairly matched and excel alike in rhetorical abilities. Through the interplay of arguments representing more than

---

[13]Brucker-Enfield, p. 126; cf. Brucker, *Historia*, I, 666.
[14]Ulm, 1751, 2nd ed., p. 84.
[15]*Wielands Briefwechsel*, I, 75.
[16]*Literarische Zustände und Zeitgenossen. In Schilderungen aus Karl Aug. Böttiger's handschriftlichem Nachlasse*, ed. K. W. Böttiger (Leipzig, 1838) I, 239. One of Wieland's fictive figures echoes this censure of Platonic dialogue in a most revealing fashion. The epistolary novel *Aristipp und einige seiner Zeitgenossen* (Bk. IV, letter 4) contains Aristipp's extensive discussion of Plato's method and reiterates the criticism leveled against the imbalance of the dialogues.

one side of the issue at hand and the expression of multiple and almost equally valid opinions, Cicero creates the impression of unbiased communication of information and disinterested searching after truth.

Undoubtedly the *dramatis personae*, their verbal elegance and persuasive powers, served as models for not a few of the fictitious figures in Wieland's dialogues. An apt characterization of the method and purpose of Cicero's dialogues in the *Academica* describes equally well the technique and intentions of Wieland's figures, who are often involved in philosophical discussions: "the sole object of our discussions is by arguing on both sides to draw out and give shape to some result that may be either true or the nearest possible approximation to the truth."[17] The contentious ideas of several dialogues foreshadow some of Wieland's favorite topics. The controversy concerning Epicureanism contained in the *Tusculan Disputations*, the various theological views of the three schools of philosophy that were of chief importance in Cicero's days, as shown in his *De Natura Deorum*, and the inquiry into different theories of knowledge in the *Academica* may well have been a stimulus toward formulating central thoughts and essential ideas in Wieland's novels.

While debating controversial doctrines of sense perception and attempting to arrive at a valid theory of knowledge in the *Academica*, Lucullus and Cicero naturally touch upon questions of sight and vision. In his attack on skepticism Lucullus even alludes to the advantage of observing matters from multiple points of view. The resulting parallel or divergent perspectives will complement each other and broaden man's still limited knowledge: ". . . in my judgement the senses contain the highest truth, given that they are sound and healthy and also that all obstacles and hindrances are removed. That is why we often desire a change of the light and of the position of the objects that we are observing, and diminish or enlarge their distances from us, and take various measures, until mere looking makes us trust the judgement that it forms."[18]

One of Wieland's later essays, *Ueber eine Stelle des Cicero, die Perspectiv in den Werken der Griechischen Mahler betreffend*, may be taken as evidence of his particular alertness to questions of artistic perspective. A French art historian, Abbé Sallier, had attempted to prove that the ancients were not as ignorant of the principles of perspective as some, such as Charles Perrault, had claimed. However, in his documentation he had overlooked a crucial reference in Cicero's *De Oratore* which seemed to indicate the acquaintance of Greek

[17]*Academica* II, iii, 7-8. (For the English translations of Cicero I have for the most part relied on the editions of individual works in the Loeb Classical Library.)
[18]*Academica* II, vi, 19.

artists with matters of perspective. Sallier, Wieland believed, could
have splendidly supported his argument by citing the relevant lines in
Cicero: "pictoris cuiusdam summi ratione et modo, / formarum
varietate locos distinguentis."[19]

Yet Cicero was not actually concerned here with perspective in the
pictorial arts. Contextually interpreted, these lines are of a more profound significance to the verbal artist, the orator, and the poet.
Relating an event in the life of the Greek poet Simonides of Ceos,
who is said to have been the first to teach the art of remembrance,
Cicero mediates his discovery "that the best aid to clearness of
memory consists in orderly arrangement."[20] To those wishing to
develop their powers of recollection Simonides recommends the
attentive observation of reality and the perspective arrangement of
images in the mind so that objects, events, and human beings can
be recalled to memory in their accurate relation to each other. The
broader implications of such principles for the creative writer attempting to recollect and represent aspects of empirical reality in
literature, and their possible symbolic extension, certainly did not
escape Wieland, whose own memory was a rich source for literary
motifs and configurations.

Of Simonides Cicero tells another relevant story in *De Natura
Deorum*. Hiero of Syracuse asked the poet to explain the being and
nature of God. Simonides requested a day's grace for consideration;
the next day he asked for two, and continued in this fashion multi-
plying the number of days by two. When asked to give the reasons for
his delay he replied: "Because the longer I deliberate the more obscure the matter seems to me."[21] Since Simonides was, it is reported,
a man of learning and wisdom, so many acute and subtle ideas came
into his mind that he could not decide which of them was nearest the
truth, and therefore despaired of truth altogether.

In two of his last contributions to philosophical literature, in the
Academica and in *De Officiis*, Cicero explicitly discussed his own
epistemological principles. Attached to the New Academy and as a
disciple of the Skeptic Carneades he accepted the doctrine that the
senses, the understanding, and the imagination frequently deceive us,
and therefore cannot be infallible judges of truth; he subscribed,
however, to the principle of probability and stressed the necessity
of conviction. "The wise man," he stated in the *Academica*, "will

[19]Christoph Martin Wieland, *Sämmtliche Werke* (Leipzig, 1857), xxxiv, 109-114;
the note was first published in Wieland's *Teutscher Merkur* (1774), vi, 2, 218 ff. For
Cicero see *De Oratore* ii, lxxxvii, 358. Wieland translated Cicero's formulation as "das
Verfahren eines großen Malers . . . , 'welcher Oerter und Entfernungen durch die
Verschiedenheit der Formen unterscheide.'"
[20]*De Oratore* ii, lxxxvi, 351-353.
[21]*De Natura Deorum* i, xxi, 60.

make use of whatever apparently probable presentation he encounters, if nothing presents itself that is contrary to that probability."[22]

The epistle *De Officiis*, addressed to his son Marcus, elaborated
on this dictum: "Our school maintains," Cicero wrote, "that nothing
can be known for certain," but "we Academicians are not men whose
minds wander in uncertainty and never know what principles to
adopt . . . ; as other schools maintain that some things are certain,
others uncertain, we, differing with them, say that some things are
probable, others improbable."[23]

In the earlier eighteenth century Cicero, as a representative also
of the Middle Stoa, was probably more widely read than the Greek
philosophers,[24] and the *De Officiis* was often understood as a work
containing generally valid guiding principles. The influence of Cicero
was extraordinarily dominant, for his writings were the constant com-
panions of many a well-educated youth of the time.[25] Like Wieland,
they became acquainted with the authors of the "golden and silver
age" and may have felt as he did: "Ciceron. aber liebte ich am
meisten."[26]

The many controversies concerning epistemological problems were
not, of course, settled by the Greek and Roman philosophers; neither
were they resolved by their successors during the Middle Ages or the
Renaissance, but rather—according to Wieland and Brucker—com-
pounded and thus perpetuated in modern philosophy.[27]

Of particular interest here are the contemporary arguments concerning innate ideas and the diverging principles of sense perception.
In the early seventeenth century contrasting views were maintained
by Descartes and Gassendi. Descartes held that man cannot derive
true knowledge from sense experience; genuine knowledge is the

[22]*Academica* II, XXXI, 99.

[23]*De Officiis* II, ii, 7.

[24]The importance of Cicero for the eighteenth century, particularly for Goethe,
has been established by Harold Jantz, specifically in his article "Die Grundstruktur
des Goetheschen Denkens. Ihre Vorformen in Antike und Renaissance," *Euphorion*,
48 (1954), 153–170.

[25]Although there are numerous studies that investigate specific aspects of Cicero's
importance for later writers (cf. the annual *Bibliographie de l'Antiquité*), his significance for eighteenth-century German literature still needs a comprehensive,
thorough study. An early monograph by Tadeusz Zieliński, *Cicero im Wandel der
Jahrhunderte*, 3rd ed. rev. (Leipzig/Berlin, 1912), does not treat this broad subject.
The author mentions Wieland only once, Frederick the Great in connection with
French writers, and Goethe not at all; there is no recent scholarly work that bridges
this considerable gap. One particular subject, Wieland's translation of Cicero's letters
(1806), has received some attention; see Gerhard Hay, "Zu Wielands Cicero-Über-
tragung—Mit bisher nicht publizierten Briefen," *Jahrbuch der deutschen Schillergesellschaft*, XIII (Stuttgart, 1969), 13–32.

[26]*Wielands Briefwechsel*, I, 50.

[27]Cf. Wieland, *Die Natur der Dinge* (1751), 2nd book; Brucker, *Historia*, Book VII
(on scholastic philosophy).

result of reasoning from fundamental concepts, and these are inherent in the mind itself; ideas are innate or a priori. An intentionally opposing thesis was developed by Gassendi who undertook to construct a consistent scheme of Epicurean doctrine. He reinstated the theory of the Greek atomist that knowledge begins with sensation: "Nihil est in intellectu quod non prius fuerit in sensu." Yet he was no mere sensationalist, for he too believed that the intellect plays a significant part in the gaining of truth.[28]

Gassendi's theory of knowledge clearly foreshadows the epistemological realism of the eighteenth century, specifically the viewpoint of John Locke.[29] The central doctrine of Locke's theory contained in the first chapter of the second book of his *Essay Concerning Human Understanding* was extensively discussed not only in England but in Germany as well. Locke opposed the doctrine of inborn truth. The mind is in its first state "white paper, void of all characters, without any ideas." The question now is, how does it come to be furnished? "Whence comes it by that vast store which the busy and boundless fancy of man has painted on it with an almost endless variety?" To this Locke answers in one word, *"experience."* All our knowledge is founded on, and ultimately derived from, experience. The two sources of ideas are sensation and reflection: "our Senses . . . convey into the mind several distinct perceptions of things, according to those various ways wherein those objects do affect them," and thus the mind is furnished with sensible qualities. The second source, reflection, or internal sense, supplies the mind with ideas of its own operation, such as perception, thinking, doubting, believing, reasoning, knowing, and willing. There are then no innate ideas nor any a priori knowledge in the mind.[30]

The controversy between Descartes and Gassendi and the anti-Cartesian views of Locke were well known to Leibniz, and they became an important issue in the formulation of his own concepts. The *Monadology* and the *Nouveaux Essais* present his views. Rather than reject entirely either one of the contrasting theories, he attempted to reconcile them and to establish a *via media* between two extreme positions. His conception of the human mind as a Monad leads to a theory of knowledge which combines valid principles of both philosophies. He accepts the Cartesian ideal of genuine knowledge as a system of universal and necessary truths based on principles

[28]See Richard I. Aaron, *John Locke*, 2nd ed. (Oxford, 1955), p. 31.

[29]For an extensive discussion of epistemological realism see Maurice Mandelbaum, *Philosophy, Science, and Sense Perception; Historical and Critical Studies* (Baltimore, [1964] 1966).

[30]John Locke, *An Essay Concerning Human Understanding*, ed. Alexander Campbell Fraser (New York, 1959), I, 121–127.

and not derived from experience; it is "the knowledge of necessary and eternal truths that distinguishes us from the mere animals and gives us *Reason* and the sciences, raising us to the knowledge of ourselves and of God."[31] Leibniz rejects, however, the notion that human knowledge consists exclusively in the perception of universal and necessary truths. Although he does not agree with Locke's theory that the human mind is a *tabula rasa* void of innate ideas, he acknowledges the significant role experience plays in the clarification of knowledge. Even though experience does not create knowledge, innate ideas are made explicit by the stimulus of experience. Thus human knowledge is at once a priori and a posteriori.[32]

At a very early age Wieland became well acquainted with the writings of Leibniz. His first philosophical poem, *Die Natur der Dinge*, completed in August 1750, shortly before his seventeenth birthday, is in its portrayal of "die vollkommenste Welt, welche möglich ist" meant as a defense of Leibniz' *Théodicée*. Although Wieland explicitly subscribes to major ideas as expressed in the *Essai . . . sur la bonté de Dieu, la liberté de l'homme et l'origin du mal*, he does not uncritically accept every one of the principles contained in the *Monadology*; in the third book of the *Natur der Dinge* he refutes in particular the notion of innate ideas and rejects Leibniz' explanation of the relationship between mind and matter.

Wieland's critique is remarkable not for its profound philosophical thought or accurately scientific acumen but because it foreshadows the artistic techniques that are characteristic of his more mature works. In the habitual manner of his later writings Wieland sets out to contradict the brilliant illusions, "das schimmernde Blendwerk," of Leibniz in a perspective presentation of arguments, clearly announced in the earliest version of the poem, subtly suggested in later editions. A rhetorical question introduces the philosophical proposition: "Was hält den ewgen Geist an seinen Leib gebunden?" He does not attempt to reply immediately or directly, but invokes "Truth" to present two prevalent views, the opinion of Leibniz and her own perspective:

O Wahrheit, zeig uns erst, wie Leibnitz dieß erklärt,
Und sprich ein Urtheil aus, das deine Macht vermehrt.[33]

The final judgment of "Truth" will, of course, conform to the ideas of the young poet, who hopes to correct what he sees as the erroneous views of an eminent philosopher.

[31]Section 29 of the *Monadology*; for the English translation I have consulted Gottfried Wilhelm Leibniz, *The Monadology*, ed. and trans. Robert Latta (Oxford, 1898), p. 233.

[32]*Ibid.*, p. 124.

[33]*Die Natur der Dinge*, Book 3, ll. 389–390.

It is no mere coincidence that in his analysis of Leibnizean doctrine Wieland should use the perspective method of argumentation. Leibniz himself had employed the method in the refutation of one of his adversaries, Pierre Bayle, the author of the *Dictionnaire historique et critique*. In the article "Rorarius" Bayle had directed his main criticism against the theory of pre-established harmony and the possibility of multiplicity in the Monad, particularly the concept of variety in its operation.[34] Leibniz defended his principles in the *Théodicée* and did so by offering, though not objectively, a double perspective; in a systematic rebuttal of Bayle's attack he alternately presented lengthy quotations excerpted from the "Rorarius" and his own critical analysis of these statements.

Beyond this the *Théodicée* and *Monadology* mediate essential insights into questions of point of view and pertinent references to the phenomena of perspective.[35] Leibniz' concern with these matters was no doubt stimulated by his interest in optical theories and systems; he was well acquainted with the *Dioptrique* of Descartes and discussed at length the principle of refraction in the *Discours de métaphysique*.[36] In his extensive treatment of sense perception and the geometry of vision Descartes was specifically concerned with the point of view of the observer, and in the fourth and sixth discourses, *de sens en génerale* and *de la vision*, he comments upon the perspective appearance of objects. Similarly, optical and mathematical principles, the metaphor of perspective, and the concept of point of view figure prominently in the *Théodicée*. The imperfect perception of man, for example, and resulting from it his mistaken impression of disorder in the universe can be explained through the analogy to perspective art; the contemplation of relevant principles will lead to an understanding of order and harmony in the universe and to a recognition of its inherent beauty:

> C'est comme dans ces inventions de perspective, où certains beaux desseins ne paroissent que confusion, jusqu'à ce qu'on les rapporte à leur vray point de veue, ou qu'on les regarde par le moyen d'un certain verre ou miroir. C'est en les plaçant et s'en servant comme il faut, qu'on les fait devenir l'ornement d'un cabinet. Ainsi les deformités apparentes de nos petits mondes se reunissent en beautés dans le grand et n'ont rien qui s'oppose à l'unité d'un principe universel infiniment parfait.[37]

Long before Leibniz scientific investigations had revealed that the representation of a figure depends on, in fact betrays, the physical

[34]Leibniz-Latta, *Monadology*, p. 272.
[35]Claudio Guillén, "Metaphor of Perspective," *Literature as System* (Princeton, 1971), pp. 318–325.
[36]Gottfried Wilhelm Leibniz, *Die philosophischen Schriften*, ed. C. J. Gerhardt, IV (Berlin, 1880), 427 ff.
[37]Leibniz-Gerhardt, VI (Berlin, 1885), 197–198.

position of the artist; and the form of the recreated object, seemingly different from its actual shape, reflects the point of view of the observer. Leibniz affirms these insights when he states that "la même chose peut être representée differemment." Experiments with perspective drawings demonstrated that a circle can be represented by many different figures, an ellipsis, a parabola, or a hyperbola, indeed even by another circle, a straight line, or a point; to be sure, "rien ne paroit si different, ny si dissemblable, que ces figures."[38]

Like the artist, who creates an apparently subjective image of an object, the soul creates for itself a subjective image of the universe: "Aussi faut il avouer que chaque ame se represente l'univers suivant son point de vue, et par un rapport qui luy est propre; mais une parfaite harmonie y subsiste tousjours."[39] This rather limited perspective of the universe characterizes the individual Monad as Leibniz explains in the *Monadology*:

> Et comme une même ville regardée de différens côtés paroît toute autre et est comme multipliée perspectivement, il arrive de même, que par la multitude infinie des substances simples, il y a comme autant de différens univers, qui ne sont pourtant que les perspectives d'un seul selon les différens points de vue de chaque Monade.[40]

Although Leibniz describes the qualities of simple substances and applies the metaphor of perspective to metaphysical relations, the concrete example explaining the subjective view of "created things" could well be used as an analogy to describe a more mundane, yet still parallel relationship, that of man to the world.

Christian Wolff, the commentator of Leibniz and his best-known successor, shared many of the views expressed in the *Théodicée* and *Monadology*. He especially supported the criticism of the Lockean concept of the mind as a *tabula rasa* and rejected the notion that "die Begriffe der Dinge / die ausser uns sind / in die Seele als in ein leeres Behältniß hinein getragen werden"; he accepted the rationalistic theory that the mind possesses innate ideas, "die . . . in dem Wesen der Seele gleichsam vergraben liegen / und bloß durch ihre eigene Krafft auf Veranlassung der Veränderungen / die auswärtige Dinge in unserem Körper verursachen / hervor gebracht werden."[41] Negative evaluations of Lockean principles, comparable to those of Leibniz and Wolff, were also expressed by well-known

---

[38]*Ibid.*, p. 327.
[39]*Ibid.*, p. 327.
[40]*Opera Philosophica*, ed. Johann Eduard Erdmann (Berlin, 1840), p. 709.
[41]Christian Wolff, *Vernünfftige Gedancken Von den Kräfften des menschlichen Verstandes Und ihrem Richtigen Gebrauche*, 5th ed. (Halle, 1727), p. 13.

English writers such as Arbuthnot, Swift, Pope, and Prior who made the concept of the *tabula rasa* an object of parody and satire.[42]

In contrast to the unfavorable attitude of Leibniz, Wolff, and the English critics, some contemporaries accepted the ideas of Locke with remarkable enthusiasm: a most sympathetic response was expressed in the early moral weeklies. Of central interest to their editors was the controversial concept of the mind as a "white paper" and the theory that all knowledge is founded on, and ultimately derived from, experience. Three of the early periodicals—the English *Spectator*, Bodmer and Breitinger's *Discourse der Mahlern*, and Gottsched's *Vernünftige Tadlerinnen*—played a significant role in the dissemination of Lockean principles. Since Wieland in 1750 urgently recommended Addison's *Spectator*, albeit in its French translation, and Gottsched's *Tadlerinnen* as edifying reading to Sophie Gutermann,[43] he most certainly was familiar with the content of these *Wochenschriften*. Although he did not specifically mention the *Discourse* he no doubt became acquainted with the Swiss collection of dialogues not later than 1752, when he came to live with Bodmer in Zurich.

The most ardent champion of Locke in England was Joseph Addison, one of the editors of *The Spectator*; he reproduced entire sections of the *Essay Concerning Human Understanding* and applied Locke's theory in an extensive treatment of the "Pleasures of the Imagination." The article asserts rather categorically the predominance of the sense of vision: "Our Sight is the most perfect and most delightful of all our Senses. It fills the Mind with the largest Variety of Ideas, converses with its Objects at the greatest Distance, and continues the longest in Action without being tired or satiated with its proper Enjoyments." We cannot indeed, the author continues later, "have a single Image in the Fancy that did not make its first Entrance through the Sight."[44]

In direct commentary or indirect allusion, Addison intimates that factors governing the sense of sight ultimately determine the extent of man's imagination. It is checked by the limits of his physical vision or the bounds of his perspective; it is circumscribed by maintaining a fixed position, but enriched by the frequent shifting of his point of view. If, for example, an observer views a stately garden, his imagination will be checked by the "narrow compass" of the object, whereas in the wide field of nature his sight "wanders up and down without

---

[42]Kenneth MacLean, *John Locke and English Literature of the Eighteenth Century* (New Haven, 1936) pp. 7-12.

[43]*Wielands Briefwechsel*, I, 8.

[44]*The Spectator*, No. 411, June 21, 1712; ed. Gregory Smith (London, [1907] 1967), III, 276-277.

confinement" and is provided with a great variety of images. Both kinds of views are often represented with pleasing similitude, but with more perfect patterns, in works of art; the receptive scrutiny of these recreated natural scenes will without fail add significant dimensions to the empirical experience of the observer.

The editors of German *Wochenschriften* were familiar with the controversy over the philosophical theories of John Locke. Amazingly enough they did not follow Leibniz and Wolff in their rejection of his principles but subscribed rather eagerly to his philosophy, particularly as it was expressed in the posthumously published *Of the Conduct of the Understanding*.[45] The very title of the Swiss weekly, *Discourse der Mahlern*, suggests the interest in perspectivism so prevalent in the journal and reflects the influence of Locke, whose writings had inspired the selection of painters as the fictive figures involved in dialogue and discourse. Every contributor to the periodical was to play the role of a painter who should think of the imagination of his readers as white paper upon which he was to paint whatever he felt should be impressed on the *tabula rasa*.[46] Several discourses, particularly those written by Breitinger—for example the essays "Die Kunst des Denkens" and "Der Mensch ist verpflichtet zu denken"—distinctly reflect the theories of Locke, and the nineteenth discourse, entitled "Imagination," echoes, probably intentionally, the appropriate essay of *The Spectator*, for the Swiss authors thought highly of the English periodical.

Gottsched, who was otherwise a loyal follower of Leibniz and Wolff, disagreed with them on the presence of innate ideas in the mind: "Meines Erachtens ist uns nichts angebohren, als eine große Schwachheit des Verstandes; ein Mangel alles Erkenntnisses; eine Unwissenheit aller Wahrheiten." In contradiction to the eminent philosophers he subscribed to Locke's theory: "Den Augenblick, da wir gebohren werden, wissen unsere Seelen noch von sich selber nicht. Die Sinne machen die allerersten Eindruck in die leeren Tafeln unsers Gemüthes, und legen den Grund zu allem unserm künftigen Erkenntnisse."[47] Like Locke he considered this insight of the greatest significance for the education of the young. The fully developed personality, mind and body, always reflects childhood experiences and activities, and the mature man is a product of influences exerted upon him during the early years of his life:

[45]The German edition, *Johann Lockens Anleitung des menschlichen Verstandes zur Erkäntniss der Wahrheit nebst desselben Abhandlung von den Wunderwerken*, appeared in 1755 in Königsberg; the translator was Georg David Hypke.

[46]Hans Bodmer, *Die Gesellschaft der Maler in Zürich und ihre Diskurse* (1721–1723) (Frauenfeld, 1895), pp. 44–45.

[47]*Die Vernünftigen Tadlerinnen. Der andre Theil* [1726] 3rd ed. (Hamburg, 1748), pp. 450 and 448.

Hier bildet sich diejenige Beschaffenheit unsers Wesens, welche man das Naturell zu nennen pflegt. Hier leget man den Grund zu allen Gemüthsneigungen und Begierden; zur Gesundheit und Krankheit; zu Tugenden und Lastern. Die Seele weiß sich noch selbst nicht zu helfen: darum läßt sie sich ganz durch äußerliche Dinge lenken, die, vermittelst der Sinne, in sie wirken.[48]

A further step toward the popularization of Lockean doctrines was the introduction of his concepts into the fictive realm of the novel. One example with which German readers were very well acquainted is Samuel Richardson's *Pamela*. The philosophical principles of course undergo poetic interpretation by the author and a subjective adaptation by the heroine of the novel. She has received Locke's *Treatise on Education* from her husband so that she may raise their children according to its rules. Pamela is so delighted with the *Treatise* that she establishes a school for seven or eight children, applies Locke's theories to their education, and closely observes the efficacy of his principles. She is eagerly looking forward to the time when "the little buds of their minds will begin to open, and their watchful mamma will be employed, like a skilful gardener, in assisting and encouraging the charming flower, through its several hopeful stages, to perfection."[49] She agrees with Locke that parents should not "indulge their children in bad habits, and give them their head, at a time when, like wax, their tender minds may be moulded into what shape they please." The early influences are of great consequence, for the initial molding of the mind is "the foundation on which the superstructure of the whole future man is to be erected," and wrong impressions will "hardly ever be eradicated."[50]

Whereas Richardson treats these matters in a very serious manner, the authors of humorous novels exploit the philosophical principles, particularly the notion of the *tabula rasa*, for comic effect. They sometimes portray a youth who receives an almost unmanageable variety of impressions during his formative years; actual experiences inscribe "true" impressions on his mind, and the reading of highly improbable literature, such as fairytales or stories of superstition, fictional biographies of idealized characters, or daring adventures, brings about "false" inscriptions. With a lively imagination the young hero, who often lacks proper guidance, indiscriminately reflects upon the "true" and "false" impressions as if both were real, and as a result

[48]*Ibid.*, p. 450. See also F. Andrew Brown, "Locke's 'Tabula Rasa' and Gottsched," *GR*, 24 (1949), 3-7; "Locke's 'Essay' and Bodmer and Breitinger," *MLQ*, 10 (1949), 16-32; and "German Interest in John Locke's *Essay*," *JEGP*, 50 (1951), 466-482. In these studies Brown makes no mention of Wieland.

[49]*Pamela; or Virtue Rewarded* [1740], ed. Ethel M. M. McKenna (London, 1902) IV, 234.

[50]*Ibid.*, p. 270.

his mind receives a confusing mixture of ideas. Life itself with its complex interaction of experiences and the intervention of a responsible mentor usually exerts a corrective influence. However, some of the more profound early impressions, albeit "false" ones, remain in his mind permanently; they are never completely eradicated and their emergence, sometimes at the most inappropriate moment, causes the hero no little embarrassment, needless to say to the delight of the reader.[51]

In their attempts to establish viable theories of knowledge and to prove the competence of the human mind to discern truth, Leibniz and Locke had to defend the diverging principles of their own dicta in analytical comparisons against others upholding somewhat different theories; they also had to suffer the criticism of the contemporary philosophers of doubt, the modern skeptics. Leibniz' controversy with Bayle was well publicized. The author of the *Dictionnaire* not only attacked the apparent inconsistencies of the Leibnizean theory of preestablished harmony, he was equally skeptical of man's ability to use his reason effectively to arrive at true knowledge. Influenced by Montaigne, who was one of his favorite authors, Bayle held the view that man's reason leads him more often into error than toward the recognition of truth. The skepticism of Bayle and his predecessors was, however, not esteemed by Brucker, whose views were often accepted by those—among them Wieland—who considered him a reliable authority. They often shared his judgment: "in whatever form Scepticism appears, or from whatever cause it springs, it may be confidently pronounced hostile to true philosophy; for its obvious tendency is to invalidate every principle of human knowledge, to destroy every criterion of truth, and to undermine the foundations of all science, human and Divine."[52]

Not yet known to Brucker were the writings of a younger philosopher, David Hume of Scotland. In his own time Hume was considered a representative of modern skepticism standing in the tradition of Sextus Empiricus and Bayle.[53] Not all of his views were equally well-known or fairly evaluated by German men of letters, and his philosophic position is, of course, more complicated than modern readers and earlier interpreters had realized.[54] Among Wieland's

[51]The best early examples in German literature are Wilhelm Ehrenfried Neugebauer, *Der teutsche Don Quichotte oder die Begebenheiten des Marggraf von Bellamonte* (1753), and Christoph Martin Wieland, *Der Sieg der Natur über die Schwärmerei oder die Abenteuer des Don Sylvio von Rosalva* (1764).

[52]Brucker-Enfield (Book IX), p. 562; Brucker, *Historia*, Part IV, p. 609.

[53]Wieland, *Sämmtliche Werke*, XXIX (Leipzig, 1857), 142.

[54]The interpretation of Hume as a skeptic, which was still prevalent at the beginning of this century when T. H. Green's critique of Hume was taken as standard, has undergone a radical reappraisal in the last decades. One important work in the

friends he was best known, perhaps even notorious, as the "most subtle doubter," who had "misused his talents against religion"; but he was also esteemed for the excellent qualities of his writings, "seine Feinheit, seinen Tiefsinn und seine Eleganz," and recognized as an outstanding historian.[55] His philosophical works, at the time of their publication apparently more favorably received on the continent than in England, were, like those of Locke, vitally concerned with epistemological problems and treated most extensively the importance of sense experience as the origin of ideas and knowledge.

Hume's thesis was, however, fundamentally different from that of his predecessor. Locke was essentially a "critical realist," who held "that the actual qualities of physical objects resemble some of the types of qualities with which we are familiar in sense experience"; yet he also held "that what we are capable of perceiving is never identical with what exists independently of us."[56] Hume, as a representative of a "cautious phenomenalism," held that "*if* there were anything outside of experience we could not know its nature, and that, in fact, we cannot offer adequate reasons for either affirming or denying that anything of the sort exists."[57] His phenomenalistic approach to the analysis of the physical world and the nature of man probably served many a novelist of the later eighteenth century as a guiding principle or as a thesis supporting previously held notions. It most certainly struck a sympathetic chord in Wieland, whose fictive figures often observe man and events from strangely subjective points of view but nevertheless think of their limited perspective as having universal value. These writers do, perhaps less intentionally and more coincidentally, verify Hume's theory:

> It seems evident that men are carried by a natural instinct or prepossession to repose faith in their senses, and that without any reasoning, or even almost before the use of reason, we always suppose an external universe, which depends not on our perception but would exist though we and every sensible creature were absent or annihilated.

It also seems evident to Hume that whenever men follow their "blind and powerful instinct of nature" they "always suppose the very images presented by the senses to be the external objects, and never entertain any suspicion that the one are nothing but representations of the other."[58]

---

reevaluation—although its interpretation is often challenged—is Norman Kemp Smith, *The Philosophy of David Hume* (1941).

[55] Johann Georg Zimmermann, *Ueber die Einsamkeit*, 1 (Leipzig, 1784), 81–83.

[56] Mandelbaum, *Philosophy, Science, and Sense Perception*, p. 119.

[57] *Ibid.*, p. 121.

[58] David Hume, *An Inquiry Concerning Human Understanding*; in V. C. Chappell, *The Philosophy of David Hume* (New York, 1963), p. 379.

Of perhaps even greater importance to the creative writer intending to treat philosophical questions in fiction was the literary method by which Hume made some of his principles known. The form of two works—a collection of four essays, "The Epicurean," "The Stoic," "The Platonist," and "The Sceptic," designed to present classical philosophic attitudes, and the *Dialogues Concerning Natural Religion*—was undoubtedly inspired by traditional dialogue literature. Like so many of his contemporaries, Hume was very fond of Cicero, a major writer of this genre. "I found," he admits in his autobiography, "an unsurmountable aversion to everything but the pursuits of philosophy and general learning; and while [my family] fancied I was poring upon Voet and Vinnius, Cicero and Vergil were the authors which I was secretly devouring."[59]

Each one of the four essays presents the views of a representative philosopher, but it was not Hume's intention to "explain accurately the sentiments of the ancient sects of philosophy"; his aim, although not expressed in these terms, was to have each speaker offer from his point of view the perspective he represents in the complex realm of philosophy. The *persona* was to "deliver the sentiments of sects that naturally form themselves in the world, and entertain different ideas of human life and happiness."[60] Since all four spokesmen are, like Cicero and Hume, masters of rhetoric and present their opinions with conviction and eloquence, the discovery of Hume's own attitude, naturally not overtly expressed, but perhaps allusively implied, demands a most attentive reading of the essays. The artistic techniques of Augustan satire, most skillfully used by Hume, do however reveal his antipathies. Each first-person speaker unwittingly characterizes himself as an overzealous defender of his views and betrays the weakness of his theories, not unlike the central character of Alexander Pope's *Dunciad*, but of course much more subtly.

The later *Dialogues Concerning Natural Religion*, although not lacking in ironic dissimulation, are a much more serious attempt to present diverging views in dramatic form. The interlocutors are so fairly matched and the argumentation so well balanced that attempts to identify the individual speakers with contemporary figures or to determine the extent of Hume's own views possibly expressed in the discussion have led to countless speculations.[61]

The serious presentation of multiple, almost equally valid points of view on a controversial philosophic topic exemplifies Hume's theory that man's knowledge never reaches absolute certainty, but

[59]Hume, *My Own Life, ibid.*, p. 4.
[60]Hume, *Of the Standard of Taste and Other Essays*, ed. John W. Lenz (Indianapolis–New York, 1965), p. 100.
[61]John Valdimir Price, *The Ironic Hume* (Austin, Texas, 1965), p. 127.

that he may arrive at an approximation of genuine knowledge by a comparative analysis and critical acceptance of well-founded concurring views. This method of presentation, the discussion of a particular theme from different yet equally convincing points of view was used not only by philosophers but also by creative writers and literary critics; it was employed in all types of writings and applied in the treatment of unusually variegated topics, and it became in fact one of the favorite artistic devices of eighteenth-century literature.

2 ‖ Literary Background: Classical and Foreign Literatures

The literary dialogue, whether independently published or part of a larger unit, is perhaps the most prominent genre that consistently uses the point-of-view method of presentation and beyond that often treats the theme of perspectivism in a serious manner or in satiric fashion. Of all the classical authors of dialogues, Wieland's favorite was Lucian of Samosata, whom he admired long before he published his German translation of the works in 1788. According to Wieland, Lucian's innovation was the result of a fortunate idea of combining aspects of Socratic dialogue with those of the dramatic dialogue of Eupolis and Aristophanes, a method by which he created

> eine neue Gattung von Composition . . . , die ihm einen weiten Spielraum gab, alle Fähigkeiten seines Geistes zu deployieren, und ihn in den Stand sezte, alle Endzwecke, die er sich als Schriftsteller für das feinere Publicum vorsezte, auf eine desto gewissere Art zu erreichen, da er, (eben so wie die alte Comödie) sein Vorhaben, durch Kritik und Satyre zu bessern oder zu strafen, hinter den Anschein, bloß zu scherzen und zu belustigen verbergen wollte.[1]

It is this very kind of writing which Lucian defends, though with ironic obliqueness, in one of his satiric dialogues, ΔΙΣ ΚΑΤΗΓΟΡΟΥ -

[1] Lucian von Samosata, *Sämtliche Werke*, ed. and trans. Christoph Martin Wieland (1788; rpt. Darmstadt, 1971), I, 1, xxv. Wieland's reading and knowledge of Lucian is treated in Julius Steinberger's dissertation *Lucians Einfluss auf Wieland* (Göttingen, 1902). For a comparison of the two writers, particularly their historical situation and their ideas on philosophy, religion, and politics, see Paul Geigenmüller's "Lucian und Wieland," *Neue Jahrbücher für Wissenschaft und Jugendbildung*, III (1927), 35–47.

ΜΕΝΟΣ (*The Double Indictment*, or as Wieland translated the title, *Der doppelt Angeklagte*).

A Syrian writer, easily identifiable as the spokesman of Lucian, is called before the gods to testify in his defense against the accusations of two plaintiffs. He is charged by Rhetoric, his early consort, with neglect and desertion. Pleading her case she presents an adulatory portrait of herself in a grandiloquent oratory which is nothing less than an exalted "Praise of Rhetoric." Her speech is, of course, to be understood as a mock encomium, for she delivers her testimony in an excessively ornamented style that ironically exposes the absurdities of her turgid rhetoric. Dialogue, the companion of his later days, accuses the Syrian of having impaired his dignity: he made him play the comedian and buffoon, exposed him to the rudeness of Menippus, and forced him to adopt the practice of Menippus of mingling verse and prose which turned Dialogue into a "surprising blend . . . , a strange phenomenon made up of different elements, like a Centaur."[2]

In his defense the Syrian reveals the immoderation of Rhetoric. He left her because she had debased herself, adorning her body with repulsive finery, conducting herself like a courtesan, and bestowing her favors without discrimination even on drunken lovers. Dialogue too was a rather pompous and conceited fellow, overly melodramatic and tedious; like Plato's speakers he wanted to discuss only serious questions or profound ideas and refused to acquire a sense of humor. The Syrian therefore attempted to strip Rhetoric of her affectation and to protect her from being misused for undignified purposes; he tried to change Dialogue into a less serious and more congenial, perhaps even witty companion. The defendant argues his case with persuasion and is able to convince the judges of his honorable intentions. Hermes announces the verdict: "You win by all of ten votes!" and unwittingly forecasts the fate of Lucianic dialogue: "Well, go your ways, and good luck to you."[3]

A not unusual configuration in Lucian's dialogue is that of an uninformed but by no means unintelligent interlocutor and a mentor who generously shares his knowledge with a less experienced companion. The dialogue ΧΑΡΩΝ exemplifies Lucian's predilection for this configuration and also reveals his concern with questions of viewpoint and perspective. It is a conversation between Charon and Hermes, two *Weltbeschauer*, as Wieland cleverly translated the subtitle ΕΠΙΣΚΟΠΟΥΝΤΕΣ.

Charon, the ferryman of the underworld, and therefore naturally a man of limited perspective, desires to acquire some knowledge of the

---

[2] *Lucian*, ed. and trans. A. M. Harmon, Loeb Classical Library (London and New York), III (1921), 147.

[3] *Ibid.*, III, 151.

world and requests Hermes to be his guide for the day. Their immediate concern is the search for a superior point of view: "Charon, we want a high place of some sort, from which you can look down upon everything. If it were possible for you to go up into Heaven, we should be in no difficulty, for you could see everything plainly from on high."[4] Yet Charon is not permitted to enter Jupiter's realm, and the two spectators must be content with a view from the highest mountain. Hermes is confident that they will find a suitable post of observation: "I will see what is to be done, and will find the proper coign of vantage."[5] None of the existing peaks, however, seems high enough, and so, in imitation of the poets who achieve such feats in a few lines, they roll mountain upon mountain only to discover that they are now too far removed from the world of men. His present perspective, Charon complains, is not much better than his past view of the world. He wishes to observe man from a closer point of view, he wants to see what man does and hear what he says. His wish, Hermes promises, will be fulfilled: "I . . . will make you sharp-sighted in a minute by getting a charm out of Homer for this purpose."[6] Whatever they cannot closely observe from their high vantage point will be brought into focus through their recollection of literary scenes and configurations.

While they are gazing down upon the valley Hermes mentions the name of Croesus and identifies him for Charon: "Look over there towards the great acropolis with the triple wall. That is Sardis, and now you see Croesus himself sitting on a golden throne, talking with Solon of Athens. Would you like to listen to what they are saying?" "By all means," answers Charon,[7] and the conversation they now over-hear is an imaginative reproduction of the dialogue between Croesus and Solon as reported by Herodotus in the first book of the *Histories*. Here and at other occasions Charon's limited view is expanded by poets and historians who have portrayed all possible aspects of man and his life on earth. Through their works they have provided suf-ficiently rich materials to stimulate the imagination and widen the

[4]*Ibid.*, II (1960), 401; Wieland's translation of the text contains two particularly characteristic formulations: "Charon, wir brauchen zu unserm Vorhaben einen hohen *Standpunkt*. Wenn du den Himmel besteigen dürftest, so wäre uns auf einmal geholfen: denn von da aus könntest du, *wie von einer Warte*, alles gar schön übersehen." Cf. Lucian von Samosata, *Sämtliche Werke*, ed. and trans. Christoph Martin Wieland (1788; rpt. Darmstadt, 1971), I, 2, 166 (italics are mine).
[5]Lucian-Harmon, II, 403; Wieland's formulation: "Ich denke bald einen tauglichen Standort ausfindig zu machen." *Ibid.*, p. 167.
[6]Lucian-Harmon, II, 409; Wieland's formulation: "Vermittels einer kleinen von Homer entlehnten Zauberformel [will ich . . . dich] so scharfsichtig machen als du nur verlangen kannst." *Ibid.*, p. 171.
[7]Lucian-Harmon, II, 415.

horizon of their readers. If every reader, like Charon, were able to convince himself of the reality of poetic portrayals and descriptions, literature would serve him well as an extension of his modest perspective and a vivid augmentation of his limited experience.

For centuries to come, Plato, Cicero, and Lucian were to provide diversified, at times highly controversial models for the art form of the dialogue and the presentation of various subject matter from multiple points of view. Most of the later writers perpetuated the tradition, of course not uncritically, and contributed their own innovational features toward perfecting the genre and adapting it to modern demands.

One of the most eminent mediators of classical models in the Renaissance and an eloquent advocate of perspectivism was Erasmus of Rotterdam. During a time of profound transvaluation of values and of crucial religious controversies he often chose a *via media* rather than commit himself without reservations to any one specific cause. In doing so he disappointed many contemporaries who expected him to take a firm stand and interpreted his flexibility as an inconsistent attitude, irresolute and even cowardly. They did not acknowledge, perhaps did not even recognize, the judicious principle underlying his position.

Like so many of his predecessors Erasmus inquired into the nature of truth, but he did not provide generally valid answers or sharply defined solutions to particular questions. To the consternation of many he attacked both the Church and the attackers of the Church at the same time, and he urged the princes to protect Luther but refused to side with him. His biographer Johan Huizinga explains his attitude: "If Erasmus . . . hardly ever gives an incisive conclusion, it is not only due to cautiousness, and fear to commit himself. Everywhere he sees the shadings, the blending of the meaning of words. The terms of things are no longer to him, as to the man of the Middle Ages, as crystals mounted in gold, or as stars in the firmament." He likes assertions so little that he would "easily take sides with the sceptics wherever it is allowed by the inviolable authority of Holy Scripture and the decrees of the Church."[8] Rather than ask "What is truth?" Erasmus would pose the complementary question: "What is free of error?" He realized that truth was rarely simple and that a permanently fixed standpoint was not a desirable, in fact not even a defensible position. His readiness to change his point of view and consider different aspects and divergent perspectives enabled him to see many facets of individual problems. Such apparent vacillation does not necessarily indicate an irresponsible inconsistency; rather it is "a

[8]Johan Huizinga, *Erasmus of Rotterdam* (London, 1952), p. 116.

quality of the maturest minds," and the ability to see at least two sides of a question "implies a particularly high order of wisdom."[9]

With Erasmus the consideration of multiple perspectives, each having its validity as an integral segment of a larger, more comprehensive view, was a habit of mind that is reflected in every one of his works. The very first one, the *Collectanea adagiorum* (1500), expanded in later editions to 4251 adages, presents a magnificent panorama of classical learning and wisdom, interspersed with reflections and observations, amusing anecdotes and stories. Variegated thoughts on every topic are juxtaposed in such a fashion that parallel, diverging, and sometimes even contradictory views are presented. Occasionally an adage served as the stimulus for a longer essay in which Erasmus expressed his personal views on a controversial topic. Some of the essays, for example the treatise on war based on the adage *Dulce bellum in expertis,* have had a lively history of their own; they were printed separately, published in several, often altered editions, and were repeatedly translated.

It should not come as a surprise that the most frequently quoted authority in the *Adagia* is Cicero.[10] Along with other humanists Erasmus became deeply involved in the controversy about Cicero, and he exposed in his satiric dialogue *Ciceronianus* (1528) the insensitive imitations of Cicero's style; yet he approved of the artistic emulations of the timeless qualities, the urbane spirit and excellent method, the pure language, the candor, and the graceful manner of Cicero's works.

Echoes of Greek and Roman authors are perceptible in all the writings of Erasmus, and the techniques employed in his *Colloquies* distinctly recall those of Cicero and Lucian. The contemporary reception of this work foreshadows in its criticism the superficial interpretation of so many of the later dialogues. The method was sadly misunderstood. Erasmus was often naively identified with every one of the spokesmen and then rebuked for impudent or heretical statements. He therefore deemed it necessary to explicate the principle according to which the *Colloquies* should be judged and did so in the

[9]Walter Jacob Kaiser, *Praisers of Folly,* Harvard Studies in Comparative Literature, No. 25 (Cambridge, Mass., 1963), p. 39.

[10]Margaret Mann Phillips, *The 'Adages' of Erasmus* (Cambridge, England, 1964), pp. 393–403. The total number of references to Cicero's works is 892, followed by Homer with 666, and Plutarch with 618; in a more comprehensive study of perspectivism in the writings of the ancients, Plutarch (who was widely read in the eighteenth century) would also deserve consideration. The *Moralia,* for example, treat diverse topics from multiple points of view; monologues, dialogues, letters, lectures, narratives, quotations, and proverbs introduce different perspectives, and numerous allusions refer the reader to the views of well-known authorities.

epistle *To the Divines of Louvain* (supposedly written in 1531). One of his major arguments is basically an expansive definition and defense of the point-of-view technique. Before the critic arrives at negative conclusions he should, Erasmus insists, inform himself of the personality of the speaker. If, for example, the immature views of a sixteen-year-old boy on church dogma are presented, no one should ever mistake them for the opinions of the author; and if an interlocutor condemns the Indulgences of the Pope in a larger context, the author of the dialogue should not be held responsible for such a debatable view.[11]

The *Colloquies* generally present, like Cicero's and Lucian's dialogues, two or more figures in conversation with another who discuss diverse matters often in a serious tone and in an instructive manner. Probably the best-known work of Erasmus, the *Moriae encomium* of 1509, offers a different, uniquely biased perspective. Its introductory heading, "Stultitia loquitur," names the persona of the monologue and establishes the point of view from which human acts of folly are seen and evaluated. Erasmus' mock encomium continues the classical tradition which is evoked in the dedicatory epistle addressed to Sir Thomas More. The particular pattern, a fool praising foolishness, the mocker being mocked, is also grounded in tradition and is not as original with Erasmus as has been assumed. But then originality was not as highly regarded during the Renaissance as in a later century. An early example from Lucian was previously cited: Folly praising folly is analogous to Rhetoric lauding rhetoric. In a subjective presentation of their personal qualities both female speakers expose their weaknesses, and as a consequence, praise is turned into mockery.

Fifteen years before the *Encomium* was published, another work of a similar nature appeared in Basel and almost immediately became popular. It was Sebastian Brant's *Narrenschiff* (1494). A recent description of Brant's method contrasting it with the *Encomium* is not completely accurate in its emphasis on differences: "In Brandt's book it was Wisdom who occupied the pulpit and preached admonishingly to the fools sitting beneath her."[12] To be sure, the introductory line of the *Protestation*, "Das Narrenschiff hatt ich gedichtet," identifies the poet and names the major spokesman of the work; but in an ironic admission of guilt, perhaps equal to that of others, the author characterizes himself not without satiric overtones as a fool:

---

[11]*The Colloquies of Erasmus*, trans. N. Bailey (London, 1878), I, xxiii.
[12]Kaiser, *Praisers of Folly*, p. 35.

Es kan nit yeder narren machen
Er heisz dann wie ich bin genant
Der narr Sebastianus Brant.[13]

Brant, however, does not speak consistently in his own voice through the entire work. The very first chapter, "Von vnnutzen buchern," introduces another first-person speaker, a fool praising folly, who presents the subjective perspective of one depending for his wisdom on books and notes which he does not fully understand. Significantly, three of the last five lines play with the central image of fools' literature:

Ich weysz das vinū heysset win
Gucklus ein gouch, stultus eyn dor
Vnd das ich heysz domne doctor.[14]

The fifth chapter of Brant's work introduces yet another spokesman, an old fool who describes the acts of folly of the aged; chapter thirteen, "Von buolschafft," has Venus as the speaker, and only the twenty-second chapter presents Wisdom delivering her praise of wisdom while fools are sitting at her feet. The *Narrenschiff* thus offers several distinctly different perspectives of which at least one clearly foreshadows the *Encomium* of Erasmus.

Although the pattern of a fool's perspective was prefigured in earlier works, it was not as consistently presented as in *The Praise of Folly*. The *Encomium* is a difficult work and has often been misunderstood. Its first critic, Martin Dorp, who suggested to Erasmus that he also publish a "Praise of Wisdom" to counteract the "Praise of Folly," is representative of many who did not understand the complex method but only considered the surface value of the moralistic message. And still today, even the most sensitive interpreters cannot entirely refrain from identifying the voice of the *persona* as that of Erasmus.[15]

The Praise of Folly is, of course, to be understood ironically. But the simple inversion of values based on the assumption that whatever Stultitia praises is actually to be condemned is not sufficient for the understanding of the work. The more complex intention of the author is expressed in the dedicatory letter: "I have praised folly, but not altogether foolishly." One of the masterful strokes by which the significance of the *Encomium* is extended beyond the surface meaning is the combination of several points of view from which particular topics are treated. A brief discussion of the section on friend-

[13]Sebastian Brant, *Narrenschiff*, ed. Friedrich Zarncke (Leipzig, 1854), p. 1.
[14]*Ibid.*, p. 5.
[15]Kaiser, *Praisers of Folly*, p. 55.

ship may serve as an example. The formal pattern of Stultitia's presentation follows the rules of classical rhetoric; she has a particular preference for the *exemplum* and the *allusio*, devices which reveal important depth perspectives to the well-informed, creative reader. Her discussion of friendship begins with the reference to "some" who call friendship the most desirable of all things, "a more essential element than air, fire, or water."[16] This passage is customarily annotated with a reference to Cicero's *Laelius, a Dialogue on Friendship*; it would appear that Stultitia's views conform to those of an acknowledged authority and should therefore be taken seriously. To be sure, her generalizing remark about the high esteem in which certain philosophers hold friendship is acceptable as a sound evaluation. Yet how reliable is the particular assertion? The *Laelius* does indeed contain a comparable statement. But Laelius does not really say that friendship is "a more essential element than air, fire, or water." The actual formulation is: "itaque non aqua, non igni, ut aiunt, locis pluribus utimur quam amicitia" ("therefore we do not use fire and water, as they say, on more occasions than we use friendship").[17] Stultitia is, it seems, an unreliable speaker and inclined to exaggerate; this is, despite the serious overtones, another sign of her folly.

The *Laelius* is not the only literary source that serves as an extension of Stultitia's discussion of friendship. Allusions also refer to a fable of Phaedrus and an idyll of Theocritus, and for much of her argumentation she relies on Horace. The frequent references to his satires add a parallel perspective to her own derision of human folly. Yet the thoughts and formulations of Horace are not accurately reproduced. With an ironic twist the satiric overtones of the model are perverted into serious notes. Whereas Horace had ridiculed the frailties of man with ironic good humour, Stultitia, the fool, paradoxically castigates them in a moralizing diatribe.

For a long time Erasmus remained a misjudged man, "that great injured man" as Alexander Pope called him. Among the few who understood the man and his work was Wieland. The unequivocal spiritual kinship between the two is strikingly manifest in Wieland's *Fragment über den Charakter des Erasmus von Rotterdam*, a most sensitive and sympathetic portrayal of the humanist. Erasmus, "the king of but," is eloquently, though not impartially, exonerated by the German "prince of however."[18] Wieland's profound understanding

---

[16]Desiderius Erasmus, *The Praise of Folly* [1509] trans. Leonard F. Dean (Chicago, 1946), p. 57.

[17]Cicero, *Laelius*, ed. E. S. Shuckburgh (New York, 1894), p. 13.

[18]Georges Duhamel felt that "le roi du *mais*" would be a most appropriate term to describe Erasmus. See *Deux Patrons* (Paris, 1937), p. 33.

of one who distinguished himself by his ability to observe man and
events from diverse points of view, who acknowledged with tolerance
the validity of different perspectives and preferred to walk the *via
media* attests to the affinity between the Dutch scholar and the
German writer.

During the seventeenth and eighteenth centuries dialogue literature following the classical models increased prodigiously and was
accompanied by influential theoretical tracts. The contributions of
Bernard de Fontenelle, his *Nouveaux dialogues des morts* (1683) and
the *Entretiens sur la pluralité des mondes* (1686), are unquestionably milestones in the development of the genre. The references
to Cicero in the *Entretiens* and the dedication to Lucian at the beginning of the dialogues testify to his connection with a tradition that
was still very much alive, though vigorously debated, particularly
in the quarrel between the ancients and the moderns. The prefatory
remarks of the *Entretiens* express Fontenelle's concern with questions
of method and indicate his awareness of an unusual departure from
tradition. Contrary to common practice in dialogues treating philosophical and scientific theories, he has matched a woman, a somewhat naive, unknowing, and admittedly fictitious *Marquise*, with a
well-informed scholar in a discourse that is meant to instruct an interlocutor who has never conversed about such matters. Implications
and allusions indicate that her experience is limited and her perspective accordingly narrow. Literature has, however, served as an extension of her reality, and the mediated experience may well be of
advantage in her contemplation of philosophical or scientific problems. If, for example, she has delved into the complexities of Madame
de la Fayette's novel *La Princesse de Clèves* she should have no
difficulty comprehending a similarly complex system of philosophy,
provided of course she applies her analytical abilities equally well.

Throughout the dialogue the literary perspective serves as a frame
of reference, and configurations or events of the fictitious world are
compared or, more often, contrasted with the phenomena of empirical
reality: day and night are likened to beautiful heroines of the novel,
one fair and brilliant, the other auburn and charming. The instructive entertainment derived from scientific discourse is contrasted with
the delightful albeit superficial amusement provided by the comedies
of Molière, for example. Nature, *un grand spectacle*, is compared
with an opera, and the observer of the universe is likened to the
spectator in the theater whose perspective is limited by external
factors; from his point of view he can see neither the entire stage nor
the machinery, the moving force behind the mechanical operation,
which is hidden from sight for aesthetic reasons.[19] Toward the end

[19]Bernard le Bovier de Fontenelle, *Entretiens sur la pluralité des mondes* [1686],
ed. Robert Shackleton (Oxford, 1955), pp. 62–63.

of the discourse the *Marquise* realizes that her former eccentric perspective has been corrected, her limited views broadened, and that now she has a true philosophical understanding for "tout le système de l'univers."[20]

The form of the dialogue was to assume an important function in the periodical literature which had its rise at the end of the seventeenth century. An early English collection of dialogue papers was edited by Roger L'Estrange, the translator of Erasmus' *Colloquies.* Its title, *The Observator in Question and Answer* (1681–1687), recalls Lucian's ΕΠΙΣΚΟΠΟΥΝΤΕΣ. L'Estrange presents in his papers political criticism from multiple points of view, occasionally letting the flip of a coin decide which role, Tory or Whig, he will assume in the dialogue. Once a role has been assigned to a speaker, the editor insists that the chosen point of view be presented consistently and faithfully so that the reader is assured of well-balanced and fair argument.

Another early periodical appearing in 1698 significantly carried the title *English Lucian* and published, clearly in imitation of the classical dialogues, "weekly discoveries of the witty intrigues, comical passages, and remarkable transactions in town and country, with reflections on the vices and vanities of the times."[21]

Best known for a consistent point-of-view presentation of the most variegated topics is the periodical literature of the eighteenth century. The English *Spectator*, which began in March 1711 and appeared daily, was widely popular and was read with great interest on the continent. A major concern of its principal authors, Richard Steele and Joseph Addison, was to be diversified, to have various perspectives represented, and to publish instructive and entertaining essays.

The contemporary reader obviously realized that the personality of the writer, his attitude and opinions, his temperament and humor would color his presentation. In recognition of this insight Addison precedes his first essay in *The Spectator* with relevant observations: "I have observed, that a Reader seldom peruses a Book with Pleasure, 'till he knows whether the Writer of it be a black or a fair Man, of a mild or cholerick Disposition, Married or a Batchelor, with other Particulars of the like nature, that conduce very much to the right understanding of an Author."[22] To gratify the curiosity of the reader,

---

[20]*Ibid.*, p. 143. The German editions of Fontenelle's dialogues (1st ed., 1726; 4th ed., 1751) are accompanied by a history and theory of dialogue acquainting the German reader with the development of the genre and its criticism, including contemporary views, edited and translated by J. C. Gottsched.

[21]Walter Graham, *The Beginnings of English Literary Periodicals* (New York, 1926), p. 39.

[22]Joseph Addison, Richard Steele, and others, *The Spectator* [1711–1714], ed. Gregory Smith (London/New York, 1967), No. 1 (1711), I, 3.

the "editor" then describes himself and indicates the possible bias of his own contributions.

The second essay, on the Spectator Club, introduces the six members who according to the original though not fully executed plan were to share the burden of the editor. Each one of these men was to narrate his unique experiences, to report from his subjective point of view, and to give insights into his own segment of social life, thereby expanding the limited perspective of his readers. A favorite method of adding yet other perspectives was the publication of letters to the editor. Most of the correspondence was of course fictitious and invented for the particular purpose of presenting specific matters from subjectively biased points of view.

The first set of letters was included in the eighth issue of *The Spectator*. Like every other number this one was accompanied by a motto from classical literature. Three lines from Virgil's *Aeneid* are quoted:

At Venus obscuro gradientis aere sepsit,
Et multo nebulae circum dea fudit amictu.
Cernere ne quis eos . . .[23]

Thus fragmented and taken out of its original context the motto sets the stage for the topic to be discussed in the following letters. The first correspondent introduces himself as a director of the Society for the Reformation of Manners, a man who is acquainted "with the predominant Vice of every Market-Town in the whole Island." For his particular criticism he has singled out the "Midnight Masque," a society whose purpose, he believes, is the advancement of "Cuckoldom." His vitriolic denouncement of the "lawless Assemblies" is meant to induce *The Spectator* to offer "publick Advice and Admonition" in order to prevent these clandestine meetings.

The second letter was written by "some young Templer," identifying himself as a man "guilty of any Vice or Folly," who has participated in the "Midnight Masque" and is therefore able to present the views of an insider. Not overly concerned with morals, rather with ethics, he feels cheated because he has been deceived by a servant girl who impersonated a noblewoman, and his account is meant to warn other "vain young Coxcombs" who might easily be entrapped by similar deceptions.

---

[23]*The Spectator*; No. 8 (1711), 1, 25–28; trans.: "But Venus shrouded them, as they went, in a mist of darkness, and, with celestial power, shed round them a great mantle of cloud, that none might see them. . . ." *Virgil*, ed. and trans. John Jackson (Oxford, 1908), p. 118. In the original text "them" refers to the ramparts of the city, whereas in the motto the reference remains unclear so that a different meaning could be read into the fragment.

The editor realizes that these essentially different, highly subjective views do not offer a fair evaluation of the "Tuesday Masquerade," and he suspends his judgment until he has had an opportunity to visit the next masquerade and form his own, presumably more objective, opinion. His views, however, are not presented. A third perspective is added instead, for in another letter to the editor the "Undertaker of the Masquerade" (the notorious Swiss Count Heidegger) is permitted to report his observations.[24] He is fully aware of the criticism leveled against the enterprise and is eager to explain apparent inadequacies. It is his opinion that not everyone is suited for this sort of diversion but that the participation in the masquerade presupposes either an excellent acting ability or a distinct affinity with the chosen role. Yet experience has disclosed that quite a few participants want sound judgment in the selection of their role or lack the necessary adaptability to perform convincingly: "People dress themselves in what they have a Mind to be, and not what they are fit for." Their insensitivity to decorum causes deplorable discrepancies. At the last masque, for example, a nymph conversed with a "Crook," and both spoke in vulgar language; a judge danced a minuet with a Quaker; a philosopher was speechless; a Turk drank two bottles of wine and a Jew ate "half a Ham of Bacon." Such inconsistencies could be avoided if the participants would study their roles with greater care and strive for empathy with their chosen alter egos. A young girl, for instance, who assumes the character of a shepherdess could benefit from reading the *Arcadia* or "some other good Romance" before she appears at the masque. The observation of these simple requisites should lend elegance and grace to the masque and make it more acceptable to the town.[25]

This pattern of multiple perspectives, often extended beyond the frame of one particular work, is characteristic of many a later periodical. A quotation, usually from classical literature, accurate, fragmented, or perverted; artless reporting, relatively objective and trustworthy; and personal letters containing highly subjective and often unreliable views are frequently combined so that the reader becomes acquainted with many aspects of affairs then standing at the center of interest.

Among the diversified essays of *The Spectator* there were, of course, some that treated purely literary matters. One work of con-

[24]*The Spectator*; No. 14 (1711), I, 44–45.
[25]The masque was also satirized by Hogarth in his engravings "Masquerades and Operas," in the "Taste of the Town," and in the "Large Masquerade Ticket." Fielding attacks this type of entertainment in his *Masquerade* of 1728, and Pope alludes to Heidegger, the "strange bird from Switzerland," in *The Dunciad*.

siderable lasting importance was several times either briefly mentioned or extensively treated. It is Alexander Pope's *An Essay on Criticism*. The presentation in poetic form of his own ideas, as well as the reiteration of classical thought on criticism, also attracted many German readers of a later period, among them young Wieland. Pope was not primarily concerned with questions of point of view and perspective, yet his essay does not lack incidental allusions to related principles and particular aspects of the complex phenomenon. Although no skeptic but an advocate of normative values, he nevertheless realized that individual critics will deviate from the ideal norm and evaluate literature from a slightly biased point of view; and yet they are often firmly convinced of the correctness of their judgment:

> 'Tis with our *Judgments* as our *Watches*, none
> Go just *alike*, yet each believes his own.[26]
> (9–10)

A conscientious critic, one was soon to realize, will not judge an author by standards formulated for another literature, but will assume the historical point of view by projecting himself into the writer's period and circumstances. Although Pope himself did not yet formulate such strict principles, he expected the critic to adopt a sympathetic attitude and presumed that he would at least try to recapture the spirit of his author and evaluate the work with a measurable degree of empathy:

> A perfect Judge will *read* each Work of Wit
> With the same Spirit that its author *writ*.
> (233–234)

A fair critic will also consider the intentions of the author; he will not prescribe designs alien to the aim of the writer and then unjustly condemn individual aspects of the entire work because it does not achieve the purpose erroneously established by the critic:

> In ev'ry Work regard the *Writer's End*,
> Since none can compass more than they *Intend*;
> (255–256)

The *Essay on Criticism* is especially rich in comparisons that illustrate and illuminate Pope's precepts and theories. A central section, the famous Alpine simile, is a vivid metaphorical representation of man's endeavor to broaden the perspective of his knowledge and widen the

---

[26]*The Poems of Alexander Pope*, Vol. I, ed. E. Audra and Aubrey Williams (London and New Haven, 1961); the references in parentheses here and those that follow indicate the lines of the *Essay on Criticism*.

panorama of his intellectual vistas through the frequent shifting of his point of view:

Fir'd at first Sight with what the *Muse* imparts,
In *fearless Youth* we tempt the Heights of Arts,
While from the bounded *Level* of our Mind,
Short Views we take, nor see the *Lengths behind*,
But *more advanc'd*, behold with strange Surprize
New, distant Scenes of *endless* Science rise!
So pleas'd at first, the towring *Alps* we try,
Mount o'er the Vales, and seem to tread the Sky;
Th'Eternal Snows appear already past,
And the first *Clouds* and *Mountains* seem the last:
But *those attain'd*, we tremble to survey
The growing Labours of the lengthen'd Way,
Th'*increasing* Prospect *tires* our wandring Eyes,
Hills peep o'er Hills, and *Alps* on *Alps* arise!
(219-232)

During the early years of his life the mental outlook of a youth is severely limited, but the persistent attempts of the maturing man to rise above the lowlands gradually expand his perspectives and help him survey hitherto unknown territories. Yet the realization that the elevated position he has attained after an unremitting struggle only exposes larger areas to be conquered is rather frightening and leads to the awareness that the ultimate peak of achievement may well remain beyond the reach of even the most ambitious and able ascender.

Throughout the essay Pope guides the reader's imagination by activating his sense of sight through the extensive use of visual imagery and recurring allusions to color and light. To be sure, these images and poetically depicted scenes in external nature are not presented for their own sake but as an embodiment of his critical doctrines. The combination of useful didacticity with decorative imagery, essentially the blending of the Horatian *utile* and *dulce*, was particularly attractive to the German readers of Pope. It is certainly no mere coincidence that the German translation of *An Essay on Criticism*, the *Versuch über die Critik* (1745) by Gottfried Ephraim Müller, is accompanied by the translator's epistle "Abschilderung einer schönen Gegend" and his "Ode über eine schöne Aussicht," in which instruction and adornment are similarly intermingled.

In the same year *An Essay on Criticism* appeared, an older contemporary of Pope, Anthony Ashley Cooper, third Earl of Shaftesbury, published his major work, *Characteristicks of Men, Manners, Opinions, Times*. From a very early period Wieland was attracted to Shaftesbury for obvious reasons. Kindred in spirit

(Goethe thought of them as *Zwillingsbrüder*), both were profoundly influenced by the ancients, sharing to the full many of the antipathies and upholding many of the same ideals. More influential than Shaftesbury's philosophical ideas, many of which were reiterations of traditional principles, were his exemplary techniques and the theoretical remarks on dialogue and soliloquy contained in the *Characteristicks*.

In a central comparison of classical and modern dialogue literature Shaftesbury approved of the manner in which the ancients treated the very gravest subjects: "Their Treatises were generally in a free and familiar Style. They chose to give us the Representation of real Discourses and Converse, by treating their Subjects in the way of *Dialogue* and free Debate."[27] Shaftesbury later observes that the method was frequently imitated by his own contemporaries but that their adaptations often seemed deplorably poor. Although they assigned different roles to every one of the speakers they did not really offer multiple well-balanced points of view: " 'Tis by their Names only that these *Characters* are figur'd. Tho they bear different Titles, and are set up to maintain contrary Points; they are found, at the bottom, to be all of the same side." Quite obviously their views echo those of their creator: "notwithstanding their seeming Variance [they] cooperate in the most officious manner with the Author, towards the display of his own proper Wit, and the establishment of his private Opinion and Maxims. They are indeed his very legitimate and obsequious *Puppets*." An author who presents his subject in the form of a dialogue must delineate his characters carefully and "naturally." If, for example, the antagonist of the dialogue is a Skeptic (Shaftesbury may well have thought of Cicero's method), he should be furnished with sound arguments, "shreud a Turn of *Wit* or *Humour*," and be allowed to demonstrate his "full Reason, his Ingenuity, Sense and Art." Only the superior literary artist is able to create a chief character who will prove a match for an admirable protagonist; only the writer who masters such delicately balanced portrayals may dare to forego the advantages of descriptions and reflections and employ the more direct method of dialogue.

A related topic particularly attractive to Wieland was Shaftesbury's theory of the soliloquy. The essential thought is prefigured in Plato's *Theaetetus*. According to Socrates thinking and contemplation may well develop into an inner dialogue, a "conversation which the soul holds with herself in considering of anything." The soul "when thinking" appears "to be just talking—asking questions of her-

[27]Anthony Ashley Cooper, Earl of Shaftesbury, *Characteristicks of Men, Manners, Opinions, Times*, 4th ed. (n. p., 1727); Vols. I-III; see particularly II, 73; III, 292-295.

self and answering them, affirming and denying."[28] Such a "dialogue" often finds its expression in a soliloquy, frequently employed by the dramatists to reveal the innermost thoughts of their protagonists. Shaftesbury presents a sensitive treatment of the technique in the first part of his *Advice to an Author* and sees revealing connections between soliloquy and counseling. Giving advice, that is dictating rules, teaching manners, and prescribing "good sense," is a painful operation that should only be performed by a skilled surgeon possessing the essential requisites, tenderness of hand, feeling, and compassion. But even under the best of conditions few will voluntarily submit to the treatment by a stranger. It is therefore fortunate *"that we have each of us* OUR SELVES *to practise on."* This simple solution, Shaftesbury feels, will meet with objections: "For who can thus multiply himself into *two Persons,* and be *his own Subject?"*[29] The answer has been given by poets who present excellent examples of this process of "Self-dissection" in their dramas. A person alone upon the stage takes himself to task without sparing himself in the least. "By virtue of this SOLILOQUY he becomes two distinct *Persons.* He is Pupil and Preceptor. He teaches, and he learns." Shaftesbury knew that the technique of soliloquy had been attacked by contemporary critics as an unnatural device, and he felt compelled to defend the poetic use of the soliloquy: "For whether the Practice be *natural* or no, in respect of common Custom and Usage; I take upon me to assert, that it is an honest and laudable Practice; and that if already it be not natural to us, we ought however to make it so, by Study and Application."[30]

These thoughts on dialogue and monologue provided imaginative stimuli for Wieland, who became aware of the extensive ramifications of theory and method for the artistic portrayal of man in literature, and the soliloquies of fictive figures in his novels were to add one more revealing perspective of their personalities which are observed from so many different points of view.[31]

Wieland paid tribute to Shaftesbury many times and considered his writings "allezeit ein Muster feiner Composition." One of his own works, the dialogue *Timoklea,* was intended to disseminate "die Lehren des Shaftesbury über diese Art von Werken des Geistes unter den Deutschen."[32] In a review published in his periodical *Der Neue Teutsche Merkur,* Shaftesbury's *Moralist* was favorably compared

---

[28]Plato, *Dialogues,* ed. and trans. B. Jowett (New York, 1892), IV, 252.
[29]Shaftesbury, *Characteristicks,* I, 157.
[30]*Ibid.,* I, 158.
[31]See Marga Barthel, *Das "Gespräch" bei Wieland,* Frankfurter Quellen und Forschungen, No. 26 (Frankfurt, 1939).
[32]*Werke* (Akademieausgabe), II, 277.

with Galianis' *Dialogues sur le commerce des blés*,[33] and during a conversation with Goethe, Wieland contrasted the dialogues of Plato, Lucian, and Shaftesbury to the advantage of the last. Plato's dialogues, he felt, suffered from an unfair bias toward one group of interlocutors: he often had the Sophists answer "als dumme Jungen." Lucian greatly improved the literary form, but even more perfect are the dialogues of Shaftesbury, because "in seinem *Philosopher* [ist] es jedem der Colloquirenden v o l l e r Ernst."[34] This evaluation clearly reveals Wieland's preference for fairly balanced dialogues in which dual or even multiple points of view are intelligently presented and the resulting perspectives are almost equally valid.

Many a European novelist of the eighteenth century shared in the contemporary concern with viewpoint and perspective in literature. The omniscient narrator of the seventeenth century Romance is gradually replaced by a more personal, often ironic or even fictive third-person narrator who betrays a subjective point of view and frankly, or inadvertently, admits the limits of his insights. The range of the first-person narrator, the hero or anti-hero who allegedly relates his own experiences without the intervention of a fictitious commentator or editor, is even more limited. In fact, the constant necessity to circumscribe his perspective, to present his prejudices and perhaps manifest his unreliability may well account for an author's decision to select this type of narrator for the story he wants to have told. A form that was superbly suited for the artistic manipulation of narrative perspective was the epistolary novel, and Montesquieu's *Lettres persanes* (1721) was an important landmark in the development of this genre. In addition to the two principal writers, Rica, the younger traveler, and Usbek, the older and more experienced man, seventeen other correspondents participate in the depiction of European and Oriental societies, their members and their customs. Dialogues, reports, fables, and tales are interpolated, and countless literary allusions are interjoined to produce a broad spectrum of perspectives. Most revealing are the Parisian reports of Rica and Usbek, for they demonstrate the adaptability of men who enter a society as outsiders and gradually adjust their point of view until it coincides almost exactly with that of the insiders.

The pattern, perfected by Richardson in England, Rousseau in France, and Wieland in Germany, became the model for countless epistolary novels. In every one of these works the events are narrated by various distinctly different personalities whose background, edu-

[33]*Der Neue Teutsche Merkur* (Weimar, 1800), No. 12, p. 245.
[34]*Literarische Zustände und Zeitgenossen. In Schilderungen aus Karl Aug. Böttiger's handschriftlichem Nachlasse*, ed. K. W. Böttiger (Leipzig, 1838), i, 239.

cation, experience, moral fibre, and mood color the presentation of episodes and influence the evaluation of other characters. Thus the reader is confronted with a variety of perspectives and is induced to look at events and figures from points of view approximating those of the correspondents. He will do well to assume a critical attitude and attempt to penetrate the veil of subjectivity that envelops each individual narrative.

3 | German Echoes and Innovations

Even a casual perusal of eighteenth-century German writings, with particular though not exclusive attention given to works certainly known to Wieland, reveals the conspicuous concern with point of view in literature and criticism. Like their English counterparts, German periodicals reflect a lively interest in these matters and demonstrate a distinct preference for the perspective method in their presentation of man and events, themes and ideas. One of the very first, the *Monatliche Unterredungen*, edited by Wilhelm Ernst Tentzel and published from 1689 to 1698, thus a predecessor of *The Tatler* and *The Spectator*, made extensive use of the dialogue and exploited its advantages with considerable skill: individual speakers, whose personality traits are carefully delineated, present and defend their distinctly biased, sometimes even eccentric opinions, and illuminate an unusual perspective of a given topic from their subjective point of view. The relatively neutral presentation of different or even contrasting views without any clarifying, approbatory, or admonitory remarks by the author occasionally puzzled contemporary readers and otherwise discerning critics simply because they were used to relying on mediators either explicating diverging views or taking a firm position in the defense of a specific stance. Since the perspective method was at times misunderstood, Tentzel found it necessary to remind his readers of the motto *"Sine Censura & approbatione Auctoris"* that accompanied every one of the monthly issues. He had hoped to make it abundantly clear that the opinions of others were offered, "daß gleichwie die darinnen abgehandelte Geschichte und gegebenen *Censuren* nicht so wol nach meinem eigenen / als anderer

Leute Gutachten und Zuneigung eingerichtet / also auch darnach geurtheilet und verstanden werden müsten."[1] Consequently, at least two sides of an argument are presented in juxtaposition. Since such clearly conflicting opinions cannot possibly represent the views of one man, an astute critic should recognize the dialectic of the interlocution and should have no difficulty deciding which of these contrasting opinions, if any, might possibly be shared by the author of the dialogues.

Although Christian Thomasius had employed the perspective method in his earlier *Monatsgespräche* (1688–1689), he published in 1711 an unsparing critique of Tentzel's *Unterredungen*, which he considered an inferior imitation of his innovational periodical, and he rebuked Tentzel for his persistent, allegedly unfair attacks on matters and theories presented in the *Monatsgespräche*. More specifically, however, he criticized the dialogical technique, a *Schreib=Art* which he himself, guided by the Horatian dictum *"ridetur, chordâ qui semper oberat eâdem,"*[2] had soon, and he believed wisely, abandoned. Yet his most vigorous attack was directed against the apparently neutral attitude of the editor. Tentzel, he felt, should have committed himself more deliberately, selecting one specific character to be his spokesman, or perhaps another to present distinctly negative views in such an unambiguous manner that no one could possibly mistake them for the editor's opinions.[3] Thomasius' condemnation of the substance of the dialogues was bound to be undermined by Tentzel's presentation of multiple points of view; it was, to be sure, rather ludicrous to assault fictitious figures for defending opinions that admittedly were at least in part untenable.

During the early part of the eighteenth century the traditions of dialogue and of the moral weekly were carried on in Germany with significant variations that led to uniquely artistic developments in later periods. One of the most widely circulating collections, David Fassmann's *Gespräche im Reiche derer Todten* (1718–1739), echoes Lucian's *Dialogues of the Dead* and reveals the stimulating effects of

[1]Wilhelm Ernst Tentzel, *Monatliche Unterredungen Einiger Guten Freunde* (January 1690), p. 5.

[2]A separate publication by Thomasius, *Weitere Erleuterung durch unterschiedene Exempel des ohnlängst gethanen Vorschlags wegen der neuen Wissenschafft / Anderer Menschen Gemüther erkennen zu lernen . . .*, 4th ed. (Halle, 1711), contains two lengthy chapters concerned with Tentzel: Chapter 1, "Von des Herrn *Tenzelii* vielfältigen Zunöthigungen zu dem *Autore*" (pp. 1–82); and Chapter 2, "Von den vielfältigen Schnitzern womit Herr *M.* Tentzel seine Monate angehäuffet" (pp. 83–281); see specifically p. 3.

[3]The first paragraph of the second chapter constitutes Thomasius' theory of literary dialogue; the second paragraph contains his criticism of Tentzel's method; see specifically p. 87.

Fontenelle's *Nouveaux dialogues des morts* (1683) as well as Fénelon's *Dialogues des morts* (1712).

Whereas Fassmann presents primarily well-known figures of the past in serious conversation, most of the moral weeklies portray fictitious characters conversing about contemporary matters and often satirizing the foibles of society. Many an editor indicated in the title of his periodical that the views of a particular personality, perhaps a dreamer, a bride, a pilgrim, or a hermit, were presented. Invariably, these figures offered a relatively narrow perspective. Complementary letters to the editor often challenged the intentionally biased presentation and defended opposite, yet at times equally controvertible, views.

The perspective pattern prefigured in the English *Spectator* was selected as the model for the *Discourse der Mahlern* (1721-1722). The first discourse outlined the plan to have a variety of contributors participate. Individual authors would submit their essays to the society of painters who in weekly editorial meetings were to examine and evaluate the manuscripts: "man discourirt, man critisirt darüber pro und contra" so that the final decision to publish an article would reflect the conscientious consideration of every manuscript from diverse, sometimes even contrasting points of view.[4] This was meant to insure the excellent quality of a periodical that did not address itself to the "gröste Hauffen" but to discerning readers. The intended arrangement remained a fiction, however, for with one exception Bodmer and Breitinger were the sole contributors and the only authors of the first twenty-four discourses.

Fictitious characters relating their experiences often expressed their awareness of the tradition in which they stood. They proudly adhered to beneficial aspects but departed critically from the negative features of their models. *Die Deutsche Zuschauerin* (1747), for example, one of Justus Möser's periodicals, contains generally valid remarks on tradition and innovation. The reporting female figure alludes to Addison's *Spectator* and discusses the relative advantage of her different circumstances, for as a woman she is able to relate experiences normally not accessible to men. In contrast to Addison's figures, who report from a coffee-house, Drury Lane, or Grub Street, her post of observation—the house of Lady Wilkins—is more strictly fixed, yet her understanding of human nature is not unduly limited by these external factors. Observing every visitor closely, she hopes to gain more profound insights than those she could impart were she to alter her vantage point frequently. Occasionally,

---

[4]*Die Discourse der Mahlern 1721-1722*, ed. Theodor Vetter (Frauenfeld, 1891), p. 8.

however, she will change her post of observation. Like Lucian's *Weltbeschauer*, she will by some kind of magic ascend to greater heights and observe the world from above. Like Charon and Hermes she may well find herself too far removed from empirical reality and have to rely on imagination and memory to supplement the distant vistas. Philosophical reflections and mental observations are meant to add complementary views, a *moralische Perspektive*, as she calls it, which she will gladly share with her readers.[5]

In a later essay entitled "Von dem moralischen Gesichtspunkte" Möser discusses in a significant context the question of point of view and perspective. Following the example of scientific analysis in which minute particles are enlarged and viewed in isolation with the aid of a microscope, writers have sometimes emphasized negative human peculiarities too exclusively and have created a distorted image of man through unfair generalizations. Human beings, Möser maintains in accordance with the contemporary defenders of the mixed character, are neither divinely perfect beings nor completely evil creatures. Just as the color grey is a composite of black and white, so is man a mixture of good and evil; the magnification of a small detail—perhaps the lamp-black in the grey—and the evaluation of the microscopic section as being representative of the whole are entirely misleading. Only an appropriately distant point of view affording a complete image is suitable for a fair appraisal of the object (or man) and the appreciation of its complex beauty: "Es hat also jede Sache ihren Gesichtspunkt, worin sie allein schön ist; und sobald Sie diesen verändern . . . : so verfliegt mit dem veränderten Gesichtspunkt die vorige Schönheit."[6]

German poetry of the period also reveals a marked effect of the contemporary concern with relevant questions and contributes further informative insights into the phenomena. The poems of Barthold Heinrich Brockes, one of Wieland's favorite poets, probably intensified the young man's interest in these matters. In his collection *Irdisches Vergnügen in Gott* (1721-1748), Brockes celebrates the gifts of God to man; one of the poems is dedicated to the sense of vision, and in several others the principles of viewpoint and perspective are predominant structuring devices. The poem "Das Grosse und das Kleine," for example, depicts a meditating young man standing at early dawn on a high hill surveying from this superior point of view the still shadowy landscape beneath and the luminous sky above. As the sun slowly rises, distinct forms are accentuated, and the

---

[5] Justus Möser, *Sämtliche Werke*, I, ed. Werner Kohlschmidt (Oldenburg, 1944), 297.

[6] *Ibid.*, IV, ed. Ludwig Schirmeyer and Werner Kohlschmidt (Oldenburg, 1943), 97.

beauty of nature immediately surrounding him becomes visible. Deeply touched by the dazzling splendor, the observer abandons the broad perspective and concentrates on a limited area nearer his eyes. He suddenly notices a tiny creature moving at his feet and decides to watch it more closely. He therefore sits down, thus changing his point of view, and uses a magnifying glass in order to adjust his perspective. Observing the seemingly insignificant creature he is impressed by its complex structure and by its obvious similarities to more sublime beings. The final section of the poem must of course be read symbolically; it is a noble tribute to God and an enthusiastic encomium to his creation.[7]

A second poem, "Die Allee," demonstrates even more clearly the poetic application of perspective principles. The poet himself is the spectator who relates exciting visual experiences and speaks of fascinating spatial observations:

> Wenn man bey'm Garten=Teich der, voll von schnellen Fischen,
> Und rings umher umpflanzt mit Taxus=Bäum= und Büschen,
> Sich im geraden Viereck zeiget:
> Die breite Stieg' hinunter steiget;
> Erblickt man einen grünen Gang,
> Deß Seiten Linien so lang,
> Daß die darob fast müden Augen
> Gespitzt mit Müh' ihr Ziel zu finden taugen.
> Des grünen Kerkers holde Länge
> Treibt den gefang'nen Blick in eine schöne Enge;
> Er hofft, voll süsser Furcht, daß gar kein Ende sey,
> Und wird, wie matt er gleich, dennoch mit Unmuth frey.
> In diesem angenemen Steige
> Gehorcheten nicht nur
> Die schlanken Bäume, Stämm' und Zweige,
> Nein, gar die Blätter selbst der gleich=gezog'nen Schnur . . .[8]

The opening lines of the poem show the speaker in motion through space. Leaving behind him the geometrical pattern of a square garden pond with its well-defined boundaries, he descends to a lower plateau and is confronted by a most natural exemplification of a basic phenomenon in perspective, the apparent diminution in width of a straight road as it approaches the vanishing point. On either side the poet's view is blocked by full-branched trees and dense foliage. Now and then a ray of sunlight penetrates the wall of greens and offers a glimpse of life beyond the range of his sight. While he is standing near the steps, his children cross the road in the distance, and looking

[7]Barthold Heinrich Brockes, *Irdisches Vergnügen in Gott*, 2nd ed. (Hamburg, 1724), pp. 133 ff.
[8]*Ibid.*, p. 218.

through the grove it seems as if they came from nowhere and disappear like shadows in the dark. The phenomenon so vividly confronting him causes the poet to meditate and reflect; it is, he concludes, truly symbolic of man's life on earth which so often is characterized by chance encounters and fleeting images, by limited perspectives and the inability of the observer to see or judge from his point of view whatever lies beyond the boundaries of his vision.

Albrecht von Haller, a younger contemporary of Brockes, whom Wieland also greatly admired, uses comparable techniques in one of his best known poems, *Die Alpen* (1729). In a central section he describes, allegedly in authentic imitation of reality, the main events and popular games at an Alpine festival:

> Hier ringt ein kühnes Paar / vermählt den Ernst dem Spiele /
> Umwindet Leib um Leib / und schlinget Hufft um Hufft.
> Dort fliegt ein schwerer Stein nach dem gestekten Ziele
> Von starker Hand beseelt durch die zertrennte Lufft;
> Den aber führt die Lust was edlers zu beginnen
> Zu einer muntern Schaar von jungen Schäfferinnen.
>
>   *   *
>   *   *   *   *
>
> Dort fliegt ein schnelles Bley in das entfernte Weisse /
> Das blizt und Lufft und Ziel im gleichen nu durchbohrt;
> Hier rollt ein runder Ball in dem bestimmten Gleisse /
> Nach dem erwählten Zwek mit langen Säzen fort:
> Dort tanzt ein bunter Ring mit umgeschlungnen Händen /
> In dem zertretnen Gras bey einer Dorff=Schallmey.[9]

The speaker seems to stand close to the villagers assembled under the oak trees, and yet he is outside the circle. From this point of view he successively observes small groups of players, and a repeated change in perspective, verbally indicated by the frequent shift from *hier* to *dort*, enables him to present contrasting views of their activities. Occasionally his glance moves beyond the circle; his eyes follow an object projected into space, obliterating for a fleeting moment the activities in the village square.

The more general significance of perspective and point of view in literature becomes apparent in Haller's critical writings. In one of the most searching contemporary reviews of the English novel *Clarissa,* he specifically indicates the advantages of narration from multiple points of view. The events in Richardson's earlier epistolary novel *Pamela* are too frequently presented by the heroine herself. In

[9]Albrecht von Haller, *Versuch von Schweizerischen Gedichten,* 2nd ed. (Bern, 1734), pp. 5–6.

Clarissa, however, different voices are heard more often, and each account is convincingly colored by the personality of the individual correspondents. The resulting variety in descriptions, reflections, language, and style is, the critic feels, artistically a considerable improvement over the monotonous presentation of Pamela's story.[10]

Haller himself is the subject of an eighteenth-century biography in which the principle of point of view is almost consistently applied and the term *"Gesichtspunkt"* frequently reiterated. The author, Johann Georg Zimmermann, was a close friend of Wieland, and one may assume that his work acquainted the young writer with effective techniques which, slightly modified, were to prove very useful in the artistic portrayal of man in fiction. Zimmermann's dedication and preface indicate the author's intention and method. With conventional modesty he speaks of his mediocre abilities and of the accordingly limited perspective of his portrayal: "Die engen Schranken meines Geistes erlauben mir nicht über den Rang eines Geschichtschreibers mich zu erheben." In his attempts to become well acquainted with the character and personality of Haller, he has observed his teacher in diverse situations and from multiple points of view: ". . . ich wollte den Wehrt meines Lehrers von mehreren Seiten einsehen."[11]

The first part of the biography relates the major events of Haller's life in chronological order. The structure of the second part, however, is determined by the frequent shifting of viewpoint. Zimmermann finds it necessary to announce the changes in perspectives and explain the reasons for the modification of his approach. Following the example of Plutarch as well as the "rules of reason," he will derive "seinen Character aus den ächten Quellen . . . und denselben in den vornehmsten Gesichts=Puncten darstellen, die die Züge des Ganzen auf das allergenaueste entdecken."[12] In swift succession Zimmermann then enacts the roles of different expert observers. As physician and psychologist he describes Haller's physical condition and state of mind; as physiognomist he delineates and interprets his features; as a critic of the arts he evaluates the portraits of the Swiss scientist; and as a man of letters he offers sensitive critiques of his poetry and his writings. At the conclusion of his portrayal he writes: "Am allerangenehmsten ist mir der letzte Gesichtspunct, in dem ich

---

[10]Albrecht von Haller, "Beurtheilung der berühmten Geschichte der Clarissa," in *Sammlung kleiner Hallerischer Schriften*, 2nd ed. (Bern, 1772), I, 293–315; the essay was previously published in English in *The Gentleman's Magazine*, XIX (London, 1749), 245–246, and 345–349. For a more comprehensive treatment of Haller's literary criticism see Karl S. Guthke, *Haller und die Literatur* (Göttingen, 1962).

[11]Johann Georg Zimmermann, *Das Leben des Herrn von Haller* (Zurich, 1755), dedication and preface, unpaginated.

[12]*Ibid.*, pp. 361–362.

den Herrn Haller betrachten werde." He admits that his emotional involvement will color the presentation, but he feels that his subjectivity is justifiable: ". . . wer kan meinem Herzen seine Empfindungen hemmen, wer soll mich hindern, meinem grossen Lehrer sein Recht widerfahren zu lassen."[13] The pupil then presents an image of his teacher that does indeed betray his admiration.

The poetry of Brockes and Haller was treated in a significant context by Johann Jacob Breitinger, the Swiss critic with whom Wieland had personal contact for many years while he was living in Zurich. Breitinger praises the *Irdisches Vergnügen in Gott* and *Die Alpen* in a section of his *Critische Dichtkunst* that is essentially an eloquent defense of the point-of-view technique in art and literature.[14] All things, he maintains, have at least two sides, a beautiful one and an ugly one. The true artist, if it is his intention, will be able to minimize negative aspects and emphasize positive characteristics without detriment to the truth of his portrayal. To accomplish this the poet might learn from the three ancient artists who faced the task of painting Antigonus, the one-eyed king of Macedonia. The first painter portrayed him in a naturalistic manner with only one eye; he violated, of course, the rules of decorum. The second artist painted an idealized image of the king showing him with both eyes; he violated the demand for truth in art. But the third and most clever artist, Apelles of Greece, created a portrait every one admired; he painted the king in profile, showing only the healthy side of his face. This "fable" is intended by Breitinger as an instructive lesson not only for painters but also for poets. It demonstrates that the portrayal of disfiguring features can be avoided without the distortion of truth, by presenting the model from the most advantageous point of view.

The artistic depiction of man, a topic widely and intensely discussed at this time, was of considerable importance also to the Swiss critics, who in their theoretical writings analyze diverse techniques for the successful portrayal of individual figures and for the convincing representation of society in literature. One specific method, the indirect yet effective depiction of contemporary man, particularly his foibles and iniquities, in the animal fable is treated in Bodmer's *Critische Briefe* of 1746 and earlier in Breitinger's *Critische Dichtkunst* of 1742. The classic models, Aesop's fables, particularly the versions of Babrius and Phaedrus, their later adaptations and translations, and the seventeenth-century collections of La Motte and La Fontaine were well received among German writers. In fact, the genre experienced an amazing popularity in the earlier decades of the

---

[13]*Ibid.*, p. 413.

[14]Johann Jacob Breitinger, *Critische Dichtkunst* (Zurich, 1740), I, 379–380.

eighteenth century when countless fables were published in periodicals, numerous collections appeared in book form, and influential
theories were formulated. Together with the allegorical quality of the
fable the pattern of parallelism and the interrelation of perspectives
were frequently examined. Considerations of point of view were,
however, of greater importance to the Swiss than, for example, to
Gottsched in his more limited, predominantly historical treatment of
the genre contained in the *Versuch einer Critischen Dichtkunst.* As an
allegory the fable should ideally present "parallele Sitten," customs
that are evidently analogous to the practices of men.[15] In the best examples the animals will act according to their very own natures, save
that they have speech. Yet at the same time they are symbolic of men,
and the depiction of their attitudes must be understood as a delinea-
tion of typically human bias and behavior. The transposition of the
fable's moral meaning onto this second level of reference establishes
the parallel perspective for which the paraenesis of the tale is intended. The implied or expressed thesis can be understood as generally valid, yet a sensitive interpreter will devise a third, an interior
perspective; he will "gleichsam *per Reflexionem* einen Blick in
[seinen] eigenen Busen . . . thun" and extract a personal message
from the fable which may stimulate a desire to improve his morals
and perfect his character.[16]

Most fables reflect the human point of view, for attitudes and
events are observed and explicated by the poet-narrator. Yet this is
not the only possible method; a clever fabulist, Bodmer reports,
invented a unique kind of tale in which the vantage point is reversed.
In his stories animals tell fables to each other, not about themselves
but about human beings. These fables have a double function, one of
which is, of course, fictional: the allegorical tales convey a lesson to
the animals listening to stories about human folly; but they also offer
moral instruction for the reader of the fable. The *Critische Briefe*
contain three fables that are designed to exemplify Bodmer's theory,
and they do so rather successfully. The departure from the pattern of
the conventional fable is, however, not equivalent to a complete break
with tradition. Consequently, the new kind of fable has a double
structure, a frame and an inserted tale; the fabulist is the principal
narrator, and the dialogue of the animals containing the central story
is interpolated.

There are still other possibilities for the experimentation with point
of view in the fable. There is, for example, a third type in which an

---

[15]Johann Jacob Bodmer and Johann Jacob Breitinger, *Critische Briefe* (Zurich,
1746), p. 166; letters 9, 10, and 11 (pp. 146-198), treat the fable.
[16]Breitinger, *Critische Dichtkunst*, I, 179; the entire seventh section of the first
volume treats the fable; see pp. 164-262.

animal acts as the fabulist and the tale is told without any outside intervention. This kind of fable was introduced by Wilhelm Ehrenfried Neugebauer in his collection *Die Fabeln des Fuchses* (1761).[17] In ironic dissimulation the author pretends to be merely the editor of the work. Significantly, it is not the preface but the first fable that announces the method of narration and establishes the identity of the speaker so that the placement of this information underscores the fictionality of the unusual arrangement. The alleged narrator is Reynard the fox. In a conversation with the fabulist he criticizes the blatant lack of verisimilitude in most fables, whose authors portray not animals but simply exchange names, Phylax for Harpax, or Fox for Tartuffe, and do not accomplish a very convincing depiction of animal life. If stories of animals have to be told, they should be related by a member of their own society whose views are much more reliable than the observations of a poorly informed outsider. The fabulist readily agrees with Reynard's argument; the fox is permitted to tell his tales, and he does so in a sustained presentation of his personal perspective. Although the actions and attitudes of his characters are evaluated from his subjective point of view, his critical interpretation of their behavior has universal validity; to be sure, he does not state the epimythion commonly expressed in the conventional fable, but he does indeed "cunningly" imply a moral lesson that is directed at human society.

The most widely read among the German fabulists were Friedrich von Hagedorn, whose *Versuch in poetischen Fabeln und Erzehlungen* appeared in 1738, and Christian Fürchtegott Gellert, who published his *Fabeln und Erzählungen* in 1746. Their works share many characteristics, yet the poetry of Hagedorn is particularly rich in artistic devices that permit the skilful manipulation of perspectives. In his *Erzählungen* he often employed the method of adaptation and presented new arrangements of poetic artifacts borrowed from classical or modern literature. Although creative imitation of exemplary models was a venerable custom, it seemed nevertheless intermittently necessary to explain, indeed even to defend the principles underlying the practice. Hagedorn does so in a *Schreiben an einen Freund* that was published as part of the *Poetische Werke*.[18] The epistle is a justification of the seemingly excessive annotation that accompanies his text, but the admission of having used the property of other writers, implied in overt references to his sources, causes

---

[17]The fables are reprinted as a supplement to Neugebauer's novel *Der teutsche Don Quichotte* (1753), ed. Lieselotte E. Kurth and Harold Jantz (Berlin, 1972), pp. 251–318.

[18]The letter is dated 1752; cf. Friedrich von Hagedorn, *Poetische Werke*, 1st part (Hamburg, 1769), pp. xvii–xl.

Hagedorn to discuss the convention of poetic imitation and compare it with independent originality.[19]

There are, he realizes, critics who see no difference between unimaginative copying and the creative use of sources. They would even consider Alexander Pope a mere imitator, for when he stated in the *Essay on Criticism*

> Fear not the anger of the wise to raise:
> Those best can bear reproof who merit praise,

he simply "copied" Plinius who long ago had expressed the same thought in a comparable formulation: "Nulli patientius reprehenduntur, quam qui maxime laudari merentur." Common imitation, *gewöhnliche Nachahmung*, is of course not a characteristic of Pope's poetry: "Keiner ist reicher an eigenen, neuen Gedanken, glücklicher im Ausdrucke, edler in Gesinnungen. So gar seine Nachahmungen aus dem Horaz sind meisterhafte, freye Originale. Er ist ein Muster der besten Nacheiferung." Excellent emulation then is a perfectly honorable, indeed a recommendable practice. Pope himself had a fitting answer for those among the critics who negated the principle of creative imitation and insisted on absolute originality; in his "Observations on Homer" he wrote: "It is generally the fate of such people, who will never say what was said before, to say what will never be said after them," a dictum which Hagedorn elevated to a basic truth that deserved to be translated into German:

> Wer nimmer sagen will, was man zuvor gesagt,
> Der wagt, dieß ist sein Loos, was niemand nach ihm wagt.

An excellent example of creative emulation, artistic adaptation, and the application of the combinatory principle is Hagedorn's verse narrative *Adelheid und Henrich, oder die neue Eva und der neue Adam* (1747). The sources for this work, explicitly acknowledged by the author, are Cerceau's verse tale *La nouvelle Eve* (1732) and a prose narrative relating the story of a "new Adam" published in 1746 in the Swiss periodical *Mahler der Sitten*. In satiric fashion Cerceau tells the story of a modern Eve who is the living example of the proverbial belief that be it ever so tasteless, fruit becomes irresistibly sweet when forbidden. The main figures of the tale, husband and wife, quarrel about the extent and implication of Eve's guilt. The wife unmercifully condemns Eve, who for nothing more than a bite from an apple brought unutterable misery upon herself and Adam. Her husband holds a different opinion: it was certainly not the petty desire for the apple that caused the fall of Eve; it was her inability to

[19]*Ibid.*, pp. xxiii–xxix.

resist the temptation of transgressing the law of God. An unimportant object, even something ugly, can become attractive if it is forbidden. To prove the validity of his argument he challenges his wife to refrain for the next four weeks from stepping into the muddy pool that she passes on her way to the bath. For a while she does indeed resist the temptation to wade through the dirty water, but the pool becomes increasingly more attractive so that she finally succumbs and steps with both feet into the mud, mischievously enjoying her misdeed. Her husband has secretly witnessed the incident; he is delighted that his theory is affirmed and hopes that his wife will now have compassionate understanding for Eve's transgression. This is the end of Cerceau's story.

The tale seems to have been well known among contemporary readers; the *Mahler der Sitten* refer to the "Erzehlungen von der neuen Eva" without detailed explanation. The story is discussed in a social circle and denounced as being unfairly biased against women, for men are just as easily tempted to transgress. One of the women promises to find a clever mind, "einen geschickten Kopf," who will tell a story of the fall of a modern Adam and thus exonerate the fair sex. Her tale is published in the eighty-eighth and eighty-ninth issues of the Swiss periodical.

Each installment is introduced by a quotation from Latin literature which adds a meaningful perspective in depth. The first,

Siquidem hercle possis, nil prius, neque fortius,
Verum si incipies neque perficies fortiter,
Peristi.[20]

is from Terence. As is so often the case with a motto, the lines surrounding it in the original text are just as important as the quoted verses. Bodmer, whom Hagedorn identified as the author, borrowed the motto from the *Eunuch*, and the lines immediately preceding it express the dilemma of a man who, like von Weiden, the "new Adam" of the modern tale, is shut out by his beloved and verbalizes his inner conflict caused by indecision: "What am I to do then . . . would it be better . . . not to put up with the insults of such women?"[21] Courageously he determines not to return to the woman even if she should implore him to come back to her. The execution of his decision will demand resolute self-control. Even his servant Permano realizes that: "Certainly, Sir, if you could do it, there's no better or more valiant course. But if you attempt and don't stick stoutly to it, . . . you

[20]*Der Mahler der Sitten*, ii (Zürich, 1746), 450–472.
[21]*Terence*, ed. and trans. John Sargeaunt, Loeb Classical Library (London/New York, 1931), i, 241.

are done for." The motto thus suggests intriguing possibilities and does indeed promise a most entertaining story.

The wife, Adelheid, rather illogically holds her husband responsible for her transgression; she plans to seduce him into committing a misdeed that will make him equally guilty, and she designs a perfidious scheme that will force him into submission. In penance for her wrongdoing she will withdraw into solitude for a year and deny herself the pleasure of his love, intending of course, to punish him by withholding her affection. He naturally objects to her plan and she therefore suggests a compromise: if he will commit a deed thought to be unworthy of a man she will be reconciled. For her sake he should sit at the distaff and spin twelve threads. Although he considers her request so unreasonable that an honorable man would have to contemplate it for at least a month, he at once decides to take spinning lessons to prepare for his surrender.

The second installment of the narrative is introduced by a quotation from Ovid's ninth *Heroid*. Seven verses from Deianira's epistle to Hercules are cited. She has heard that Venus has his "neck beneath her humbling foot" and that he acts effeminately among the Ionians spinning wool with the handmaidens of Omphale:

> – – Inter Ionicas calathum tenuisse puellas
> Diceris & dominae pertimuisse minas.
> Non fugis, Alcide, victricem mille laborum
> Rasilibus calathis imposuisse manum?
> Crassaque robusto deducis pollice fila,
> Aequaque formosae pensa rependis herae?[22]

The motto sets the stage for the coming event. If none other than Hercules demeaned himself and performed a woman's task in order to gain the favor of his mistress, von Weiden may well gratify his wife's wish and do what even the most powerful hero of the Greeks did long ago. These are then the components that went into the making of Hagedorn's tale.

Cerceau's verse narrative and Bodmer's prose tale are artistically combined into one work. Although divided into three parts, Hagedorn's verse tale is excellently unified: the anonymous characters of Cerceau are transformed into Adelheid and Henrich; the transition from one episode to the next is elegantly smooth, and the

---

[22]Ovid, *Heroides and Amores*; for trans. see Grant Showerman, Loeb Classical Library (London/New York, 1921); "They say that you have held the wool-basket among the girls of Ionia, and been frightened at your mistress' threats. Do you not shrink, Alcides, from laying on the polished wool-basket the hand that triumphed over a thousand toils; do you draw off with stalwart thumb the coarsely spun strands, and give back to the hand of a pretty mistress the just portion she weighed out?" (pp. 112-114).

events follow in logical succession. Diverse perspectives were, to be sure, prefigured in the sources, but Hagedorn's manipulation of points of view is more complex than the modest experiments of his predecessors.

The first line introduces the proverb of central importance to the action: "Nichts schmeckt so schön, als das gestohlne Brodt."[23] A first person speaker affirms the validity of the maxim, "Ein Sprichwort sagts, das ich nicht falsch befinde," and reflects at length upon its implications. At this point there is no indication whose views are presented, and one could easily infer that these are the thoughts of the narrator. But the thirteenth line identifies another as the speaker: "So sprach ein Mann," who is not much later introduced as Henrich, the husband of Adelheid. The initial reflections are thus revealed as the subjective opinion of a fictive figure. In a similar manner and in swift succession other perspectives are given: Adelheid presents her opinion and then views the ominous mudhole. Reflections by the narrator are followed by observations of Hannchen, the maid, who describes a tempting perspective of the pool. Taking her lady to the scene of the crime, she marvels at the delight with which the ducks are playing in the mud

> . . . und zeigt ihr mit der Hand
> Der Enten Zug, die schwimmend näher kommen;
> Wie diese taucht; wie jene schnatternd ruht;
> Wie im Morast die gelben Schnäbel spielen.[24]

The final act of transgression is observed and related by the narrator who seizes this opportunity to express his admiration for the beautiful sinner:

> Pantoffel, Band und Strumpf wird abgeleget.
> Der schönste Fuß, der je die Welt betrat,
> Der einen Leib, der seiner werth ist, träget,
> Entblösset sich, und rennet durch den Koth,
> Vertiefet sich, und plätschert in der Lache,
> Und wühlt und forscht, ob Vorwitz und Verbot
> Den Ekel selbst zur Lust und Freude mache.[25]

The greater part of the second section is a dramatic dialogue in which Henrich and Adelheid express their thoughts and reveal their feelings without any intervention by the narrator; it is externally marked as a dramatic interchange, for the name of the speaker heads each segment of the conversation.

---

[23]Hagedorn, *Poetische Werke*, 2nd part (Hamburg, 1769), pp. 273-292.
[24]*Ibid.*, p. 277.
[25]*Ibid.*, p. 278.

The third section introduces two new aspects. Having listened to the advice of his father confessor and the implorations of his mother-in-law, Henrich goes into seclusion and contemplates his dilemma in a dramatic monologue that recalls Greek tragedy or Shakespearean drama and is reminiscent of Shaftesbury's theory of soliloquy. The hero analyzes his feelings, weighs his options, and finally rationalizes his impending submission:

> Ein weiser Mann ist Schöpfer seiner Sitten;
> Und immer hat ein unerschrockner Geist
> Den Wahn getrotzt, das Vorurtheil bestritten.
> Egypten war die Zuflucht der Vernunft,
> Wo Griechen selbst, als Weisheitschüler, lebten;
> Und weiß man nicht, daß dort der Weiber Zunft
> Geschäffte trieb, und ihre Männer webten?[1]
> Zu meinem Glück ist mir mein Evgen gut:
> Sie hat mir ja nichts schweres aufgeladen.
> Es hätte mir ein Weib von stolzerm Muth
> Leicht auferlegt, im Schlamme mich zu baden.
> Am Manzanar[2] müsst ich itzt ritterlich,
> Zu ihrem Ruhm, mit Rittern mich zerfetzen,
> Und liesse selbst, so wie ein Roderich,
> Den stärksten Stier auf meine Lanze hetzen.[26]

Hagedorn employs here another characteristic technique. In two notes he adds instructive information that pretends to expand in a significant manner the perspective of the presentation. The "perspective of the footnote" traditionally permitted the addition of important views in non-fictional literature. In new editions of older works and translations of foreign texts it also performed an important function because it enabled the editor or translator to present his own, occasionally quite different ideas; sometimes he even developed a contrasting theory in a comprehensive set of *Anmerkungen* as Johann Adolf Schlegel did, for example, in his translation of Batteux' poetics.

Hagedorn's notes are, of course, not seriously meant, and his reasons for such annotations, given in the *Schreiben an einen Freund*, are undeniably parodistic. He confesses that it is a deep-rooted habit of his to try to anticipate questions his audience, particularly the female readers, might have and to volunteer the answer before a question is asked. Perhaps he should offer a satisfactory explanation for his eccentricity, but he does not feel justified to discuss at great length these personal matters; yet in a facetious manner he does so anyway for he lists all the details he allegedly does not really want to mention.

[26]*Ibid.*, p. 288–289.

The brief textual statement (1) that in Egypt women attend to business while men stay at home and do the weaving is supported by no less than three authorities. The allusion to the river Manzanar (2) is explicated by references to travel literature that affirms the existence of the river. One source, however, is cited that negates the actuality of the river, maintaining that it is only to be found in the imagination of poets. And finally, a third lengthy note, added in a later edition and allegedly copied from a letter of a friend, affirms again the geographical reality of the river. To be sure, these notes must be understood as entertaining, whimsical ornamentation, but reaching beyond this function they importantly broaden the parodistic perspective of the work.

The effectiveness of ironic annotations was readily confirmed by the satirists of the age who often used notes as an integral part of their fiction. Gottlieb Wilhelm Rabener, author of a collection of *satyrische Schriften* (1751), even went a step further when he published *Hinkmars von Repkow Noten ohne Text*, a sixty-page collection of footnotes.[27] The fictive author maintains that *Anmerkungen*, preferably those to the works of others, are an unfailing method of becoming famous: "Noten also sind der rechte Weg, zu demjenigen Zwecke zu gelangen, welchen alle Gelehrte auf verschiedne Arten, aber mit ungleichem Erfolge, suchen." A literary work in itself is often an incidentally created and unimportant object; but notes are undeniably essential, they are "das vornehmste und wichtigste." The destruction of a text is a trifling matter, but the loss of notes is tragic because they are irreplaceable. Repkow therefore would rather compile a collection of *Anmerkungen* than toil over a text which could without much difficulty be produced by a writer less talented than the author of the *Noten*. The parodistic presentation is designed to ridicule certain practices and thus constitutes literary criticism that is seriously meant. Among the devices mocked are unsuitable quotations from classical writing that serve as mottos, and unnecessary footnotes that perform no other function than to sprinkle the pages with ostensibly learned information.

The nonexistent text of Repkow was to be introduced by two Latin words: *farrago libelli*. The author confesses that these words are quoted out of context and are part of Juvenal's verses

Quidquid agunt homines, votum, timor, ira, voluptas,
Gaudia, discursus, nostri est farrago libelli.[28]

[27]*Sammlung satyrischer Schriften*, Part 2 (Leipzig, 1751), pp. 109-168.
[28]*Ibid.*, p. 124; G. G. Ramsay, *Juvenal and Persius*, translates the lines as follows: "... all the doings of mankind, their vows, their fears, their angers and their pleasures, their joys and goings to and fro, shall form the motley subject of my page,"

Repkow admits that he could not use these two lines in their entirety
as his motto, for their reproduction would create wrong impressions
and lead his readers to expect a book entirely different from the one
that should eventually accompany his notes. His argumentation suggests, however, that the informed reader will habitually, perhaps even
involuntarily, recall the context of a motto and contrary to the intention of the author cause the larger context to play upon the interpretation of the work. This inference is sufficiently affirmed by Repkow's
listing of quotations from classical literature that are allegedly useful
as sentential titles. Most of them are unreasonably fragmentized and
virtually every one is highly suggestive if the larger context is
remembered or the sources are consulted; the seriously implied
demand is that a motto be most carefully chosen so that not only the
lines reproduced further the interpretation of the work but that the
context of the quotation contribute in equal measure to the understanding of it.

Repkow's "note on notes" is equally facetious. His definition is
synonymous with criticism of the occasional irrelevancy of footnotes:
"Anmerkungen heißen diejenigen Zeilen, welche der Buchdrucker
unter den Text setzt. Mit diesem haben sie keine Verbindung weiter,
als daß sie auf eben der Seite stehen, . . . wo die Worte des Textes
zu finden sind."[29] Footnotes, he reasons, should be obvious and
"müssen in die Augen fallen." They should state what others have
said before, should refer to ancient authorities, or cite well-known
scholars preferably from all corners of the world. The irony of this
advice carries over into the rule that a footnote should also present
the unexpected and contain matters nobody would anticipate. "Zum
Exempel: Im Texte steht das Wort; *Cicero*, und in der Anmerkung
untersuche ich die Frage: Ob Nebucadnezar auch wirklich Gras
gefressen habe, wie ein Vieh?"[30]

Rabener's parodistic *Noten ohne Text* probably provided a stimulus for the writers of the following decades, for they suggest a pattern
that is easily identifiable in the satiric novel of the period: the narrative works of Johann Timotheus Hermes, for example, the novels of
Friedrich Nicolai, and of course the fiction of Wieland, all add in
humorous fashion and with ironic pretense supplementary perspectives in their footnotes which seem to reflect Repkow's ironic advice
to state the obvious and bring the unexpected in *Anmerkungen*.

---

describing a more ambitious enterprise than Repkow had planned. See Loeb Classical Library (Cambridge/London, 1950), p. 9.
[29]*Sammlung satyrischer Schriften*, p. 120.
[30]*Ibid.*, p. 120.

A second work of Rabener, the *Satyrische Briefe* contained in his *Schriften*, is of particular relevance to a discussion of literary perspectivism. Many of the letters of this collection are written by knaves or fools, each of whom looks at the world from his egotistically limited point of view and judges men and events with personal bias and arrogant prejudice. There are, for example, letters of recommendation for preachers, tutors, and teachers which place the candidate for a position in a very peculiar light; and there are the letters of the applicants which, unintentionally of course, reveal the strangely distorted images of those among the characters who are seeking a position. Several other letters are written by an old prudish spinster who in a final attempt to catch a husband assiduously courts every man who owes her a favor, be it ever so modest, and in the process involuntarily paints a pathetic portrait of herself. A considerable number of letters quite different in content offer advice on bribery and corruption, as does the "Schreiben, wie ein ungewissenhafter Vormund es machen soll, wenn er den Richter bestechen will," or the "Recept, wie eine schöne Frau den Richter gewinnen soll."[31] The central topic of still another group of letters is the dilemma of a young girl who is in love with both a grandfather and his grandson; every one of the correspondents regards some aspect of the problem from his vantage point and combined they offer the strangest, most diverse solutions for the conflict.

The more progressive critics among the younger generation were equally concerned with questions of perspectivism. Lessing, for example, was fully aware that the viewing of a multilateral object from a restricting point of view would invariably cause misconceptions and result in incorrect evaluations. One of his early satiric poems, *Die Schöne von hinten* (1747), exemplifies this insight in a humorous manner:

> Sieh Freund! sieh da! was geht doch immer
> Dort für ein reizend Frauenzimmer?
> Der neuen Tracht Vollkommenheit.
> Der engen Schritte Nettigkeit,
> Die bey der kleinsten Hindrung stocken,
> Der weiße Hals voll schwarzer Locken,
> Der wohlgewachsne schlanke Leib,
> Verräth ein junges art'ges Weib.
>   Komm Freund! komm, laß uns schneller gehen,
> Damit wir sie von vorne sehen.
> Es muß, triegt nicht der hintre Schein,

---

[31]*Ibid.*, Part 3 (Leipzig, 1752); see specifically pp. 71-74 and 96-98.

Die Venus oder Phyllis seyn.
Komm, eile doch!–O welches Glücke!
Jetzt sieht sie ungefähr zurücke.
Was wars, das mich entzückt gemacht?
Ein altes Weib in junger Tracht.[32]

Despite its frivolity the poem is symbolic in intention, for it depicts the dangers inherent in the assessment of any object or event from an inadequate point of view.

Lessing's awareness of the phenomenon was expressed in his other writings as well. In his reviews published in contemporary periodicals he repeatedly warned, at least inferentially, against the critical fallacy of judging a work of literature by absolute, often irrelevant standards. He generally attempted to discover the poet's stance or intention and evaluated the product from the appropriate point of view. Formulations in which the term *Gesichtspunkt* is used were not infrequent. A controversy concerning the German adaptation of Charles Coffey's *The Devil to Pay*, for example, caused Lessing to contradict those critics who had not considered the dramatist's intentions, "daß das angeführte englische Stück, bey allen seinen Fehlern noch immer von einem großen komischen Genie zeige, welchem es gefallen hat, die Natur aus dem Gesichtspunkte eines holländischen Mahlers nachzuahmen."[33]

An essay of 1754, *Abhandlung von dem weinerlichen oder rührenden Lustspiel*, expresses a like respect for the somewhat subjective motivations of innovators who attempted to produce new dramatic genres. Many a French bourgeois dramatist was obviously annoyed to see "sich immer auf der lächerlichen Seite vorgestellt . . . ; ein heimlicher Ehrgeitz trieb ihn, seinesgleichen aus einem edeln Gesichtspunkte zu zeigen."[34] Yet considerations of viewpoint are of a still greater significance to the essay than these brief remarks may indicate. The point-of-view technique is the basic structuring principle that underlies the presentation of the arguments. In the introduction Lessing himself offers general observations on recent dramatic innovators. He then presents the views of a French critic who attacks apparently inferior features of the "new comedy." Immediately following is the antithetical *Abhandlung für das rührende Trauerspiel* by Christian Fürchtegott Gellert; and lastly the two views are evaluated and synthesized by Lessing, who attempts to judge from an objective point of view the contrasting opinions which are clearly representative of a larger controversy.

[32]Lessing, *Sämtliche Schriften*, ed. Lachmann-Muncker, I (Stuttgart, 1886), 69.
[33]*Ibid.*, v (Stuttgart, 1890), 185.
[34]*Ibid.*, vi (Stuttgart, 1890), 7.

Another observation of Lessing from the early period of his literary career is of relevance here. In May 1755 his review of *Das Leben des Herrn von Haller* was published in *Berlinische privilegirte Zeitung*. Zimmermann is praised for his unusual approach to the writing of biography, and the departure from the conventional chronological presentation is explicitly approved: "Der Herr D. Zimmermann ist keiner von den trocknen Biographen, die ihr Augenmerk auf nichts höhers als auf kleine chronologische Umstände richten."[35] Lessing apparently sanctioned Zimmermann's technique and implicitly endorsed the artistic portrayal of the author's hero from multiple points of view.

Other instances of Lessing's scrutiny and application of relevant principles could easily be cited and traced on to the *Laokoon* (1766), his classic contribution to aesthetic theory. In section xix, for example, he discusses perspective in ancient art and its poetic representation in epic literature with reference to previous critics, among them Alexander Pope whose views were expressed in the "Observations on the Shield of Achilles." Here and throughout the essay Lessing takes considerable advantage, in all seriousness of course, of allusions and footnotes which significantly broaden the perspective of his argument.

The advantages of carefully selected, occasionally even highly unusual points of view are overtly mentioned and tacitly implied, and the importance of the proper *Gesichtspunkt* from which to observe an object to be reproduced in art is discussed in the third section, in which the principle of the most pregnant moment is combined with the dictum of the singularly appropriate vantage point. In the representation of his subject the artist should ideally select a single moment in ever-changing nature and observe this moment from the most meaningful point of view. It is therefore evident "daß jener einzige Augenblick und einzige Gesichtspunkt dieses einzigen Augenblickes, nicht fruchtbar genug gewählet werden kann."[36]

The same care with which the artist selects the most appropriate point of view should be exercised by the critic of literature, and it is above all advisable that he not adhere to a fixed, limiting vantage point but adjust it according to the demands of the artistic aspect to be evaluated. If this rule, an obvious departure from normative theories, is observed, even the "loathsome introduction" of the Harpies in Virgil's *Aeneid* (xxv) and ancient tales commonly rejected as "lies" (ii) become acceptable as artistic features.

[35]*Ibid.*, vii (Stuttgart, 1891), 30.
[36]*Ibid.*, ix (Stuttgart, 1893), 19.

It would not be difficult to cite more examples of Lessing's concern with questions of perspectivism in literature and criticism; and beyond that it would be easily possible to multiply instances relevant to the topic from the writings of others and to expand the presentation into a comprehensive, more richly documented study. Such an investigation would uncover the intricately woven web of interconnected threads that vertically span the proverbial three-thousand years for which the well-educated man of the eighteenth century was held accountable,[37] and would link horizontally the artistic achievements and intellectual interests of contemporary Europe.

Although the three introductory chapters on background may seem inordinately long, they actually offer only a modestly limited view of a most complex and intricate system of references from which eighteenth-century writers derived the wealth of knowledge and information that characterizes most of their works. Virtually every one of the well-known writers expected that his works would be interpreted in this historico-cultural context and implicitly demanded a creative reader who was equally familiar with the world of ancient philosophy and classical literature. Even a brief examination of modern annotated editions of eighteenth-century works and a casual scrutiny of their indices reveals a substantial section of the panoramic fabric. A close reading of each work would expose further classical echoes and supplementary connections. These complex interrelations should caution against the assertion of the exclusive influence of any one individual writer on his contemporaries. To be sure, men like Shaftesbury played decisive roles in the establishment of the intellectual atmosphere of their time, but their influence was less original and not as exclusive as modern studies tend to indicate.[38] In contrast, the impulse that came from classical and Renaissance writers has sometimes been unduly neglected. It is, perhaps, no exaggeration to say that the figure of Cicero dominated the cultivated world of Europe in the eighteenth century; and yet there is no study that

---

[37]Cf. Goethe's *West=östlicher Divan*, "Buch des Unmuts," which contains the frequently quoted quatrain

Wer nicht von dreitausend Jahren
Sich weiss Rechenschaft zu geben,
Bleib' im Dunkeln unerfahren,
Mag von Tag zu Tage leben.

In: *Werke*, vi (Weimar, 1888), 110.

[38]The studies of Charles Elson, *Wieland and Shaftesbury* (1913), Herbert Grudzinski, *Shaftesburys Einfluss auf Chr. M. Wieland* (1913), and Oskar Walzel, "Shaftesbury und das deutsche Geistesleben des 18. Jahrhunderts," *Germanisch-romanische Monatsschrift* 1 (1909), 416–437, do not discuss the common background and thus overemphasize the importance of Shaftesbury. There is no recent study that corrects their bias.

delineates accurately and comprehensively the profound significance of the intellectual stimuli he provided for so many who studied his writings early in life with care and profit. Similarly underestimated, to offer only one further example, are the mediative efforts of Erasmus. Virtually every eighteenth-century writer knew his works and was particularly well acquainted with the famous collection of Adages; but again, his importance for the development of literature has not yet been sufficiently recognized, and still requires, as do so many other aspects of tradition and background, a detailed study. The evidence presented in this introductory section, though selective, is intended to offer a glimpse of the broad and colorful tapestry that was the actual backdrop for the formative works of eighteenth-century literature; it is meant to support the assertion that a profound concern with questions of point of view and perspectivism was a salient element of the contemporary climate, with firm roots in long tradition; and it is designed to set the stage for the analysis of the perspective method in the early writings of Wieland.

4 || Personal Views and Critical Perspectives

From the beginning of his career Wieland was aware of the significance of perspectivism in literature. Many of his writings reflect a more than casual interest in it; he successfully utilized the point-of-view technique in his creative works as well as in his contributions to criticism, and his private letters show that he even approached personal and intimate questions from diverse points of view and expected of others that they be equally flexible.

In October 1751 the young Wieland initiated his correspondence with Bodmer and Schinz in Zurich, hoping to establish a lasting, intellectually beneficial friendship with them. A letter of February 29, 1752, expresses his emotional need for mature friends and exemplary mentors; it also shows that he was inclined to idealize his elders and create a favorable image of them which clearly betrays an intentionally felicitous point of view: "Ich sehe Sie und alle meine unbekannte Freunde . . . aus dem schönsten Gesichtspunct an."[1] Although the young man idealized others, he tended to view himself critically. Whenever he doubted his own worth and desired a more profound insight into his own character he would, perhaps guided by Shaftesbury's "Advice," play the role of an impartial observer and contemplate his faults and virtues from, so far as possible, an objective point of view. Whereas he was willing to accept a slightly negative self-image, he emphatically rejected the unjustified criticism of others and neutralized it by attaching the subjective element of mood to the point-of-view technique of self-evaluation: "In meinen muntern

[1]*Wielands Briefwechsel*, i, 42.

Stunden sehe ich mich in einem solchen Gesichtspunct, daß mir
Urtheile, wie ich schon viele habe hören oder lesen müßen, Ver-
brechen zu seyn scheinen."[2]

Mood is not the only unstable factor determining a man's point of
view; time is another decisive component; diversified experiences
gathered as life goes on often cause a shift in his standpoint and expand his perspectives. Therefore, the analyses of the immature reflections of a youth on philosophical ideas and systems may well prove
rather futile if such an examination is meant to reveal the stance of
the mature man, for in the course of time he has acquired more profound knowledge and has consequently changed his views, perhaps
even fundamentally. With prophetic sagacity the eighteen-year-old
Wieland unsuspectingly predicted his own intellectual development
when he expressed his aversion to senseless disputes over ephemeral
philosophical ideas and ridiculed his immature attempts to construct
his own philosophical system: "Etwa nach 40 Jahre, so werden wir
die Welt aus einem gründlichern Gesichtspunct ansehen, und über
unsere Systeme lachen!"[3] At every period of his life Wieland's conclusions, drawn from his inquiries into problems of philosophy, determined his individualistic, occasionally even idiosyncratic *Weltanschauung*, which in turn is reflected in his poetry. It is, he believes, the
right of the poet to depart from generally accepted thought and present
his own subjective ideas, though they may be eccentric, perhaps even
false: "Und gesezt, der Gedanke wäre unrichtig; muß denn ein
Dichter allemal philosophisch wahr denken? Ist es nicht genug, wenn
seine Aussprüche von einer Seite her betrachtet, den Schein der
Wahrheit haben?"[4]

Comparable considerations should also guide the critic, because
every work of literature, Wieland suggestively intimates or explicitly
states, is created from a particular point of view and presents a
unique perspective of its subject matter. A sensitive and fair critic
will therefore try to recognize the principles by which the poet was
guided and judge a work accordingly. Since most critics, however,
would much rather establish their own biased canons, young Wieland
was particularly grateful to one perceptive commentator who did not
apply alien standards to his early works but evaluated them with true
understanding: "Sie, mein Wehrtester Freund," he wrote to Schinz
in March 1752, "sind unter den Wenigen welche meine *Cosmologie*
. . . aus dem wahren Gesichtspunct ansehen. Sie ist und soll nichts
anders seyn als ein *philosophischer* Roman."[5] And later, expressing

[2]*Ibid.*, I, 114.
[3]*Ibid.*, I, 80.
[4]*Ibid.*, I, 33.
[5]*Ibid.*, I, 54.

his gratitude for a particularly sensitive appreciation of his odes, he thanked Schinz once more: "Sie sehen meine Ode aus einem so richtigen Gesichtspunct und zugleich mit so freundschaftlichen Augen an, daß auch dieser Zug Ihres Characters Sie mir schäzbarer macht."[6]

Such sensitive evaluations are of course exceptional. Even the best of literature is often unfairly judged because of the critic's deplorable disregard for the writer's intention and point of view. "Warum," Wieland queries in exasperation, "haben doch die besten Bücher das Unglük so schlecht gelesen und aus einem falschen *point de vüe* beurtheilt zu werden?"[7] Meaningful criticism must transcend the limits of empathic appreciation, of course, and young Wieland advocates a more complex critical approach: the perspective evaluation of literature. An excellent work of verbal art will acquire even greater significance if it is analyzed and explicated from diverse points of view. Klopstock's *Messias*, for example, should be interpreted by several critics each one illuminating different aspects:

> Es würde für mich ein recht lebhaftes Vergnügen seyn, Beurtheilungen von verschiednen Kennern über den *Messias* oder dergleichen Werke, zu lesen. Es ist zu vermuthen daß eine jede besondere Anmerkungen enthalten würde, und es würde dem Leser ein Vergnügen verschafft werden das demjenigen ähnlich wäre, wenn uns einerley Figuren eines Gemähldes aus verschiednen Gesichtspuncten gezeigt werden.[8]

These were not merely transient opinions designed to please the young poet's correspondents; the approach suggested here was to become Wieland's favorite method of literary criticism, actual and fictive.

His first generative experiment with the perspective method in criticism was part of a broader controversy in which a particular type of poetry, the modern biblical epic, and later a specific poem, Johann Jacob Bodmer's *Joseph und Zulika*, were evaluated from multiple points of view by several real and fictive critics. It will be remembered that Milton's *Paradise Lost* for some time stood at the center of an acrimonious quarrel between the literati of Leipzig and Zurich. Bodmer's opposition to the French and German censures of the poem and his tracts in the defense of the marvelous in religious epic poetry were a major element in the feud, and his own contribution to the genre did not escape the censure of Gottsched.

A discussion of the topic, "Herrn Prof. Joh. Chr. Gottscheds bescheidenes Gutachten, was von den bisherigen christlichen

---

[6]*Ibid.*, I, 98.
[7]*Ibid.*, I, 381.
[8]*Ibid.*, I, 59–60.

Epopeen der Deutschen zu halten sey?", appeared in 1752 in *Das Neueste aus der anmuthigen Gelehrsamkeit*.[9] Despite an assurance that the argument would deal in generalizations, it was particularized by an unobtrusive reference to one of the "zürcherischer Kunstrichter"—that is Bodmer—who in the *Critische Briefe* of 1746 had commended his predecessors for their artistic embellishment of biblical materials. It is precisely this quality that was questioned by Gottsched; he rejected the imaginative and often highly improbable inventions of the poets in their adaptation of biblical stories, and he did not sanction the inclusion of undocumented events or the portrayal of unbelievably ideal characters and supernatural creatures. The combination of sacred truth with falsehood and fiction, "Lüge und Fabel," was bound to produce inferior works, "geistliche Romane," whose authors would certainly cause church and religion considerable harm:

> Denn außer dem, daß sie der Einfalt und Leichtgläubigkeit des Pöbels, den sie in Irrthum stürzen, misbrauchen; geben sie den Freygeistern Anlaß, an den wichtigsten Wahrheiten zu zweifeln, und sie boshafter Weise mit dieser Art von Erdichtungen zu vermengen.[10]

Gottsched's critical evaluation of artistic aspects, particularly the verse form of these biblical poems, reiterates a judgment previously expressed in his *Critische Dichtkunst*; the German hexameter still lacks the "charming harmony" of Greek and Latin verse, it sounds "gar hart und rauh," and has not yet reached the perfection of classical models.

As a response to his criticism Gottsched was soon to receive three comprehensive answers from Wieland: two implicit replies and one direct rebuttal, a rather insolently ironic letter probably composed with the approval of the Swiss critics. Since the end of 1752 the young poet had been writing an elaborate defense of Bodmer's biblical epic, the *Abhandlung von den Schönheiten des Epischen Gedichts Der Noah*, which appeared in Zurich in 1753. Wieland frankly admits that his is not an impartial evaluation of the work, but that it presents the views of a close friend of the author who intends to praise the poet and reveal the beauty of the poem. Accordingly, Bodmer and his work are lauded, whereas Gottsched and his theories are ridiculed and decried. Despite its bias, the major section of the analysis is a most sensitive *explication de texte*, quite possibly one of the first, understandably still imperfect, models of this modern critical method. Particularly revealing is Wieland's attempt to interpret every significant section of the epic in its larger context. Underlying the entire poem is a tissue of biblical and classical echoes, and Wieland explains

[9]Leipzig, 1752, pp. 62–72.
[10]*Ibid.*, p. 68.

many of the overt and subtle allusions to literary themes, motifs, and configurations, thus revealing the rich interplay between the author's text and the full context it allusively suggests.

In the autumn of the same year Wieland's own biblical epic poem in hexameters, *Der gepryfte Abraham,* was published. Its artistic intention, expressed in a preface dated September 8, 1753, was at the same time a justification of poetic idealization of man and events:

> Die Poesie soll nach ihrer natur und nach ihrem wahren verhaeltniß zu dem menschlichen herzen, das lob Gottes, unsers Schoepfers und Erloesers, und den Menschen in seinen vornehmsten gesichtspuncten und bestimmungen, folglich, religion, tugend und sitten zum gegenstand haben.[11]

The poem was doubtlessly also meant as an affirmation of the viability of the genre and a demonstration of the adaptability of the German language to the verse form of the classical epic.

Six days after the preface was signed Wieland wrote a puzzling, apparently complimentary letter to Gottsched, albeit without giving his name. Interpreted in isolation it could easily be understood as one of the letters young poets were accustomed to write to eminent men from whom they expected support and patronage for their literary works. But this letter was meant ironically; it reveals the author's ability to argue an issue from a point of view apparently opposed to his true conviction; it manifests his gift for literary impersonation and as a mock encomium demonstrates his talent for satire. Despite its parodistic nature the letter testifies to the controversy between Leipzig and Zurich. Irreverently the young Wieland plays the role of an ardent admirer of Gottsched and his disciples and pretends to be a severe critic of the Swiss and their followers. Although a deceptive mixture of truth and falsehood, the letter seems so convincingly honest that it was taken seriously. To be sure, the discrepancy between the correspondent's scornful rejection of contemporary biblical epics, particularly Klopstock's *Messias,* and the artistic techniques employed in his own *Hymne auf die Sonne,* which was attached to the letter for a critical appraisal, did not escape Gottsched, and he justifiably inferred that the author was indeed not as hostile toward Klopstock as he pretended. Nevertheless, Wieland's challenge to publish part of the letter in Gottsched's periodical *Das Neueste aus der anmuthigen Gelehrsamkeit* was accepted, and sections of it appeared in the December issue of 1753. This is exactly what Wieland—and doubtlessly Bodmer, who at this time was always well informed about his companion's plans and undertakings—hopefully expected, so that the impending identification of the correspondent would reveal the

---

[11]*Werke* (Akademieausgabe), Vol. II, Part 2, p. 103.

parodistic intent of the letter, shamefully humble Gottsched, and publicly ridicule him.

Gottsched's criticism did not, of course, divert Bodmer from his path. He published other epic poems based on biblical materials, among them *Joseph und Zulika*, one of several imaginative contemporary versions of the scriptural episode of seduction. A neutrally descriptive review of the poem appeared in 1753 in *Göttingische Anzeigen von gelehrten Sachen*.[12] Its author, Albrecht von Haller, singled out two particular aspects for explicit approval: the classical meter of the poem and the portrayal of supernatural beings, among them Simri, the guardian spirit of Joseph, and Chemos, the most carnal of the fallen angels and the evil tempter who together with his creatures, the "sensuous phantoms of love," was permitted to exercise his powers over Zulika so that she might successfully seduce the slave of Potiphar.

These details were bound to meet with exacting criticism from Bodmer's adversaries, and the very same year a critique echoing Gottsched's sentiments, a "Schreiben eines Junkers vom Lande an Herrn*** in Z." did indeed appear in the *Zürcher Freymüthige Nachrichten*.[13] The country squire sarcastically censures the artistic features of the epic poem, the pattern of verse, the exotic style, the manneristic metaphors, and specifically the sublime and marvelous qualities reflecting English influence; with particular emphasis he criticizes the unrealistic portrayal of man: the depiction of a temptingly beautiful sinner and an improbably virtuous hero who are both entirely unsuitable to fulfill the primary function of literary figures, namely, to serve as models for emulation in life. As a man of the world the squire can do without the kind of "seraphic creatures" beheld, for example, by the "abentheuerliche Verfasser der Briefe der Verstorbenen in seinem *Itinere ecstatico*"—the allusion refers to Wieland, the author of the *Briefe*. The critic's most serious protest, however, is directed against Chemos, whose intervention he compares to the unartistic operations of a *deus ex machina*. This type of criticism echoes the poetic principles of Gottsched; it reiterates his objections to *Paradise Lost* and recalls his unfavorable reaction to the enthusiastic acceptance of Milton's poem among the Swiss.

The epistle must have puzzled contemporary readers; Gottschedian criticism in a Zurcher periodical of which Bodmer was the editor seemed a contradiction not readily understood. Yet the "Schreiben" was so persuasive in tone and argument that it was taken seriously by many of those who read it. The seriousness of the letter

---

[12]P. 1189; Karl S. Guthke in his study *Haller und die Literatur* (Göttingen, 1962) identifies the Swiss scientist as the author of the review.

[13]The letter is reprinted in Wieland's *Werke* (Akademieausgabe) IV, 22-25.

is suspect, of course, and a close reading of the text reveals its parodistic quality. The squire is a fictitious figure, and none other than
young Wieland was the author of the epistle. The ironic overtones
escaped the readers, however; even those who were informed of Wieland's authorship obviously misunderstood his intention and considered the derogatory evaluation of the poem a betrayal of a benevolent patron. Bodmer himself mentioned the unexpectedly ambivalent reception of the epistle in a letter to Hess:

> Das Schreiben eines Junkers vom Lande wegen des Chemos und der
> Zulika würde von einigen Freunden für so verführerisch gehalten,
> daß Wieland genug zu tun bekomme, dieses Gedicht zu verteidigen. Er
> habe nicht wenige Briefe geschrieben, in denen er sich weitläufig
> erkläre.[14]

Wieland's satiric design is in retrospect more easily identifiable
because the "Schreiben" foreshadows the technique of his more
mature satiric writings and reveals his penchant for wit and irony at
an early period when the most unkind of his many critics still considered him an overly serious pedant. The figure of the fictive correspondent was purposefully chosen: country squires were notorious
for their lack of true *Bildung* and their want of sensitivity to aesthetic
values, but they were nevertheless inclined to pose as critics of the
arts. Invariably, they were attracted to neoclassic poetics and would—
as contemporary satires reveal—naively simplify the complex principles of criticism to suit their limited comprehension. Introduction
and conclusion of the letter underline the derogatory image. Initially
the squire expresses his appreciation of Bodmer's poems because they
have helped him while away time on a vexatiously boring evening
and have thus fulfilled what he considers an important function of
literature. After he has finished his long letter he almost regrets his
undertaking as a waste of time and effort; his fingers hurt from the
unusual strain of writing, the uncommonly intensive contemplation
has made him as tired as if he had been threshing all day, and he
finally realizes that his energy would have been much better spent
had he gone hunting; at least he would have shot a few hares.[15]
    Although the literary criticism of the epistle mirrors contemporary
theory, it becomes ludicrous through its combination of valid prin-

---

[14]*Briefwechsel*, II, 65.

[15]The formulation "Wie manchen Hasen hätte ich in dieser Zeit schiessen können"
(p. 25) may be understood as a play on the popular expression "einen Bock
schiessen" ("to commit a blunder"), which the *Junker* had most certainly done. Dis-
cussing some of his early critical writings Wieland later used the expression when
smilingly and ironically he said to Gruber: "Ja ja, da sehen Sie an meinem Beispiele,
was die j u n g e K r i t i k bisweilen für Böcke schiesst" (Gruber, *Christph. Martin
Wieland*, I, 66).

ciples with absurd opinions. For example, the squire's rejection of sublimity in poetry is supported by a preposterous description of German taste and inclinations:

Warum wollen wir in P o e s i e n d e n k e n, da uns doch die Natur kaum die Gabe gegeben hat, in P r o s e G e d a n k e n zu s t a m m e l n. Ein jeder bleibe was er ist, und rede wie ihm der Schnabel gewachsen ist. Der Deutsche hat ein angebohrnes Talent zum Fliessenden, Niedrigen, Leichten und Kriechenden.

This pronouncement reaffirms the image of the fictitious writer; he is a dunce who has set himself up for a great wit and is, as a representative type, the object of Wieland's satire. On another level the satire is once more directed against Gottsched whose critical principles, Wieland facetiously implies, seem to lend themselves readily to a *reductio ad absurdum* by the dunces of his time. And as a parody of seriously intended tracts against Bodmer, the letter mockingly invalidates much of the contemporary criticism leveled at the Swiss author.

The satiric perspective of the "Schreiben eines Junkers vom Lande" presenting ironically inverted views was augmented not much later by a personal, more favorable evaluation of the poem in Wieland's notes "Zufällige Gedanken bey Durchlesung Josephs und Zulika," in which he justifies apparently objectionable aspects of character portrayal, rationalizes the inclusion of supernatural figures, and explains their unique function in Bodmer's epos.[16] These incidental thoughts form the basis for the collection of letters "Briefe yber die Einfyhrung des Chemos und den Character Josephs . . ." which were published the following year in Bodmer's *Der erkannte Joseph und der keusche Joseph* (1754).[17] The fictive correspondents Critander and Philypsus, who exchange seven letters, share a high opinion of the poet and his work and implicitly take issue with arguments expressed in the epistle of the country squire. In his first letter Critander praises the beauty of the artistic plan, the unusual but probable nobility of most characters, the liveliness and vitality of the style, and the boldness and novelty of the imagery. Yet like the country squire he too objects to the introduction of Chemos and the portrayal of Joseph who in all his virtue and perfection is unconvincingly seraphic. Critander does not completely trust his own judgment, however; he therefore presents his views and requests that Philypsus, the wiser and more experienced philosopher, either affirm or correct his opinions. The letters, though fictive, are serious at-

[16]*Werke* (Akademieausgabe), IV, 25-27.
[17]*Ibid.*, IV, 28-50.

tempts at considering two sides of a literary problem, and the argumentation is soundly logical. Critander's objections are neither preposterous nor are they ridiculed. With psychological persuasion and some subtly sophisticated polemics, Philypsus is able to convince the younger man that the introduction of Chemos is not at all a crude trick to solve an artistic dilemma, but rather the "meisterstyk einer feinen erfindungskraft."

Of central concern to these three fictive correspondents is the artistic depiction of Joseph, a topic which echoes the contemporary controversy about the portrayal of man in literature. Of vital significance is the question whether Joseph is a representative figure and if so whether in all his chastity and virtue he is suited to serve as a model to be imitated in life. Whereas the country squire had said a categorical no to both questions, Critander is more tolerant. To be sure he questions the superior qualities of Joseph: "Was sollen wir von einem solchen sagen? Ist er ein mensch? Hat er eine sinnlichkeit? Ist er ein sohn Adams und vom weibe geboren?" Joseph's steadfast and rather inexplicable resistance toward a most charming temptress seems so unnatural that Critander must arrive at the conclusion: "Einen Joseph koennen wir nicht nachahmen. Er scheint kaum von unserm geschlecht zu seyn . . . So wie ihn der Poet gebildet hat, kann ich ihn fyr nichts anders als ein schoenes Ungeheuer ansehen," a judgment which clearly recalls Shaftesbury's rejection of perfect characters as "the greatest *Monster,* and . . . the least *moral* and *improving.*"[18] Critander is, however, willing to consider sound arguments to the contrary and does not mind being proven wrong. In his reply Philypsus attempts to demonstrate with rhetorical eloquence that Joseph is indeed human, that his chastity is not an improbable virtue, and that he is excellently suited to be imitated by young men who strive for perfection. The apparently idealizing portrayal actually verifies the complex nature of his character and if despite his human traits he approaches faultlessness he only affirms man's place near the angels in the great chain of being.

This is, however, not yet the last word spoken on the matter. The "Briefe yber die Einfyhrung des Chemos" were accompanied by a "Schreiben des Herausgebers an Herrn J.C.H.," probably a revised version of an earlier personal letter Wieland had written to Johann Caspar Hess in Altstetten.[19] Its publication must in part be seen as an attempt to counteract the misunderstood epistle of the country squire and was intended to offer yet another perspective of the many-faceted, controversial issue. In his letter Wieland discusses prin-

---

[18]*Characteristicks,* III, 262.
[19]*Werke* (Akademieausgabe), IV, 50–54.

cipally the portrayal of Joseph and his behavior at the crucial moments when Zulika, under the influence of Chemos, the evil spirit of lust, attempts to seduce him. Her loveliness, charm, and wanton passion do not even excite the slightest desire in Joseph; he is in complete control:

> seyn gemythe
> War zu bekannt mit dem hoehern reize der heiligen ordnung,
> dass unrichtige triebe sich seiner bemächtiget haetten.[20]

He is "sein selbst meister" and affirms his virtue in a protracted philosophical discourse which strangely enough calms Zulika so completely that this day her better half reigns:

> Selbigen tag behielt die bessere seele die herrschaft,
> Stillte das schaeumende blut und daemmte den aufruhr der triebe.[21]

Her second attempt is equally unsuccessful, even though Chemos and his phantoms of love, "der wilde schwarm der Liebesphantomen," inspire her with passion.

Many a critic of Bodmer felt that Joseph's imperturbably virtuous conduct lacked verisimilitude. If they are right, how then could Joseph be portrayed differently? Wieland sees at least three possibilities. Moralists and novelists are perhaps not entirely wrong when they maintain that even the most constantly virtuous youth may find himself in circumstances in which he is attracted by a beautiful sinner and sensuousness takes possession of him. The poet can, of course, easily deliver him from temptation, and the ultimate triumph of his virtue is a truly splendid victory. Second, Joseph could be depicted as a Platonic lover who is united with Zulika in affectionate but pure friendship; because of their esteem for each other and their mutual desire to increase the happiness of the beloved they would be able to withstand temptation and through their proven virtue become even more attractive. The third possibility would be the portrayal of Joseph as an Araspes, Xenophon's young hero whom Wieland was later to select as the main character of his dramatic dialogue *Araspes und Panthea*: "Er myßte zwo seelen haben, deren die eine, eine sclavin der Zulika und der sinnlichen liebe, die andere aber vernynftig und gut waere, und sich bestrebte die meisterschaft yber die sinnliche zu behalten."[22]

The three possibilities of character portrayal delineated here are, however, rejected in favor of Bodmer's version. Wieland can accept Bodmer's characterization because his interpretation of the figure

[20]Johann Jacob Bodmer, *Joseph und Zulika* (Zurich, 1753), p. 31.
[21]*Ibid.*, pp. 36-37.
[22]*Briefwechsel*, II, 68.

of Joseph differs from that of the other critics. They had tacitly treated Joseph as a representative man whose conduct should encourage and permit imitation in life. Wieland did not share this view. Joseph is a "historic" figure of heroic stature; his extraordinary virtue is an aspect of his superhuman character, and to present him any other way would simply falsify the image mediated through scriptures.

Although this last letter was intended as a defense of Bodmer's depiction of a perfect character, it foreshadows in its recognition of the many possibilities for the creation of literary figures Wieland's artistic experiments with the portrayal of man.

Gottsched and his circle were not the only ones with whom Bodmer and his followers maintained a long-lasting quarrel. Another group whose poetry did not find the approval of the Swiss were the Anacreontics, the "priests of Venus and Bacchus," among them Johann Peter Uz, Bodmer's major adversary. Wieland's involvement in the controversy began in 1752, at a time when he was establishing relations with Bodmer and professing his loyalties by promoting the cause of his patron. The documents testifying to the controversy reflect in their pattern the development of the young critic. At the beginning they disclose an intentionally biased, yet perfectly legitimate and not necessarily dishonest point of view, which he no doubt adopted to please the Swiss, and they reveal that he did not permit himself then to glance beyond the resulting, narrowly limited perspective. During the next few years, however, he gradually displayed finer sensitivities for literary values and truly penetrating insights into the complex personalities of poets. The last important work exclusively concerned with the quarrel is a scrupulously balanced dialogue which presents with pronounced fairness a dual critical perspective of the controversy.

The details of the quarrel, ruthlessly personal attacks on the Anacreontics and a blunt rejection of their poetry by the Swiss critics, and, on the other hand, Uz's retaliatory censure of the pious poets from the south and his scathing criticism of their religious epics, all expressed in various literary forms, reviews, personal letters, poetic epistles, prefaces, and verse,[23] are of less importance here than one particularly intricate topic incidentally discussed by the disputants: the identity of the *persona* of a poem and its relation to the poet, or the question of the personal responsibility of the artist for views expressed in his work.

[23]The quarrel between Uz and the Swiss critics, among them Wieland, was discussed by August Sauer in the preface to Johann Peter Uz, *Sämtliche Poetische Werke*, Deutsche Litteraturdenkmale des 18. und 19. Jahrhunderts, 33 (Stuttgart, 1890), xx–lxii.

Bodmer's feud with the Anacreontics began with an uncomplimentary review of Klopstock's "Tibullische Elegie," published anonymously in 1751. The first lines of the poem indicate unmistakably that the usually serious poet is now trying on a different costume and will play the role of an anacreontic singer:

Der du zum Tiefsinn und Ernst erhabner
   Gesänge gewöhnt bist,
Und die einsame Bahn alter Unsterblichen
   gehst,
Sing' izt, mein Geist, ein tibullisches Lied.[24]

The essential difference between a poetic description of love and the actual experience is implied in a brief address to the lovers:

Ihr fühlt mehr, als Lieder euch lehren,
   und laßt es dem Dichter,
Daß er von Küssen entfernt, anderer Küsse
   besingt.

These lines are to be understood as an affirmation of the poet's detachment, and they reiterate the motif of impersonation introduced at the beginning of the "Elegie." Bodmer, who had mistakenly hoped that Klopstock would become his loyal follower, does not sanction this experiment with a poetic *persona*; in fact, he does not even admit his awareness of the artistic dissimulation but accuses the author of indecency because he extols the delights of sensuous pleasures to gratify a young debaucher. His frivolity will undoubtedly have a demoralizing influence on youthful readers, and he will most certainly have to justify his deed before God and man. Bodmer apparently does not acknowledge the right of a poet to experiment with a *persona* that appears to be different from the image that has been accepted as his identity; a serious and religious poet may not toy with lasciviousness: "Wenn er eine strengere Morale im Herzen hat, was sollen wir von ihm halten, daß er eine so schlüpfrige lehret? Warum verthut er mit einem Liede, was er mit dem andern erbaut hat? Will er den Cato vermeiden, muß er darum ein Epikurus werden?"[25]

In his personal correspondence with Bodmer Wieland discussed the anonymous review of the "Elegie." He defended Klopstock, whom he correctly identified as the author of the poem, against the charges of indecency and immorality and sketched a more laudatory evaluation of the "Elegie" which he felt had been unfairly criticized.[26]

Although he continued to express his high regard for Klopstock, the young Wieland joined Bodmer in his attacks on the anacreontic

---

[24]*Ausgewählte Werke*, ed. Karl August Schleiden (Munich, 1954), pp. 17-20.
[25]*Wielands Briefwechsel*, II, 52.
[26]*Ibid.*, I, 33.

poets. His poetic epistle "Schreiben an Herrn*** von der Würde und der Bestimmung eines schönen Geistes," published at the end of 1752,[27] has a double function: it is a defense of Bodmer, more specifically the personality of the poet and his noble intentions; at the same time it is an indictment of the Anacreontics and their dissolute songs of wine and wanton love. The epithets designed to characterize men like Hagedorn, Gleim, and Uz are inordinately insolent; they are called "ein barbarischer Schwarm," "geistlose Brüder des taumelnden Tejers," and "Priester des Unsinns"; they are accused of poisoning the souls of the young, enticing them to leave the arms of innocence, and leading them toward the fascination of depravity.

These overt insults did not go unanswered. Uz replied with equally disparaging remarks, and the exchange of mutual criticism reached a climax in 1757 when Nicolai and Lessing entered into the controversy in defense of Uz. In the spring of 1757 Wieland's *Empfindungen eines Christen* appeared in Zurich, accompanied by a letter addressed to the *Hofprediger* A. F. W. Sack in which he again combines the defense of religious poetry with an attack on the Anacreontics. Following the example of Bodmer he does not yet discriminate between the author and the *persona*, but he insinuates that anacreontic poetry does indeed reflect the questionable morality of its authors:

> Was sollen wir also zu dem Schwarm von anakreontischen Sängern sagen, . . . Was von diesen Erzählern, die in der Schlüpfrigkeit mit *La Fontaine* eifern, von diesen schwermenden Anbetern des Bachus und der Venus, die man an der innbrünstigen Andacht, womit sie diese elenden Götzen anbeten und lobpreisen, für eine Bande von epicureischen Heiden halten sollte, die sich zusammen verschworen haben, alles was heilig und feyerlich ist lächerlich zu machen, und die wenigen Empfindungen für Gott, die im Herzen der leichtsinnigen Jugend schlummern, völlig auszutilgen.[28]

It was exactly this identification of poet and *persona* to which Uz objected when he wrote to Gleim:

> Wenn ein Dichter an seinem poetischen Charakter angegriffen wird, so kann er schweigen und der Welt das Urteil überlassen, ob seine Verse gut oder schlecht sind. Wenn hingegen sein moralischer Charakter angetastet wird, so muß er sich verteidigen.[29]

Poets who sing of wine and women are not necessarily depraved drunkards and lusty lovers:

---

[27]*Werke* (Akademieausgabe), Vol. I, Part 1, pp. 457–462.
[28]*Ibid.*, II, 2, 340.
[29]*Anakreontiker und preussisch-patriotische Lyriker*, 2nd part, Uz, Kleist, Ramler, Karschin, ed. Franz Muncker (Stuttgart, 1894), p. 95.

Manch großer Mann, von ungescholtnen Sitten,
Hat unentehrt des Tejers Bahn beschritten,
Dem Griechen gleich zu singen sich bestrebt,
Ihm gleich gescherzt und nicht gleich ihm gelebt.[30]

Uz, who was known among his friends as awkward and inhibited, chaste and virtuous, was publicly supported in his argument by other contemporaries. In the same year the *Bibliothek der schönen Wissenschaften und der freyen Künste* published an article concerned with the *Empfindungen eines Christen*;[31] it is not an evaluation of the work itself but a comparative analysis of Wieland's letter to Sack and Uz's epistle to Gleim. The substance of the article is the demand that a critic of literature should carefully discriminate between the spokesman of a work and the poet. Wieland had not made the necessary distinction but created an utterly false image of Uz when he depicted him as an "infamous scoundrel." The author pointedly objects to the improper emphasis on detail and unfair generalizations resulting from the accentuation: "Von einem leichten Scherze, von einem schalkhaften Bilde, auf ein verruchtes Herz schließen, ist die grausamste Unbilligkeit."[32] Such a conclusion is particularly objectionable if a critic does not evaluate the entire production of an author but singles out a particular kind of poetry and treats it as if it were representative of all his writings. If this approach were justified, the author implies, even the "pious Wieland" could be considered a worshipper of Venus, for in his *Briefe von Verstorbenen an hinterlassene Freunde* one of the characters, Lucinda, creates a rather sensuous image of her friend Nacissa, and the portrayal is similar to a character sketch in Uz's *Sieg des Liebesgottes*.

Many aspects of the controversy are reflected in Lessing's lengthy review of Wieland's *Prosaische Schriften* which appeared in 1759 in the *Briefe, die neueste Litteratur betreffend*.[33] Lessing also emphasizes the need for objectivity in literary criticism, but he does not follow his own dictum when he alludes to malicious rumors that Wieland played the "double role" of free-thinker and hypocrite during his student days in Klosterberge more than a decade before, when he was only fifteen years old. Although Lessing stresses the irrelevance of the private life of a poet in an evaluation of his works, he has nevertheless, to be sure rather deviously, reminded his readers of these rumors.

Wieland's immediate reaction to the derogatory criticism of his contemporaries was the drafting of a reply, "An die Leser der

---

[30]*Ibid.*, p. 97.
[31]Vol. i, 1st piece (Leipzig, 1757), pp. 415–427.
[32]*Ibid.*, pp. 422–423.
[33]*Sämtliche Schriften*, viii (Stuttgart, 1892), 14–18.

Bibliothek der schönen Wissenschaften und freyen Künste," and an equally defiant note intended as the preface to a new edition of his prose works.[34] Both notes, however, remained unpublished, for Wieland realized that nothing could be gained by a continuation of the bitter feud and the reiteration of overly subjective accusations.

A fair, even if not completely unbiased presentation of both sides of the argument, Wieland realized, would be much less offensive, and he therefore wrote the dialogue *Lysias und Eubulus, Eine Unterredung*. He was convinced of the greater effectiveness of this form of criticism "weil der Endzwek den man bey einer Critik sich vorsetzt, besser durch die Schäftesburische Manier fein und kaltsinnig zu spotten als durch die caustische Critik oder den magistralischen Ton erhalten wird."[35] The substance of the controversy engaging Wieland, Uz, and Lessing is discussed once more, here in a conversation between fictive characters. It is, however, made explicitly clear that Lysias is a friend and advocate of Lessing and Uz, whereas Eubulus— the benevolent advisor, as his name implies—represents the point of view of Wieland. Although both sides of the argument are presented and the interlocutors plead their cases with equal intelligence and conviction, the debate is weighted in favor of Eubulus, who is also the more eloquent rhetorician.

The dialogue focuses on questions of identity and the responsibility of poets. To be sure, Eubulus argues, Wieland was accused of being a hypocrite because his religious poetry has a spokesman who is evidently more ardent and idealistic than the author has revealed himself in reality. But, he asks, is there not the same kind of discrepancy between *persona* and author in anacreontic poetry? It can surely be said of both groups "daß die Moral ihres Lebens von der Moral ihrer Muse sehr entfernt ist";[36] it is therefore unjust to defend the artistic dissimulation of the Anacreontics and reject the apparent dissemblance of religious poets. Either both must be accused of hypocrisy or both should be acquitted of the charge. Wieland himself has evidently acquired these insights, and he now, it seems, tacitly agrees with Lessing, for according to Eubulus, he is not stern in his judgment of men but of their works: "Er ist es nicht gegen die Personen, denn was für eine Jurisdiction kan er über diese haben? sondern über die

---

[34]*Briefwechsel*, ii, 316–317.

[35]*Ibid.*, i, 556. An informative, more general study of Wieland's early literary criticism is Jeffrey Brent Gardiner's dissertation "Wieland's Development as a Literary Critic 1750-1760" (University of Colorado, 1970). Gardiner does not take his study beyond 1759 and imposes an artificial conclusion on the controversy with Lessing, which did not end here. He does not mention the dialogue between Lysias and Eubulus (drafted perhaps after April 1760 and published in 1763) which must be seen as Wieland's final word in the matter.

[36]*Werke* (Akademieausgabe), iv, 166.

Sache an sich selbst."[37] Poetic pretense, then, is justified. It is, however, another question whether every kind of pretension is defensible. Sacred poetry will probably stimulate Christian piety so that the poet's impersonation of a deeply religious man has a beneficial effect on the reader. Anacreontic poets, however, may well awaken sensuous desires in their readers, particularly in the fair sex for whom they profess to write, and thus exercise a harmful influence. These and related questions are amicably discussed by Lysias and Eubulus who end their conversation with an appeal to tolerance and fairness in criticism.

The ability of poets to present diverse, indeed even contrasting views and apparently conflicting arguments with a semblance of true conviction was occasionally misunderstood. Yet these poets, among them Uz and Wieland, could easily have explained and defended their method by referring the critics to classical rhetoric, to Cicero's *De Oratore* and Quintilian's *Institutio oratoria*, which contain most eloquent and persuasive justifications for experimentation with poetic *personae*. In Cicero's dialogues it is L. Licinius Crassus, the moderate and judicious aristocrat of ancient Rome, who presents a pertinent rhetorical principle: "We must argue every question on both sides, and bring out on every topic whatever points can be deemed plausible";[38] and M. Antonius, the praetor and censor, likens orator and poet to an actor on the stage who plays a role and does it well if he achieves sensitive empathy with the character he portrays.[39]

Similar principles are developed with even greater detail in the sixth book of Quintilian's *Institutio oratoria*. An orator, and by implication an actor or a poet, must identify with the person he represents. It is not sufficient to "counterfeit" grief, anger, and indignation. "If we wish to give our words the appearance of sincerity, we must assimilate ourselves to the emotions of those who are genuinely so affected, and our eloquence must spring from the same feeling that we desire to produce in the mind" of others. The process of identification can be furthered by *visions,* "whereby things absent are presented to our imagination with such extreme vividness that they seem actually to be before our very eyes. It is the man who is really sensitive to such impressions who will have the greatest power over the emotions." A potent "fire" of "fictitious emotions" that often excites an actor to perform convincingly on the stage should equally inspire the orator or the poet, for it will enable the former to sway the audience toward accepting his views, and the latter to present a per-

[37]*Ibid.,* p. 175.
[38]*De Oratore,* I, xxxiv, 158.
[39]*Ibid.,* II, xlvi, 193.

suasive impersonation, whatever the subject may be.[40] During the eighteenth century these principles were explicitly sanctioned, and comparable tenets were persistently advocated by well-known authors of poetics, among them the eminent critics of Leipzig and Zurich. Gottsched's *Versuch einer Critischen Dichtkunst* contains germane observations. At the beginning of its chapter "Von den drey Gattungen der Poetischen Nachahmung," Gottsched contrasts particularly two types of poetic imitation, mere description or very lively depiction—"bloße Beschreibung, oder sehr lebhaffte Schilderey"—and a second, less easily labeled kind of mimesis: "Die andre Art der Nachahmung geschicht, wenn der Poet selbst die Person eines andern spielet, oder einem der sie spielen soll, solche Worte, Geberden und Handlungen vorschreibt und an die Hand giebt, die sich in solchen und solchen Umständen vor ihn schicken." This "genre" of poetic imitation requires considerably greater talent and skill than straightforward description, and the poet affecting the emotions of others should ideally be a sensitive psychologist: "Man muß hier die innersten Schlupfwinckel des Hertzens ausstudirt, und durch eine genaue Beobachtung der Natur den Unterscheid des gekünstelten, von dem ungezwungenen angemercket haben."[41]

Similar views were expressed, though in a much more emotional language, in Breitinger's *Critische Dichtkunst*. The secret of an excellent poet is his adaptability and the passionate activation of his creative imagination, "eine Hize der Einbildungskraft, in die man sich selber jagt, und der man sich gerne ergiebt."[42] The successful impersonation of another being and the convincing presentation of his emotions is according to Breitinger the natural result of a close cooperation between the poet's soul and his imagination:

> Die Seele muss ihrer Einbildungs=Kraft befehlen, den vorgelegten Gegenstand zu besichtigen, alle Eigenschaften, Umstände, Zufälligkeiten desselben zu betrachten, wenn sie dann von dem Affecte mit aller Macht angespornet, und in eine starcke Bewegung gebracht worden, wird sie neue und wunderbare Bilder hervorbringen, welche, so ferne wir sie mit einer verständigen Wahl auserlesen haben, der Materie ein ungewöhnliches Licht und Leben mittheilen werden.

Paradoxically, the verisimilitude of the resultant poetic portrayal is founded on deception: "[ihre] Wahrscheinlichkeit [ist] in einem Betruge der Affecte gegründet."[43]

---

[40]*Institutio oratoria* VI, ii, 27; 29; 36.
[41]Leipzig, 1730, p. 120.
[42]Zurich, 1740, I, 331.
[43]*Ibid.*, p. 333.

Essentially, the theoretical statements of particular relevance here are intended by Breitinger as an interpretation of classical principles that effectively substantiate his own argument; he therefore quotes an appropriate line from the second book of Cicero's *De Oratore* and reproduces a lengthy section from the sixth book of Quintilian's *Institutio oratoria*.

These representative works were among the many Wieland knew well. From their authors he learned that an excellent work of literature is often the result of the poet's projection into the thoughts and feelings of others. The protean traits in the personality of a poet favoring this approach did not escape the attention of Wieland; in fact he recognized them as his own tendencies, and the criticism of his adaptability caused him no little sorrow. Two of his letters to Johann Georg Zimmermann written in March 1759 express his concern about the "impertinent verdicts" directed against him and his literary works. The imagery used to describe his dilemma is characteristically visual: "Ich erscheine noch in einem falschen Licht und werde von einigen Objecten verdunkelt die neben oder vor mir stehen."[44] The prejudiced opinions of others seem utterly unjustified, and he urgently hopes that the hour of recognition of his true self will come. The second letter to the Swiss physician and critic introduces a suggestive image that foreshadows the sensitive analyses of the personality of the poet by later writers, for example Goethe and Keats. Attempting actually to vindicate his critics and trying to explain his creative practice as well as his personal behavior, Wieland writes: "Je ressemble pour mon malheur au Cameleon; je parois vert aupres des Objets verts, et jaune aupres des jaunes; mais je ne suis jaune ni vert; Je suis transparent, ou blanc come veut Mr de la Motte."[45]

The allusion refers the reader to the fable "Le Caméleon" by Antoine Houdar de La Motte. Wieland probably expected Zimmermann to recall or verify the relevant verses and understand the equivocacy of the allusion. La Motte's fable tells of two observers quarreling about the color of the cameleon. One believes it is green, the other blue. Yet when they observe the animal against the background of a white handkerchief they discover that it now appears to be white. At this moment the cameleon is permitted to speak and in a pregnant line indicates the relativity of appearance and perception: "Vous avez tous tort et raison."[46] Any judgment resulting from personal observation is unreliable:

[44]*Briefwechsel,* I, 413.
[45]*Ibid.,* p. 415.
[46]The fable is reproduced in Wieland's *Briefwechsel,* II, 374. The French version accompanied by a German translation was also published in Barthold Heinrich Brockes' *Irdisches Vergnügen in Gott,* pp. 510–511.

Croyez qu'il est des yeux aussi bons que les vôtres;
Dites vos jugemens; mais ne soyez pas fous
Jusqu'à vouloir y soûmettre les autres.

And the concluding statement is doubtlessly meant as a universally
valid pronouncement on the subjectivity of human perception:

Tout est Cameleon pour vous.

The significant interactions between Wieland's allusive statement
and the context of the fable constitutes a symbolic extension that invites intriguing speculations: the prevalent uncertainties about the
true character of a protean personality are not only attributable to the
receptive transparency which reflects like a mirror its surroundings
and thus creates the illusion of a different identity, but they are in
equal measure assignable to the subjective perception of the observer
who is deceived by the elusive phenomenon of a merely superficial
transformation. Appearance as well as perception is then relative. Yet
ironically this very conclusion is relative too; for is it not a protean
cameleon that suggests this explanation?

Naturally Wieland was not the only poet who compared himself to
a cameleon. Ever since Aristoteles introduced the image and Plutarch
employed it in his portrayal of Alcibiades as the symbol for the
adaptability of men, writers have used it both as a derogatory symbol
to intimate the willful changeability of a man ready to deceive the
world around him and as an approbatory symbol to indicate the judicious adaptability of one ready to experiment with a second identity.

In Wieland's time the young Goethe, for example, considered the
image an appropriate symbol to characterize himself. In 1764, at the
age of fourteen, when he wanted to join the *Arkadische Gesellschaft zu
Phylandria*, he suggested that Friedrich Carl Schweitzer, called
Alexis, be asked for character references. Alexis knew him well but did
certainly not know every single aspect of his personality, for Goethe
admitted: "Ich gleiche ziemlich einem Camaeleon. Ist nun meinem
Alexis zu verdencken? Wenn Er mich noch nicht von allen Gesichts-
Puncten betrachtet hat."[47] The imagery here does not actually suggest
the changeability of the young man, but it is meant to caution against
the presentation of an oversimplified evaluation; the personality of
an individual is a complex spectrum and cannot be fully perceived
from a single point of view. Only the observation from multiple
points of view will ultimately produce a reliable portrait, a conviction
which recalls the method Zimmermann employed in his biography of
Albrecht von Haller, a work well known to Goethe.

[47]*Goethes Briefe*, ed. Karl Robert Mandelkow (Hamburg, 1962), I, 9.

A most sensitive analysis of a poet's personality using the imagery discussed here is given by John Keats in his famous letter of October 21, 1818, to Richard Woodhouse. Although this document lies chronologically far beyond the frame of the present study, it should be mentioned because Keats's confession is less limited in application than the context may suggest; it expresses succinctly and eloquently the situation of a poet who possesses innate sensibility, as Shaftesbury had called the sympathetic power of imagination that enables him to identify momentarily with the object of his attention.[48] The "chameleon Poet," Keats wrote, "is the most unpoetical of any thing in existence, because he has no Identity—he is continually in for and filling some other Body. The Sun, the Moon, the Sea and Men and Women who are creatures of impulse are poetical and have about them an unchangeable attribute; the poet has none, no identity—he is certainly the most unpoetical of all God's Creatures."[49] These observations were not merely meant as self-analysis with purely subjective overtones but may certainly be understood as a universally valid characterization of equally sensitive, gifted, and adaptable poets, an ever-present group of writers to whom Wieland, who was no stranger to Keats, unquestionably belongs.

Seen in this context, the ability of Wieland to establish sympathetic identification with the object of his attention, and the skill with which he successfully performed various literary tasks should not be considered negatively as "bedenkliches Talent," a questionable or doubtful talent; but the pliancy of his personality, which enabled him to enter almost totally into his subject with a resulting obliteration of his own identity, must be assessed as the felicitous characteristic of a superior poet.[50]

Yet sensibility alone, eighteenth-century critics realized, does not produce the most convincing portrayal of character, be it by a poet in literature or an actor on the stage. Like any other activity of the emotions it needs restraint, and although it is an innate faculty it must be improved by attentive and judicious study of human nature.[51] The earliest writings of Wieland do not yet reflect a proper study of man; they still portray, as do so many other works of the period, idealized

[48]Keats's ideas and formulations are anticipated by Shaftesbury who in the "Advice to an Author" also maintains that in the conception and portrayal of his subject the poet is ideally "annihilated," and is "no certain Man, nor has any certain or genuine Character" (*Characteristicks*, 4th ed., 1727, I, 200–201).

[49]*Complete Poems and Selected Letters*, ed. Clarence DeWitt Thorpe (New York, 1935), p. 576.

[50]Even the most sympathetic scholars occasionally express a somewhat critical attitude toward these abilities of Wieland. Cf. pp. 90 f. of this study.

[51]See Earl R. Wasserman, "The Sympathetic Imagination in Eighteenth-Century Theories of Acting," *JEGP*, XLVI (July 1947), 270.

figures that reflect the limits of his human contacts and reveal a lack of instructive experience; furthermore, they also betray his unwillingness to draw realistic images because they might conflict with his intention to present exemplary models designed to be emulated in life. Soon, however, Wieland became eager to acquire accurate and deep knowledge of man, and he kept striving, as did so many of his contemporaries, for a reliable "Kenntnis des menschlichen Herzens." All of his writings, among them the *Betrachtungen über den Menschen* of 1755 and the clearly contrasting *Beyträge zur Geheimen Geschichte des menschlichen Verstandes und Herzens* of 1770, as well as his verse and prose fiction, demonstrate his lasting and intense study of human nature. A detailed analysis of all relevant statements, which must, of course, carefully distinguish between Wieland's very own views and those of his fictive figures, would doubtlessly reveal the continuing process by which he gained the penetrating insights that considerably changed his image of man and initiated the artistically superior and convincing portrayals for which he was already commended in his own time.

5 | Wieland's Early Writings

The phenomenon of different or contrasting evaluations of all aspects of life, as they are observed from diverse points of view, evidently fascinated Wieland; it was to become one of his favorite literary topics and importantly influenced his artistic method of representation. As in his critical writings, so in his earliest creative works, his consideration and inclusion of multiple points of view affirms for him the significance of each perspective as a component part of reality. Beyond that there are subtle or probing allusions reaching over the frame of the individual work and bringing adjoining perspectives into focus; dramatic scenes and intimate dialogues demonstrate the partial accuracy of dissenting opinions or biased judgments; and the subjective narration of human experiences by fictive figures reveals the circumscribed range of man's vision or expresses the limits of his mental capacity.

Very few of Wieland's early works have been analyzed or interpreted with adequate care, none exhaustively, and there is no comprehensive study that treats them as a unit with sufficient attention to artistic detail. One reason for this may be the difference in the critical interpretation of certain crucial events in Wieland's early life. One of the first events sometimes misunderstood occurred in 1751. In June of that year the seventeen-year-old Wieland had begun to write an epic poem, *Hermann*, depicting an ancient hero who recently had been portrayed by other authors, Schlegel, Möser, and Schönaich. Wieland's decision to follow them in selecting a Germanic warrior as the main character, and his attempt to create a

great national epic could easily be seen as the experiment of a young
poet ready to test his skills in different genres, all the more since
he had in the same year published his very first works, an ode to virtue, the didactic poem *Die Natur der Dinge*, and an encomium in celebration of divine love, *Lobgesang auf die Liebe*, all of which belong
to different genres and thus testify to the exploratory nature of his
literary activities. When in August 1751 Wieland sent the first four
cantos of the *Hermann* to Bodmer in Zurich, he followed a practice
that was not uncommon among young poets who solicited evaluations
of their works from well-established and widely-recognized critics.

Yet this event has been differently interpreted by other scholars.
Even Friedrich Sengle's biography *Wieland*, an excellent and for
the most part empathic modern study, presents the matter in an unfavorable light. It is Sengle's opinion that the work does not really
reflect Wieland's desire to write a national epic poem, but was artfully designed to serve as a "morsel to bait" a patron (Bodmer "sollte
mit dieser Kostprobe geködert werden"), and he feels that Wieland's
poetic ability "jede beliebige Aufgabe mit hinreichendem Erfolg zu
erfüllen" was a "bedenkliches Talent."[1] Actually, of course, the
artistic capability that enabled Wieland to fulfill every kind of
literary task with sufficient success is not at all a questionable
talent, especially not in one so young who wished to try himself out
in every possible mood and genre, but is, rather, the felicitous
attribute of an eminently gifted poet who, with excellent results,
called upon this talent for the fashioning of virtually every one of
his works.

A second event that has been differently interpreted is Wieland's
personal association with Bodmer. Johann Gottfried Gruber, the first
biographer of the poet, sees Wieland's friendship with Bodmer as an
extraordinarily beneficial relationship that placed the young man in

---

[1]Although Sengle's interpretation of the crucial events discussed here can be questioned if they are judged from a different point of view, the value of his work as the
standard literary biography is generally acknowledged. Its intrinsic importance is
equalled by the pivotal nature of his investigation, for it brings into new focus many
of the significant contributions of past scholarship; and it has, at the same time,
informed and stimulated many a budding Wieland scholar ever since it appeared in
1949.

In his discussion of Wieland's critical writings in behalf of Bodmer's *Joseph und
Zulika*, Sengle expresses a more sympathetic understanding of Wieland's versatility.
He considers the "Briefe yber die Einfyhrung des Chemos" of seminal importance
and sees them as the "first journalistic masterpiece" of the young critic; he indicates
that they testify to the artistry of Wieland's dialectic method and exemplify his com-
mand over "die Kunst, ein Problem im konkreten Hin und Her der Meinungen dialek-
tisch zu entwickeln," a statement which is indeed an appropriate characterization of
Wieland's point-of-view technique in his early literary criticism; see *Wieland*
(Stuttgart, 1949), pp. 62–63.

a most favorable position, for it was through Bodmer that he established lasting friendships with the well-known writers, scholars, and poets, and it was here that he developed previously neglected aspects of his personality, acquired knowledge until then foreign to him, and educated his aesthetic sensibilities.[2] Gruber's descriptions and explanations unquestionably echo Wieland's very own opinions, for in the course of several years the two men had discussed many aspects of the biography in amiable and intimately personal conversation.

Although Sengle does not overlook some of the extraordinary and lasting benefits Wieland derived from his association with Bodmer, he nevertheless judges the experience less sympathetically than Gruber. He believes that the circumstances and events of the early years in Zurich are an unpleasant chapter in German literary history, and he thinks of them as disgraceful for both parties, "ein . . . recht unerfreuliches Kapitel der deutschen Literaturgeschichte, für beide Teile gleichermaßen beschämend."[3] It seems that in particular Sengle does not approve of the young man's facile adaptability during his presence in Bodmer's house. Again, however, it would not be overly difficult to look at Wieland's behavior from a different point of view and to find a more benevolent explanation for his apparently submissive flexibility. When in October of 1752 he came to Zurich, he was a lonely young man just nineteen, still uncertain about his identity, perhaps even experiencing what modern psychologists consider an "identity confusion," which seems to affect above all the gifted and creative during their late and sometimes prolonged adolescence. It is often, as in the classic case of George Bernard Shaw, "not caused by lack of success or the absence of a defined role, but by too much of both."[4] Since for a youth in search of his identity it is not unusual to try out what seem suitable roles in order to discover the one that permits the expression of his dominant faculties and accentuates his own personality, one could easily explain Wieland's behavior as conforming to a pattern that is not uncommon in the life of an "extraordinary individual"; one need not judge his actions as a "spiritual capitulation," as Sengle describes Wieland's conduct.[5]

A later series of events, Wieland's "metamorphosis," toward the end of his residence in Zurich, has also been the subject of contrasting interpretations. The first thorough investigation was undertaken decades ago by Julius Steinberger who published his findings in the well-documented article "Wielands 'Metamorphose' in seiner eige-

[2]*Christph. Martin Wieland*, 2 vols. (Leipzig/Altenberg, 1815–1816); for an extensive discussion of Wieland's Swiss period see Vol. I, pp. 52–121.

[3]Sengle, *Wieland*, p. 46.

[4]Erik H. Erikson, *Identity—Youth and Crisis* (New York, 1968), p. 143.

[5]Sengle, *Wieland*; p. 47 carries the heading "geistige Kapitulation."

nen Beurteilung," which cites revealing excerpts from Wieland's personal letters.[6] He convincingly argues that the young Wieland actually went through three phases, a period of realistic leanings before his sojourn in Switzerland, an idealistic interlude while living with Bodmer, during which time his realistic tendencies were, however, only overshadowed and not entirely obliterated, and a third phase that was characterized by a reversion to former leanings. Wieland's much debated change was thus really not as radical, sudden, and unmotivated as some of his contemporaries (and later critics) claim, with unmistakable disapproval. It was, rather, a slow development and a gradual return to inherent attitudes. Wieland himself would undoubtedly subscribe to this interpretation, for he explicitly indicates the evolutionary pattern in an autobiographical sketch included in his letter of December 28, 1787, to Leonhard Meister; there he considers the year 1757, when he began his work on the epic poem *Cyrus*, as the time of his gradual return to tendencies undeniably natural to him:

> Mit meinem Uebergang aus der Platonischen Schwärmerey zur Mystischen (Ao. 1755. 56.) und mit meinem Herabsteigen aus den W o l k e n auf die E r d e ging es natürlich und gradatim zu. Mein C y r u s, und meine P a n t h e a und A r a s p e s waren die ersten Früchte der Wiederherstellung meiner Seele in ihre natürliche Lage.[7]

The difference in the interpretation of these events by the two most eminent modern biographers of Wieland is striking. Victor Michel pointedly acknowledges the reversionary nature of Wieland's attitudes when he entitles the fifth chapter of his *C.-M. Wieland* "Le rétablissement de l'esprit en sa forme naturelle."[8] This formulation is clearly intended to recall Wieland's own description of his return to his former nature in a letter of November 8, 1762, to Zimmermann, in which he refers to his "rétablissement dans ma forme naturelle."[9] Sengle, however, entitles the section concerned with these events "Die große Wandlung," speaks of the young poet's attitude during this time as ambiguous, perhaps even improper conduct ("zweideutiges Verhalten"), and introduces as "fact" a "startlingly sudden and profound change" ("die Tatsache einer bestürzend plötzlichen und tiefgreifenden Wandlung").[10] It appears that this insistence on an abrupt and fundamental change in Wieland has been interpreted by some as an implicit value judgment of his writings, has led to

[6]*Archiv für das Studium der Neueren Sprachen und Literaturen* (1905), pp. 290–297.
[7]*Ausgewählte Briefe* (Zurich, 1815), iii, 385.
[8]Michel, *Wieland*, pp. 165–229.
[9]*Ausgewählte Briefe*, ii, 195.
[10]Sengle, *Wieland*, pp. 92–93.

scholarly concentration on his later works, and may even have caused
an uncharitable disregard for his early writings.[11]

Some of Wieland's youthful works are modest in scope and undis-
tinguished in their artistic qualities, to be sure; others, however,
warrant more attention than they have hitherto received.[12] The following discussion of a select group of these writings does not try to
rectify the omission. Its aim is more specific: the analysis of typical
sections from the more important works is for the purpose of demon-
strating the presence of perspectivism and indicating the skilful
utilization of the point-of-view technique even in Wieland's earliest
writings. Such an approach cannot do full justice to the aesthetic
values of these works, but it may show that their meaningful inclusion in more comprehensive studies will lead to new and clearer
insights.

The very first of the larger works, the didactic poem *Die Natur der
Dinge*,[13] published in 1752 (when Wieland was only nineteen), and in
substance a vindication of Leibniz' *Theodicée*, introduces perspec-
tivistic traits. The model for the poem, gratefully acknowledged by
Wieland, was Lucretius' *De Rerum Natura*, and the poet intended the
reader to notice many parallels in content, form, and style. Both men

[11]Several fairly recent studies reveal the contrasting views that are characteristic of
the controversy surrounding Wieland's early writings. Cf. Otto Brückl, "Wielands
Erzählungen [1752] . . . Ein Beitrag zur Revision des Wieland-Bildes" (unpub. diss.,
Tübingen, 1958); Wolfgang Preisendanz, "Wieland und die Verserzählung des 18.
Jahrhunderts," *Germanisch-romanische Monatsschrift*, 63 (1962), 17–31; and Cornelius Sommer, *Wielands Epen und Verserzählungen* (pub. diss., Tübingen, 1966).
Whereas Brückl and Preisendanz acknowledge the intrinsic value of the early works,
Sommer (despite his all-inclusive title and for reasons connected with Wieland's
"decisive and fundamental change") indicates that the early tales do not deserve to
be included in his analysis of form and theoretical background, and he does not treat
any that appeared before the *Musarion* of 1768.

[12]The trend promoted by Brückl and Preisendanz is continued by Hermann Müller-
Solger, the author of *Der Dichtertraum, Studien zur Entwicklung der dichterischen
Phantasie im Werk Christoph Martin Wielands* (Göppingen, 1970). He believes that a
more profound understanding of the true nature of Wieland's youthful development is
necessary before valid relationships among the early works and significant connections with those of the later years can be established. Müller-Solger does not seem
to be acquainted with the informative study of Steinberger which lends considerable
support to his thesis. As part of his extensive analysis of dream and fairytale in
selected writings of Wieland, he treats several of the early works: the fragmentary
epic poem *Hermann* of 1751, the biblical epic *Der gepryfte Abraham* of 1753, and the
extant cantos of the epic poem *Cyrus* of 1759. For the latest contribution to a better
understanding of Wieland's early works (available only after my study was completed),
see John A. McCarthy, "Fantasy and Reality: An Epistemological Approach to Wieland" (diss., University of New York, Buffalo, 1972), particularly chap. 1, pp. 9–57.

[13]*Werke* (Akademieausgabe), I, 5–128. Book and line references given in parentheses
in the text are to this edition. Scientific aspects of this poem are treated by Alexander
Gode-von Aesch in *Natural Science in German Romanticism* (New York, 1941), pp.
39–51.

attempt to prove a specific philosophical thesis and chose to do so in poetry. Each poem comprises six books, is composed in verse, and incorporates essential elements of classical rhetoric. Strikingly similar is the predominance of a vocabulary that stimulates the sense of sight; and the extensive use of visual images that are transformed into symbols or function as metaphors and similes is a common characteristic of both works.

Yet more revealing than these similarities are Wieland's departures from the model, particularly in the presentation of conflicting arguments and the ordering of supporting details. At the beginning of the poem he invokes the muses as Lucretius had done, but he requests a different kind of guidance. Inspired with divine enthusiasm by Minerva he hopes to rise above the common earthlings and plans to observe the universe from "heavenly heights":

> Ein ungewohnter Flug
> Hebt mich den Himmeln zu; von Millionen Sternen
> Umringt, lernt sich mein Blick vom niedern Pol entfernen.

$$(\text{I, } 4\text{-}6)$$

The superior point of view announced in these lines is, however, not consistently maintained, and the perspective of the poet is intermittently augmented by the views of eminent philosophers.

In the first book of the poem man is initially represented as a weary wanderer who has lost his way. Darkness and the dimness of his vision blunt his mental perception and cause him to go astray; passion, vice, and sensuousness shroud his mind, and prejudices obstruct his outlook. At times his mental range is even more narrowly circumscribed, and his image of God's universe is clouded by a deceptive haze. This deplorable condition is depicted in an almost facetious manner that may seem inappropriate in a serious poem; man is compared to a tiny fly being attached to a statue of gigantic size:

> Wie eine Fliege, die dort am Colossus hänget,
> In ihren Horizont nur wenig Puncte dränget,
> Ihr kurzer Blick, der sich in enge Zirkel schließt,
> Und kaum acht Linien vom ganzen Bilde mißt,
>
> . . . .
> So schränkt die Dummheit auch die neblichten Ideen
> In einen engen Raum; das Ganze übersehen
> Ist größrer Geister Werk.

$$(\text{I, } 603\text{-}617)$$

This extended simile, although perhaps unwittingly humorous, nevertheless reveals young Wieland's sense of the comic. At this early stage in his career, however, he did not permit his ironies to range widely, possibly because he considered the resulting mood unsuitably frivolous for a poet whose serious intention it was to edify and instruct the discriminating reader.

In his attempts to judge the entire universe by the small fragment he is able to observe, man has often fallen into error. But he does not seem wholly responsible for his mistaken beliefs, for unreliable philosophers and false prophets have often misled him, sometimes even deliberately. Both poets therefore present a *refutatio* of delusive concepts; yet whereas Lucretius reports fallacious arguments in indirect discourse, Wieland, perhaps recollecting Cicero's method in the *De Natura Deorum*, offers deceptive opinions in such a manner that they reveal more immediately the bias of their advocates. The precepts of Zoroaster, for example, are advanced in direct speech, rather conspicuously exposing their rigid limitations. Living in a dark forest, his mind filled with frightening images, the Persian contemplates the cause and nature of evil in the world; and from a dismal *Anblickspunct*—in a later edition Wieland uses the term *Augenpunkt*—he views the misery of mankind:

> Ein boshaft Wesen ists, das uns das Seyn misgönnet,
> Sein Herz ist stetes Feur, wo Zorn und Rache brennet
> Und dunkle Flammen speyt; es nährt mit unserm Blut,
> Gleich einem fetten Oel, die unglückselge Glut.
>
> (I, 671-674)

The personal experiences of the ancient prophet are necessarily limited; but Zoroaster finds his distressing visions of man's life on earth affirmed in the writings of the past, and the works of poets constitute a meaningful extension of his limited knowledge of empirical reality:

> So schließt der Perser Theut, und findt in den Geschichten
> Des grauen Alterthums, umnebelt von Gedichten,
> Was seine Meynung stärkt.
>
> (I, 681-683)

The fifth book of the poem takes up, directly and explicitly, questions of viewpoint, perspective, and relativity. A prefatory statement expresses the poet's convictions and attempts to guide the reader's interpretation of subsequent sections:

> Die Form der Dinge ist so mannichfaltig, als die Gesichtspuncte, woraus sie gesehen werden. Die Grösse, der Raum, die Zeit, die Qualitäten der Körper usw. sind bloß relative Dinge.

A major part of the book is designed to exemplify this notion and support the poet's contention that man's perception of reality is utterly subjective and depends inevitably on the position from which an object or occurrence is viewed. Although *Die Natur der Dinge* foreshadows, technically and thematically, comparable features of later works, it contains a notable contrast to the writings of the mature Wieland. In this early poem the author does not remain neutral; instead, he challenges contestable philosophic views and presents counter-arguments in which he eloquently refutes the ideas of those whom he opposes.

The next larger work, also published in 1752, is the collection of *Zwölf moralische Briefe.* The preface, virtually a formal *exordium*, announces the poet's intention to portray virtue in its most pleasing form, to acquaint the reader with its beauties and commend to him an easy manner by which he can find happiness, "Glückseligkeit." The defense of his ambitious undertaking concludes with a thoroughly confident assertion: "So sehe ich die Sache an, und ich bin gewiß, daß viele hierinn eben so denken wie ich."[14]

The self-confidence expressed in these lines and a first superficial reading of the epistles may create the impression that the events depicted in the *Moralische Briefe* are observed exclusively from the poet's point of view, by artistic design a firmly established superior standpoint. To be sure, the idealistic first-person speaker is easily identified with the young Wieland, and the interpolated moralizing reflections unquestionably advance his own values; yet a closer examination of the text reveals that the poet supports his opinions by a clever manipulation of authoritative views, for almost every one of the conclusions reached in these letters is reinforced by historic and literary perspectives. The method, employed by Wieland with remarkable skill, reflects his acquaintance with classical rhetoric and foreshadows the principles of his own *Theorie . . . der Red= Kunst* (1757), the summary of lectures which he presented when he was a tutor in Zurich. Confirming a traditional dictum of oration, he recommends that every narration be substantially supported by external proof to achieve the highest degree of probability. Convincing evidence to be incorporated in the *confirmatio* should be extracted "*a testimonio,* da man seinen Satz durch Zeugnisse, die eine große Autorität haben, und *ab exemplo,* da man ihn durch historische Beyspiele bestätigt."[15]

Exactly these are the techniques used predominantly in the *Moralische Briefe.* The first letter, for example, is preceded by a motto from Georg Ludwig von Bar's *Epitres diverses,* which in their

---

[14]*Werke* (Akademieausgabe), I, 223.
[15]*Ibid.,* IV, 309–310.

entirety served Wieland as the model for his work. Six lines, reduced in a later edition of the *Briefe* to the essential couplet

Eclairer les savans, c'est beaucoup; on fait plus,
Lorsque l'on fait aimer, et régner les vertus,

validate the young poet's intention of inspiring love and admiration for virtue, and they dignify his undertaking as he does so in poetry. The letter then introduces a symbolic simile that constitutes a significant configuration of point of view, perspective, and observer; it is doubly revealing because it indicates the attention Wieland brought to these matters and at the same time demonstrates the creativeness with which he used literary artifacts. The source is again Lucretius' *De Rerum Natura*, specifically the first lines of the second book:

SVAVE, MARI MAGNO turbantibus aequora uentis,
e terra magnum alterius spectare laborem,
non quia uexari quemquamst iucunda uoluptas,
sed quibus ipse malis careas quia cernere suaue est;
(1-4)[16]

The image is sufficiently metaphorical to function as a figurative parallel between the struggle of a sailor against the elements and that of a man against fate; the observer is implicitly identified as one who under adverse circumstances may possibly experience a similarly precarious situation but is for the moment secure and enjoys being spared such dangers.

Before Wieland incorporated Lucretius' simile into his *Moralische Briefe*, von Bar had adapted it in his *Epitres* (i, 1)[17] for a different, somewhat frivolous purpose, relegating the lines from Lucretius to a footnote and using them as a point of departure for a more narrowly circumscribed scene. The viewer is identified as a man who from a safe distance watches the unfortunate lovers shipwrecked on the "lake of tenderness," the allegorical waters of Mlle de Scudéry's *carte de tendre*, contained in her novel *Clélie*; he scorns these "galley slaves" of passion and vows rather to be damned than become the victim of such foolish infatuation. Wieland acknowledges both

[16]Ed. William Ellery Leonard and Stanley Barney Smith (Madison, Wisc., 1942), p. 311. Cf. Leonard's English translation (New York, 1957), p. 45:

'Tis sweet, when, down the mighty main, the winds
Roll up its waste of waters, from the land
To watch another's labouring anguish far,
Not that we joyously delight that man
Should thus be smitten, but because 'tis sweet
To mark what evils we ourselves be spared;

[17]Georg Ludwig von Bar, *Poetische Werke*, trans. anon. (Berlin, 1756), pp. 30-31.

sources and expands the older versions into an image of dramatic vividness:

Wie vom zufriednem Strand, gesichert vor den Stürmen,
Ein Wandrer ruhig sieht daß sich die Wogen thürmen,
Und in entfernter Höh, den segellosen Mast
Des Goldbeschwerten Schifs ein wilder Orcan faßt,
Jzt in die Wolken treibt, im Ungrund izt vergräbet,
In raschen Wirbeln dreht und wieder schleudernd hebet . . .[18]

The observer is neither a vulnerable spectator nor a cynical bystander; he is a quiet wanderer who from the sheltered beach watches the ever-changing scene inside the field of his vision. In his contemplative mood he may recall the tragic fate of Achamas, the pilot of Telemach, and thus broaden his mental perception by a literary perspective. The tranquil attitude with which the observer views the events is not, of course, characteristic of the common man who constantly must face the perils of the "Meer der Welt" and is forever torn between fear and passion; the superior point of view is that of a profoundly wise sage whose secure position "above the storms" is reinforced by intellectual knowledge and philosophical insights.

In all modesty, the young poet does not feel equally endowed with wisdom; he therefore consults the writings of others and expands the range of his own limited knowledge by including expert views of more experienced men. Every letter is framed by a supplementary perspective: a judiciously chosen motto announces the topic of the epistle and simultaneously indicates the direction of the argument; pregnant allusions to literature in the text of the letters substantiate the poet's stance; and informative glosses or footnotes pointing beyond the work marshal corroborative testimony and indicate illustrative examples. This frequent interaction of author and authorities and the poet's orchestration of several eminent voices demonstrates his dependency on reliable sources. One specific statement contained in the second letter may be understood as a more generally valid description of a characteristic method, which is here and elsewhere felicitously applied; after the poet has presented the views of well-known philosophers he explains his decision to have permitted them to speak in his stead:

"Ich beruffe mich hier auf die grössesten Philosophen, die mir bekandt sind . . . wegen der Weitläufigkeit Ihrer Einsicht, und . . . wegen Ihrer

---

[18]*Werke* (Akademieausgabe), ɪ, 224, first letter, ll. 1-6. Letter and line references hereafter given in parentheses in the text are to this edition.

besondern Kentnis der Natur wiewohl aus verschiedenen Gesichtspunc-
ten."

(ii, 50n)

Bacon, Newton, Leibniz, Bayle, and Sextus Empiricus have contributed their insights, and the young poet gratefully acknowledges
their participation in the argument.

A second didactic poem of the early period, the *Anti=Ovid* of 1752,
is concerned with more mundane problems; it treats questions of love,
sex, and eroticism. The popularity of Ovid and the contemporary
approbation of anacreontic poetry afforded the stimulus for the work,
which was ostensibly intended as a counter-perspective to the *Ars
Amatoria.* The first lines of the poem announce the poet's intention,
somewhat awkwardly in the earliest version:

> Erzehl, o Lied, die seltne Kunst zu lieben,
> Die Kunst der goldnen Zeit, da jedes weiche Hertz
> Von zärtlichen der Tugend werthen Trieben
> Noch überfloß . . . ,[19]

more explicitly in the last version of the poem:

> Die Kunst zu lieben sangst du uns, Ovid:
> Die wahre Art zu lieben sey mein Lied![20]

Although these lines seem to indicate that the poet will portray virtuous, perhaps even Platonic love, and at the same time relegate Ovid
and his followers to a position of little importance, he does not at all
silence the "singers of sensuous love." On the contrary, throughout
his work he presents a double perspective: the images of pure love,
affectionately delineated by the idealistic young poet, alternate with
the portrayal of lusty eroticism in scenes that are borrowed from
literature and are intended to serve as *exempla negativa.*

The deplorable weakness of man in permitting himself to be
seduced by the evil tempter Ariman, by the wanton songs of
Anacreon, or by the sinful teachings of Ovid, the "Meister loser
Künste," rouses the poet's indignation. Yet he is even more perturbed when he discovers that these literary representations are
imitations of reality and that, for example, Juvenal and Petronius,
who in their satires ridiculed the outrageously sordid behavior of
their contemporaries, actually took their models from life. Although
man should perhaps be held responsible for all his acts, extenuating
circumstances relieve him of part of his guilt, for personified volup-

---

[19]*Ibid.*, i, 310. Canto and line references given in parentheses are to this edition.
[20]*Sämmtliche Werke, Supplemente* (Leipzig, 1798), ii, 9.

tuousness, that is *Wollust*, dulls his awareness of evil with flattery and deceives him by creating a favorable image of herself:

Sie borgt die Farbe der Natur,
Sich uns gefälliger zu schmücken;
Verbirgt, was sie entehrt, den aufgehaltnen Blicken,
Und zeigt uns schlau die schöne Seite nur.

(I, 143-146)

A searching and critical scrutiny of her entire domain is not possible from the poet's superior vantage point; he may have to change his position, a necessity he seems to resent:

Doch wie? soll ich dann von den Höhen
. . . .
In deinen Staub herunter steigen,
O Pöbel!

(I, 199-202)

Despite his indignation, however, he descends and cannot help but mock the acts of folly he now must observe. Although it was certainly not his intention to write satire, it is literally forced out of him by the deplorable behavior of man, and with cutting sarcasm he portrays the fate of those who are enslaved by sensual pleasures and passion.

The artistic techniques used to sketch the various scenes—prefaced by the rhetorical question "Was seh ich?"—distinctly recall Albrecht von Haller's method; like the observer in *Die Alpen*, the spectator of the *Anti=Ovid* successively changes his focus and announces the different images with the appropriate adverbs of place:

Da kniet ein zärtlicher Properz,
Und klagt und zeigt sein brennend Hertz
Der tückisch lachenden Neären.
Dort siegt Ruffin, und siegt im Scherz,
Die Schöne bebt, wer kan dem Sieger wehren?

(I, 216-220).

The sketches of human folly in the *Anti=Ovid* clearly reveal the talent for satire which Wieland developed to perfection in his later writings. At this early stage, however, the young poet seems rather shocked by his inclination to expose man's weaknesses in this fashion. He suddenly realizes that he has temporarily lost sight of his intentions to panegyrize virtue; fortunately, however, love herself restrains the "Juvenalean hand" from boldly painting more scornful pictures of this sort and leads him back to his nobler task. The mediated negative perspective of the satire is again balanced by idealistic portrayals also selected from literature. Uz, Gleim, and Hagedorn are offset by Gellert, Klopstock, Haller, and Lange, who through their depiction of pure emotions encourage man to rise above the lowlands of sexual desires and physical involvement.

During the first year of his diversified literary activity Wieland also began to experiment with narrative techniques that were to become characteristic features of his later writings. The fourth larger work, the collection of *Erzählungen* (1752), introduces several significantly new modes of presentation. In contrast to the didactic poems, these verse tales belong to the genre of fiction. Although for the most part the poet enacts the role of omniscient narrator, he occasionally tries—as Henry James would much later describe such an attempt—"to get into the skin of the creature."[21] The point of view from which events and emotions are intermittently seen approximates that of the title heroes, for example Balsora, Zenim, and Gulhindy, or Melinde; in two other tales the poet's perspective sporadically converges with that of representative characters, "Die Unglycklichen" of the third story, and "Der Unzufriedene" of the fourth tale. In the earliest works, *Die Natur der Dinge, Moralische Briefe*, and *Anti=Ovid*, the voices of other authorities, that is philosophers, writers, and historians, were occasionally heard, but the poet himself was the dominant speaker. The *Erzählungen*, by contrast, present monologues and dialogues of purely fictive characters, sparingly in the first tale, most extensively in "Selim," the last of the six stories, in which at times the poet only provides stage directions and has his figures carry on an almost dramatic dialogue. Although there are three voices at work here: that of the narrator, that of Selim, the hero of the tale, and that of Selima, his beloved companion, they are not yet distinctive enough to characterize the individual speakers as being basically different from each other; all three use the same poetic and stylized language reflecting their common idealizing enthusiasm for the beauty and pleasures of nature.

In a unique manner the tale echos one of the major philosophical topics of the eighteenth century, the phenomenon of sense perception and the foundations of empirical knowledge. Selim, who was born blind, is denied the immediate vision of the beauties of nature. His

[21]Henry James, *The American* (New York, 1922), p. xxi. A detailed study of the *Erzählungen* was prepared by August Fresenius in 1885 for a new edition of the tales. Since Fresenius never completed the edition, the introduction was published after his death as an independent article in *Euphorion* (28 [1927], 519-540). In conscientious and systematic fashion the author treats the genesis of the tales, traces their sources, discusses themes and content, cites Wieland's own observations on the collection, and draws an almost complete picture of its reception among eminent eighteenth-century critics, quoting extensively from Sulzer, Ramler, Gleim, Hagedorn, Lessing, and others. Yet as is so often the case with earlier investigations, aspects of form, style, and artistic method are seriously neglected. The omission is partly corrected in the more recent study by Otto Brückl (cf. p. 93 of this monograph).

unimpaired senses, however, serve him well; he is keenly aware of the softly moving, refreshingly cool air in the valley and of the delightful fragrance of the orange blossoms; he hears the beautiful song of the nightingale, the intriguing chatter of the brook, and the crackling sound of branches breaking under the step of his beloved. As they sit under a tree, Selima describes the visual images before her eyes, hoping to mediate a scene of natural beauty to her lover; in vain, of course; he who has never seen color and light, objects or human beings, cannot possibly imagine their external appearance. Yet Selim does not really envy his beloved the ability to observe the splendors of nature. It is she, whom he truly desires to see, and it is the quiet and complete understanding of lovers gazing into each others' eyes that he wishes to experience:

> Welch eine Gunst des Himmels muß das seyn,
> Mit diesen Augen in des andern Minen
> Bloß durch das Ansehn, ohne Mund und Ohren,
> Einander zu verstehn, sich zu besprechen,
> Und, sonder Schall, die innersten Gedanken
> Der Seele anzuhören? Welche Wunder
> Von leisen Harmonien myssen nicht
> Dem Aug entfliessen, das zu gleicher Zeit
> Des Mundes und der Ohren Dienste leistet?[22]

Selim's desire is ultimately fulfilled; with the help of her benevolent guiding spirit Selima cures his blindness. As he becomes accustomed to seeing, his eyes first take possession of her beauty; gradually his perspective widens, broader vistas open before him, and every glance conveys new and splendid images to his mind. The unfamiliar experience moves him profoundly, and he describes the fascinating visions in almost rhapsodic language, concluding with an enthusiastic encomium celebrating God and his creation.

A second collection of letters, the nine *Briefe von Verstorbenen an hinterlassene Freunde* (1753) reveals—as the title indicates—a unique perspective which was actually prefigured in an earlier English work of 1728, *Friendship in Death* by Elizabeth Singer Rowe. The method of presentation is technically different from that of the *Moralische Briefe* in that the events are subjectively reported by fictive figures without the overt intrusion of the poet. Unquestionably, however, the correspondents are made to share the author's superior point of view; they obviously sanction his ideal conception of the function of literature and tacitly confirm his views on the moral obligations of writers as Wieland had expressed them in a personal letter

[22]*Werke* (Akademieausgabe), I, 416.

of March 1752: "—ich habe von der Dichtkunst keinen kleinern Begrif, als daß Sie die *Sängerin* Gottes, seiner Werke, und der Tugend seyn soll."[23]

Of particular significance here are two letters, the first written by Alexis-Junius to Daphnis, and the fourth written by Theagenes to Alcindor. During his stay in Switzerland among the Anglophiles of Zurich Wieland renewed his acquaintance with the ideas of the English empiricists—for example Hume—who held that the senses are the "inlets" through which images are conveyed to the mind, and that whatever is perceived depends on the activity of the sense organs. The images transmitted to the mind, and on a broader scale scenes of human behavior perceived in reality, may well be exemplary and thus benefit the development of the observer; on the other hand, they may be deceptive or even reprehensible and have a distinctly negative influence on a malleable young man.

The guardian spirit of Alexis, the fictive spokesman of the first letter, recognized these dangers, "schoene gefahren, in welchen die Seele willig verliehrt,"[24] for he was acquainted with the irresistible temptation through which "die holden verfyhrerinnen in ihrem triumphe" (I, 142) charm impressionable young men. To prevent Alexis from "letting in" such seductive images he decided to blind him during his stay on earth. Unlike Selim's sight, the vision of Alexis is not restored on earth but only after his death. From this moment on he eagerly observes the broad spectrum of two realms, and as he surveys the beauties of heaven and earth, he too cannot help but celebrate the creator and his universe in an eloquent encomium.

A more pronouncedly dual perspective is presented in the fourth letter "Theagenes an Alcindor." The broad visual range of one who has entered the world of spirits is contrasted—in flashback technique—with a more limited perspective of a human being living on earth. A similar emphasis on the sense of sight, now the symbol of metaphysical perception, is announced in the first lines of the epistle:

> Freund, der vorhang ist weg, die nacht ist vom tage verschlungen,
> Dein Theagenes sieht!

Beauty and truth, light and color, clear images and boundless vistas are enjoyed by Theagenes, whereas Alcindor as the representative of mankind existing in darkness must be content with an occasional glimpse of eternal ideas and an incidental glance beyond the narrow circle of his vision.

[23] *Wielands Briefwechsel*, I, 55.
[24] *Werke* (Akademieusgabe), II, 1-102; here, p. 4; letter and line references are subsequently given in parentheses.

The collections of fictive letters were succeeded by a series of *Gespräche*, formal dialogues invariably characterized by the subtle manipulation of multiple perspectives. Wieland considered the first of these dialogues, the "Gespräch des Socrates mit Timoclea von der scheinbaren und wahren Schönheit" (1754), of seminal importance, and it appeared in every edition of his collected works because it was "der erste Versuch des Verfassers in der dialogistischen Kunst."[25] As the title indicates, the topic of the dialogue is beauty, and many aspects of it, particular and general, physical and spiritual, are viewed from multiple points of view. The mirror image of Timoclea presents her beauty in a favorable light, and the slave girl attending her expresses an equally flattering opinion, yet Timoclea mistrusts both mirror and slave. Her concept of beauty has been influenced by literature, and the ideal images portrayed in poetry serve her as a means to measure her own physical qualities. The possibility that diverging evaluations of her external beauty could exist, and the seeming lack of absolute standards, puzzle the young girl. She therefore implores Socrates to tell her truthfully whether or not she is beautiful: "Sage mir doch, ob ich schön bin oder nicht."[26] He promises to grant her request but before he can do so he must express a word of caution: beauty is relative, and its appreciation depends on the beholder: "Es kömmt sehr viel auf die Augen, und die Gemüthsverhältniß des Sehers gegen dich an."[27] An envious woman will naturally find her less attractive than a man who admires her. The dialogue soon reaches beyond the limited subject of Timoclea's appearance. Socrates develops his theory of physical and spiritual beauty, interprets the body as the mirror of the soul, and touches upon Wieland's perennial topic, the nature of man. In typical socratic fashion he guides Timoclea into philosophical dialogue by asking leading questions and extracting the only possible, predictable answers. It is not by chance that at the end of their conversation their intellectual vantage points coincide and their perspectives converge.

More complex in construction is a later group of dialogues, *Theages oder Unterredungen von Schönheit und Liebe* of 1755.[28] Conversations treating the topics of beauty and love are presented in a letter addressed to a fictitious recipient written by an equally fictitious figure who willingly admits the limits of his objectivity

---

[25]*Ibid.*, II, 277. For a useful though incomplete survey of Wieland's dialogues see Marga Barthel, *Das "Gespräch" bei Wieland*, Frankfurter Quellen und Forschungen, No. 26 (Frankfurt, 1939).

[26]*Werke* (Akademieausgabe), II, 264.

[27]*Ibid.*, p. 265.

[28]*Ibid.*, pp. 423–446.

and frankly betrays the bias of his personal views. Although the work remained a fragment, the published parts do reveal the variety of views that would have been offered in the completed work. A major section of the epistle is the reproduction of a dialogue between the correspondent and his friend Nicias, an enthusiastic Platonist. Interpolated into the conversation, reported partly in direct speech, are several other dialogues, the most extensive one between Nicias and the hermit Theages, and an unusually intriguing exchange of opinions between Theages, also a Platonist, and Aspasia, who does not fully subscribe to his idealistic visions of love. Viewpoints are thus enfolded within one another and several individual perspectives are offered, even if they are not widely separated or contrasting.

Perhaps the most significant of the *Unterredungen*, the discussion of the object and the most appropriate method of love, "was und wie man lieben soll," at the end of the fragment, is promised for the next day; but since Wieland did not complete the work, the dialogue simply did not take place. Yet the direction of Theages' lesson concerning love is predictable: he would reiterate his advocation of Platonic relationships, but he might not do so uncontestedly, for as indicated in earlier remarks, Aspasia would probably challenge his views and offer a different opinion; the missing section would thus actually do no more than offer an eloquent elaboration of views essentially prefigured in the extant parts. In fact the fragmentary form of the *Unterredungen* underlines the tenuousness of the diverse arguments, and its open ending avoids, perhaps even by design, a definitive conclusion which might have forced contrasting, yet at least partially valid views into an artificial synthesis. The equivocation of an unresolved conflict was perhaps intended, and the absence of clearly defined solutions markedly foreshadows the multiplicity of possible answers presented in so many of Wieland's later works.

Among the early writings of Wieland is a group of works that reveals perhaps most distinctly the superior skill with which he made use of the *negative capabilities* he possessed. These are the poetic prayers and visions of 1753 and 1755. The first prayer, *Gebet eines Deisten*, indicates in its subtitle that it was written as a challenge to a similar, seemingly inferior work; it was "veranlaßt durch das Gebet eines Freygeistes."[29] The model for poetic appeals to a superior being in which an unorthodox believer is permitted to express his views, perhaps even utter his doubts, may have been Alexander Pope's *Universal Prayer*, well known in Germany, particularly in its widely circulating translation by Friedrich von Hagedorn;

[29]*Ibid.*, p. 188.

the mood of tolerance communicated in many of these prayers reflects the spirit of religious freedom characteristic of the Enlightenment.

The object of Wieland's implied criticism, the *Gebet des Freygeistes*, appeared at the beginning of 1753 in Hamburg as part of a trilogy of prayers which further included a *Gebet des Christen* and a *Gebet des guten Königs*. Although these prayers were published anonymously, it was correctly suspected by a few perceptive critics that their author was Friedrich Gottlieb Klopstock. The three prayers were his first important attempt at poetic prose; they do, however, echo the sublime language of his *Messias* and reflect even more distinctly the rhetorical qualities of Edward Young's *Night Thoughts*, a work much admired by Klopstock and his contemporaries. The artistic merit of the prayers was immediately questioned, and the self-portrayal of their major characters was judged to be unconvincingly artificial. The title of the first prayer is certainly misleading. The speaker is not actually a freethinker who has renounced the doctrines of the church or negated the existence of God; on the contrary, he is a deeply troubled Christian who has only temporarily lost his faith and is searching desperately for the reaffirmation of traditional religious values; he does so successfully, for he is also the speaker of the second prayer, the *Gebet des Christen*, offered "several years later" in celebration of his return to Christianity.

Two critiques of these prayers, remarkably different in form and tone, appeared soon after their publication. The first one is a parody by Johann Mattheus Dreyer; its title, *Drey Gebete eines Anti-Klopstockianers, eines Klopstockianers, und eines guten Criticus*,[30] and the arrangement of its parts parallel the caption and structure of Klopstock's *Gebete*. The first of Dreyer's prayers reflects the discrepancy between the title and the content of Klopstock's *Gebet des Freygeistes*; the "Anti-Klopstockianer" is not really opposed to the poetic values represented by Klopstock; he only temporarily questions the qualities of his literary style and attitude, and in fact does not even cease to emulate it; he never seriously considers turning against a poet whom he enthusiastically admires. The eloquent language of his prayers, parodistically intended by Dreyer, and the conception of the poet as a divinely inspired creator, reveal the devoted loyalty of the speaker to his mentor, and it does not come as a surprise that "a few weeks later" he offers an encomium of his master in a second prayer, the *Gebet eines Klopstockianers*, as evidence of his return to the fold.

Neither Klopstock's *Gebete* nor Dreyer's parody were well received; both were unfavorably reviewed in the *Berlinische privilegirte*

[30]1753, place of publication not given.

Zeitung.[31] Lessing, who was the reviewer, thought the parody rather frivolous: "sie würde sehr sinnreich seyn, wenn sie nicht so leichte gewesen wäre." He apparently did not know who had written the original prayers, but he assumed that a mediocre poet had done so in imitation of a greater man, and he explicitly objected to the insinuation that Klopstock might have been the author of the *Gebete*: "Warum läßt man den Herrn Klopstock die Ungereimtheit seiner Nachahmer entgelten? Wie kan man auf den Einfall kommen, ihn selbst zum Verfasser der parodirten Gebete zu machen?" He was too great a poet, Lessing felt, to have written such an inferior work. This same attitude is reflected in Lessing's earlier review of the three prayers, specifically in his criticism of the *Gebet des Freygeistes*, whose language he considers contrived, artificial and pretentious. Sarcastically ironic, he grants that a critic might not find the work objectionable if, contrary to good judgment, he would endorse a favorably biased premise:

> Wann Worte und Redensarten, wobey gewisse große Geister vielleicht etwas gedacht haben, widerholen, denken heißt; wann kurze und nicht zusammenhangende Perioden das einzige sind, worinne der laconische Nachdruck bestehet; wann in der bunten Reihe häufiger ? declamatorischer ! und geheimnißvoller = = = das Erhabene steckt; wann verwegene Wendungen Feuer, und undeutsche Wortfügungen Tiefsinnigkeit verrathen; kurz wann unserer Witzlinge neueste Art zu denken und sich auszudrücken die beste ist: so wird man hoffentlich wider angezeigten Bogen nichts zu erinnern haben.

Lessing not only censures the poet's style and syntax, he also criticizes the speaker's disposition, which is severely at variance with the spirit of a prayer; "Heißt denn das auch beten, müssen wir fragen, verzweifelnde Gesinnungen gegen ein Wesen ausschütten, das man nicht kennet?" The *Gebet des Christen* is even more intolerable, "[es] würde dem Unsinne eines Inspirirten viel Ehre machen"; and the prayer of the good king is so unrealistically ideal that even an "oriental Salomon" could not have prayed more piously.

Wieland, in his own criticism of the *Gebete*, points to the very same weaknesses; he is convinced that Klopstock could not possibly have been the creator of this strange figure, a man who is "so übel im Kopf beschaffen . . . , daß man uns mit seinen Schwärmereyen wohl hätte verschonen können."[32] The speaker of the first prayer seems to be an utterly absurd, foolish and confused being who prays nothing but nonsense and contradictions; he is chimerically unrealistic, for neither a deist, nor a skeptic, nor a libertine would speak the language

---

[31]Lessing, *Sämtliche Schriften*, ed. Lachmann-Muncker, v (Stuttgart, 1890); see pp. 155–156 for the review of Klopstock's work and p. 157 for that of Dreyer's *Gebete*.
[32]*Werke* (Akademieausgabe), ii, 188.

of this freethinker. To provide a better example Wieland decided to write the *Gebet eines Deisten* to present a more convincing figure who is not a "Hirngespinst," a figment of the imagination, but is eminently suited to exonerate the nature of man and that of his creator. This *Gebet*, like that of Klopstock, is not actually a prayer; it is a monologue and received in affirmation of its intended form the more appropriate title *Erstes Selbstgespräch eines tugendhaften Heiden* in a later edition of the work. The dramatic speaker is more consistently characterized than Klopstock's freethinker; as a deist he is modeled after the prototype known and defined in the eighteenth century: he believes in a God whose wise providence rules the world and who confers reward or punishment after death according to the nature of man's good or evil deeds; yet he does not believe in revealed religion, nor does he accept as truth any of the articles of faith that pass beyond reason. This deist is as different from a Christian as he is from an Atheist.[33]

In an annotation to his prayer Wieland asserts that it would be easy to substantiate the verisimilitude of the deist, for he is "nach der Natur gezeichnet." There is no reason to doubt the author, but it is conceivable that a literary figure also served, at least partially, as the model for the first-person speaker of the *Gebet*. The name of his beloved, Theoklea, immediately recalls Shaftesbury's deist Theocles, who in a dialogue with Philocles presents and defends the principles of his theology, and there are many similarities between Wieland's figure and Shaftesbury's character of the "Moralist." In close communion with nature both experience that a Deity exists, and the realization has its consummation in a mystical sense of Identity with the superior being, the "mighty Genius" of Shaftesbury's dialogue and the "Unendliche, Erste" of Wieland's *Gebet*. With divine enthusiasm both speakers express their passionate feelings in an emotional rhapsodic hymn to nature, and it can be said of each "'Twas *Nature* he was in love with: 'Twas *Nature* he sung."[34] Wieland's deist, like Shaftesbury himself, cannot be impelled by Christian dogma or logical reasoning to believe in the immortality of the soul; but he is, like his English predecessor, guided by emotion and feeling to hope for a future life; immortality is more than a simple "perhaps":

> Ja eine süße Ahnung, ein frölicher Schauer, wie meine Seele zu fühlen pflegt wenn sie einer gewissen Freude entgegenbebt, versichert mich, daß dieses mehr als ein vielleicht ist. Welch eine Aussicht? welch

[33]Johann Heinrich Zedler, *Grosses vollständiges Universal=Lexicon*, Vol. VII (Leipzig, 1734), col. 437.
[34]Shaftesbury's *Characteristicks*, II, 219.

ein Gedanke, der sich izt wie ein Gott vor meine Seele stellt? Ich darf
ihn nur halb gedenken.—Du bist unsterblich, o Seele?—[35]

This emotional expression of religious feelings and the enthusiasm for
an unchristian God who reveals himself in nature seemed so convincingly genuine that the work was judged to be "ein unanstän-
diges, ärgerliches und gottvergessenes Gebete, welches viel heil-
suchende Seelen übel verführen könnte."[36] Its publication was
prohibited by the Swiss censors, and the work had to be printed in
Berlin.

Wieland's deist, like Klopstock's freethinker, converts to Christianity, and his second prayer, *Gebet eines Christen*, later entitled
Zweites Selbstgespräch eines tugendhaften Weisen, may be understood as a response to the adverse criticism of the earlier work, and
it impressed his contemporaries indeed much more favorably than the
first prayer. The speaker now affirms his acceptance of Christian
dogma and subscribes to the articles of faith; he expresses his belief
in the incarnation of Christ and acknowledges his role as mediator
between man and God. Yet he is no less emotional and enthusiastic
than he had been as a deist; he is still a *Schwärmer*, although of a
different conviction. His gratitude toward Christ is boundless:
"Unendlich gütiger Jesu! Alles das danke ich dir! ich trage deinen
Nahmen, du hast mich erwählt und mit unzehligen Seligkeiten
begnadigt. Durch dich darf sich meine Seele freudig ihrem Schöpfer
nahen."[37] At the time of his death he will joyfully depart: "Dann
werde ich zu dir kommen, mein Erlöser, und ewig bei dir bleiben.
Dann werde ich dich sehen und Ströhme von Thränen der
Zärtlichkeit und Freude zu deinen Füssen weinen: und o Seligkeit!
dann werde ich dich weit vollkommner lieben als izt und ohne Sünde
seyn."[38] This manner of praying is strikingly similar to the fervent
language of pietism, and the wish for the *unio mystica* echos the
ardent desire of the mystics for a union with God.

The prayers do not, of course, express Wieland's own religious
convictions, and the author of the work should not be identified with
the speaker of the prayer. The *Gebete* are the products of a versatile
"chameleon poet," who is expertly "filling some other body" and does
so with persuasive empathy.

Three poetic "visions" that appeared during the next few years
follow a similar principle of composition. The first, *Gesicht von dem
Weltgerichte* (1753), has a prophet as its speaker: "Diese ganze

[35]*Werke* (Akademieausgabe), II, 191.
[36]Bernhard Seuffert, *Prolegomena zu einer Wieland-Ausgabe* (Berlin, 1904), p. 36.
[37]*Werke* (Akademieausgabe), II, 195.
[38]*Ibid.*, p. 196.

erzaehlung wird einem Propheten in den mund geleget"[39]; and the fragmentary third vision, *Gesicht von einer Welt unschuldiger Menschen* (1755), has another fictitious *persona* as its narrator. Of particular importance here is the second vision, which appeared in 1755 under the title *Gesicht des Mirza* and demonstrates a combination of Wieland's favorite techniques: it is the allegorical representation of supernatural events as they are observed and discussed from the subjective points of view of two fictive figures in conversation, and it broadens in a most significant manner the perspective of an earlier vision that must be considered the point of departure for Wieland's work.

Its predecessor appeared in one of the very first literary works Wieland mentioned in his early correspondence, the English *Spectator* which he recommended as delightful and edifying reading in August 1750 to Sophie Gutermann. The issue of September 1, 1711, contains the prototype, the *Vision of Mirzah* by Joseph Addison.[40] Although the English author promised to publish an entire "Oriental Manuscript" of several visions, *The Spectator* did not print more than one. Wieland's *Gesicht des Mirza* was unquestionably intended as a sequel to the English work.[41] The similarities between the two visions are striking, and the differences are obviously so designed that the German work contrasts in a most meaningful manner with the earlier vision. Both works bear the same title, indicating that a Persian prince is the visionary. The mediator of the English vision is a "Genius" in the worldly disguise of a shepherd playing a flute-like instrument whose "inexpressibly melodious" tunes transport Mirzah into a dream-like state and "secret Raptures" in which the vision is revealed. When he is told to "Cast thy Eyes Eastward" he perceives a huge valley, the "Vale of Misery," and "a prodigious Tide of Water rolling through it," which is part of the great tide of eternity. In the midst of the tide he sees a bridge, representing human life, with innumerable trapdoors through which men suddenly and unexpectedly disappear. Darkness and mist cover the waters, obliterating the beginning and end of the "Tide of Eternity." As the allegory ends, Mirzah requests of the shepherd that he reveal "the Secrets that lie hid under those dark Clouds which cover the Ocean on the other Side of the Rock of Adamant." Addison's "Genius" does not fulfill the request but leaves silently and secretly. It is precisely here that Wieland takes over and begins the sequel to Addison's *Vision*. The time is a

[39]*Ibid.*, p. 238.

[40]*The Spectator*, No. 170 (1711), I, 478–482. Lawrence Marsden Price, who establishes a wealth of connections between German and English literature in his *English Literature in Germany* (Berkeley/Los Angeles, 1953), does not mention this particular relationship between the vision published in *The Spectator* and Wieland's *Gesicht des Mirza*.

[41]*Werke* (Akademieausgabe), II, 298–304.

month after Mirza's first encounter with the "Genius," or the "Geist" of the German version, and the two men meet again. Mirza finds "den Geist wieder unter der jungen Ceder sitzen," and the mediator is now willing to fulfill the promise of a second vision. He again uses music to create the appropriate mood and then commands Mirza to turn towards the West, not the East where the vision of life had appeared: ". . . nachdem er mein Gemüth durch ein Lied aus einer silbernen Laute in eine sanfte Harmonie eingewiegt hatte, befahl er mir gegen Abend zu sehen." The stage is set, and in the "magic spirit of oriental philosophy" a vision is created that portrays the "Geisterwelt," the world of the spirits, as a representative of the "Zoroastic-Platonic System" would relate it to his listener. Addison had written an allegory about time, human life, and eternity; Wieland provided a fitting sequel and a supplementary perspective in his "allegorical tale of the human soul."

The early development of the point-of-view technique reaches its culmination in *Araspes und Panthea. Eine moralische Geschichte in einer Reyhe von Unterredungen* (1760).[42] It was written during the time of Wieland's "metamorphosis" and testifies to the author's descent from his *Adlerflug* to earth. In contrast to the former idealizing depiction of love, the theme of the dialogues is the question of whether the mastery of passion depends on man's free will or if there are forces at work that disable his reason when sensual desire takes possession of him. Araspes' love for Panthea is the central event, and the psychological discussion of the hero's involvement by every one of the interlocutors produces a complex pattern of analytical perspectives. The initial dialogue between Cyrus and Araspes, still a rather theoretical discourse, reveals their contrasting views. Cyrus believes that man is often helplessly enslaved by his passion for a woman and is therefore unable to control his emotions or the ultimate consequences of his action. Araspes does not agree, but is convinced that he has the capability to check his desires of his own volition. Experience, however, was to teach him differently. His admiration for Panthea, the wife of Abradates, turns into love, and he is seized with an uncontrollable desire to possess her, a development which is observed and interpreted from diverse points of view.

The first one to notice the profound change in his attitude is Araspes himself; the progression of his entanglement is intermittently accompanied by monologues of searching self-analysis and, as Shaftesbury had described the technique, Araspes becomes his own subject and undergoes a process of "self-dissection." The soliloquies are at first meant to help him understand his conflicting emotions;

[42]*Ibid.*, III, 1–88.

later, however, they serve to rationalize and vindicate his questionable behavior. Araspes is also permitted to verbalize his feelings in intimate conversations with Arasambes, who basically shares the views of Cyrus: there is no escape from passion unless the lover removes himself from the object of his desire; Arasambes therefore implores Araspes to renounce his appointment as the guardian of Panthea.

A diverging double perspective is provided through the dialogue between Panthea and her wise old servant Mandane. Whereas the young woman idealizes the feelings of Araspes and interprets them as unselfish and virtuous love, Mandane sees his infatuation as an illness which can only be cured by severe measures, at best perhaps the betrayal of his passion to Cyrus.

Still another perspective develops when the slave girls, virtually enacting the role of the chorus in Greek tragedy, voice their views and predictions. In their earthy approach to questions of love and sex they correctly analyze Araspes' behavior as typical of a man ardently desiring the woman he adores; and they interpret Panthea's obvious concern for his welfare as an expression of her own erotic feelings. It is only a question of time, they actually hope, before the lovers will gratify their desire and commit adultery. Not only has their own experience led to these insights, literature, too, portrays the fate of women pursued by passionate lovers, and at the very moment when Araspes attempts, though unsuccessfully, to seduce Panthea, they perform an antiphony of love and temptation, guilt and atonement. In the concluding dialogue with Cyrus, Araspes reveals that the experience has deepened his understanding of the nature of man. He is not any more the idealist who expects to master his passions with superior self-control; he now is aware of the complex character of human beings and concludes that man must have two souls which are responsible for his actions: "wenn die gute die Oberhand hat, dann handeln wir edel; wenn die böse, niederträchtig und schändlich,"[43] an idea which recalls Bodmer's *Joseph und Zulika.*

The story of Araspes and Panthea is presented without the intervention of a personal or fictive narrator, and the excellence of the work testifies to the success of Wieland's experimentation with philosophic and dramatic dialogue. His predilection for this artistic method also found expression in the two tragedies of the early period, *Lady Johanna Gray* (1758) and *Clementina von Porretta* (1760). Although both plays reveal Wieland's persistent and attentive study of man,

[43]*Ibid.,* p. 87. The concept was prefigured in Wieland's model, the *Cyropaedia* of Xenophon (VI, i, 41), and the related ancient concept of man being accompanied throughout his life by two spirits, one benevolent and one evil, was well known to Wieland (see also Erasmus, *Adagia* I, 1, 72).

their major characters are still idealized and their depiction does not
yet manifest the poet's descent from his superior point of view, nor
does it demonstrate the irrevocable return from his *Adlerflug*.
Wieland's presentation of perfect figures should not be censured as a
misinterpretation of human nature; on the contrary, he was sensi-
tively aware that this manner of portrayal essentially constituted a
glorification of man and did not at all conform to the principles of
psychological realism in literature that were so very earnestly advocated by many of his contemporaries; he therefore repeatedly explained his reasons for the adherence to a tradition that was much
debated at the time when his plays were performed in Germany and
Switzerland. His theoretical discussion of tragedy contained in the
Theorie und Geschichte der Red=Kunst und Dicht=Kunst of 1757
supports the poetic creation of perfect characters: "Die Personen
einer Tragödie sollen allezeit erhabne und heroische Personen
seyn";[44] and the preface to *Lady Johanna Gray* affirms his conception
that tragedy should present noble, heroic, and virtuous figures:
"Die Tragödie ist dem edlen Endzweck gewidmet, das Grosse,
Schöne und Heroische der Tugend auf die rührendste Art vorzustellen."[45] Reiterating these views in his personal correspondence, he
asserted his privilege to portray equally idealized figures in his second
tragedy and defiantly disregarded the criticism to which *Lady
Johanna Gray* had been subjected by well-known men of letters in
Berlin, among them Lessing, who had published a devastating review
in the *Litteraturbriefe* of 1759. The general public, however, had
judged differently and received the play with enthusiastic approval.
Wieland expected a similarly divided reaction to his second tragedy;
the critics, whom he did not actually care to please, would probably
condemn *Clementina von Porretta*, but the public, whose good
opinion he cherished, would most certainly like it:

> ". . . sie hat auch ihre Partey schon zum voraus genommen; sie erwartet
> und wünscht nichts von diesen Kunstrichtern, und tröstet sich wegen
> der Verfolgung, die ihr von ihnen vielleicht bevorsteht, in Demuth mit
> dem Beyfall des Publici."[46]

Lessing's criticism of *Lady Johanna Gray* was indeed severe.[47] He
ridiculed Wieland's principles as expressed in the preface of the
published work and, cuttingly sarcastic, rejected the presentation of

---

[44]*Werke* (Akademieausgabe), IV, 385.
[45]*Lady Johanna Gray* (Zurich, 1758), 2nd page of *Vorbericht* (not pag.).
[46]*Ausgewählte Briefe*, II (Zurich, 1815), 122.
[47]Lessing, *Sämtliche Schriften*, ed. Lachmann-Muncker, VIII (Stuttgart, 1892),
166–178; a more favorable review appeared about the same time in *Göttingische
Anzeigen von gelehrten Sachen . . . auf das Jahr 1759*; see p. 104. For a recent discussion of Wieland's dramas see Leslie John Parker, "Wielands dramatische
Tätigkeit" (diss., Austin, Texas, 1959).

perfect characters on the stage. Although directed against a specific work, his emphatic disapproval of idealized figures in literature must be interpreted in the larger context of a more general controversy. At mid-century the nature of man and the artistic creation of his image in literature were perhaps more ardently discussed than ever before, and some of the most reliable critics reversed their position completely in the course of a few years. Lessing's own attitude underwent an adjustment that was symptomatic of a progressive development leading to considerable changes in the literary portrayal of man. In two early reviews (1754 and 1755) of Richardson's novel *Grandison* he generously approved the depiction of an ideal hero, a "truly noble man" of religious conviction, perfection, and virtue,[48] and he praised the character of Clementina for its artistic excellence and convincing veracity; it was created "mit so viel Kunst und Wahrheit . . . , daß er unter diejenigen Phantasiebilder gehöret, die man den steifen und trocknen Nachschilderungen der Natur mit allem Rechte vorzieht."[49] At this time Lessing sanctioned the poetic idealization of man and rejected strictly mimetic depictions. Four years later, however, he voiced entirely different demands, condemned the very same method he had previously lauded, and criticized Wieland for the unrealistic representation of historical figures: "der Mann der sich so lange unter lauter Cherubim und Seraphim aufgehalten, hat den gutherzigen Fehler, auch unter uns schwachen Sterblichen eine Menge Cherubim und Seraphim . . . zu finden." Lessing was nevertheless convinced that Wieland would abandon the deceptive idealization of man at his return to earth from the "etherial regions" and recognize the true nature of a being that participates in good and evil. "Und alsdenn," Lessing predicts, "wenn er diese innere Mischung des Guten und Bösen in dem Menschen wird erkannt, wird studiret haben, alsdenn geben Sie Acht, was für vortreffliche Trauerspiele er uns liefern wird!"[50]

Not much later Wieland did indeed explicitly renounce the ideals of his youth, and it was perhaps no coincidence that in his personal correspondence he spoke of the change in his perspective, his "Herabsteigen auf die Erde," in a language that recalls Lessing's formulations.[51] He also revealed more frankly than his contemporaries would appreciate that he was well acquainted with the complexities of human nature. Yet Lessing's prediction did not come true; Wieland delivered no splendid tragedies but preferred to portray man in all his inglorious imperfection less seriously and in different genres.

[48]Lessing, *Sämtliche Schriften*, v (Stuttgart, 1890), 399.
[49]*Ibid.*, vii (Stuttgart, 1891), 18–19.
[50]*Ibid.*, viii (Stuttgart, 1892), 167.
[51]*Ausgewählte Briefe*, iii, 385.

6 ‖ Don Sylvio

Wieland's first novel, *Der Sieg der Natur über die Schwärmerei oder die Abenteuer des Don Sylvio von Rosalva*, has received considerable attention ever since its publication in 1764. Although various aspects of the work have been investigated, important and distinctly characteristic features still remain to be analyzed, among them some of those that are related to the theme of the present study.

A topic closely akin to matters of perspective and point of view is the question of *personae* in fiction; it was of considerable concern to Wieland, who knew that the indiscriminate identification of the author of a novel with the narrator of the story would invariably lead to misinterpretations. He had not been spared unjustified criticism resulting from the careless confusion of the creator of a work with its fictive speakers, and unfair personal attacks may well have stimulated him to plead the case of the misunderstood author. He did so in the brief essay "Wie man liesst,"[1] in which he presented an anecdote exemplifying the typical reaction of indolent readers who disregard the identity of the spokesman and naively believe that every thought expressed in a novel reveals the opinion of its author. At a social event the epistolary novel *La nouvelle Héloise* is discussed and its author, Rousseau, censured for his advocacy of suicide. In support of the accusation one of the guests reads aloud a letter in which suicide is indeed defended. Yet it is not Rousseau who argues in favor of it, but St. Preux, the protagonist of the novel, who presents these thoughts. Nevertheless, the critic convinces most of his listeners so

---

[1]*Der Teutsche Merkur*, January 1781, 1st quarter (Weimar, 1781), pp. 70-74.

thoroughly of Rousseau's (not St. Preux's) guilt that they are almost ready to burn the book. Only a few sensitive readers among the guests raise modest objections and cite letters in which contrasting ideas are expressed by other correspondents. Yet they are unable to exonerate the author, for it seems much more convenient to accept the prejudiced opinion of the *Vorleser* than to identify different narrative voices and contemplate the ensuing diversity of views. The anecdote causes Wieland to deliberate upon similar experiences and express his dissatisfaction with inattentive readers who do not make the necessary distinction between author and spokesman but charge the writer with intentions and opinions that do not at all reflect his personal convictions or well-established views.

Wieland's reflections on the complex author-narrator relationship and his disapproving attitude toward those who neglect a careful consideration of all its implications is a challenging invitation to a searching analysis of the narrator's identity and his function in the novel. Yet these artistic aspects have sometimes been treated too lightly. Even one of the more recent editions of his works contains the categorical statement: "Wielands Romane erzählt Wieland."[2] This formulation is an oversimplification and reflects a slight confusion of critical terms. To be sure Wieland created every single one of his novels; he selected their themes and subjects, established the order of the fictitious world, and accentuated particular ethical values. He decided upon the structure of the novel, determined its style, tone, and techniques and performed the practical task of writing the work. Yet, in none of his novels does Wieland the author narrate the events or tell the story. For this specific purpose he created an impressive variety of fictitious historians, reporters, and spokesmen. Naturally, the author himself established the identity of each narrator, prescribed his individual role, and designed the most appropriate mask and costume for him; he curtailed the extent of the spokesman's knowledge, decided upon his distinctly subjective point of view, and limited his ability to judge character or evaluate events.

Thoroughly acquainted with the traditions of the novel and with contemporary fiction, Wieland was well informed of past and current experiments with narrative techniques, and from the rich fund of available devices he freely adopted those that suited his purpose and matched his style. The classic works of prose fiction from Heliodorus to Sterne, many of them favorites of Wieland, presented a wide selection of narrator-figures that were to serve as models for later novelists. The seventeenth-century Romance generally followed the

[2]Christoph Martin Wieland, *Romane*, ed. Friedrich Beißner (Darmstadt, 1964), p. 910.

tradition established by Heliodorus in the *Aethiopica*. The events are told by an omniscient narrator, a kind of rhapsodist whose personality is perhaps best described in Goethe's and Schiller's essay *Über epische und dramatische Dichtung*:

> Der Rhapsode, der das vollkommen Vergangene vorträgt, [wird] als ein weiser Mann erscheinen, der in ruhiger Besonnenheit das Geschehene übersieht; . . . [er] sollte als ein höheres Wesen in seinem Gedicht nicht selbst erscheinen; er läse hinter einem Vorhange am allerbesten, so dass man von aller Persönlichkeit abstrahierte und nur die Stimme der Musen im allgemeinen zu hören glaubte.[3]

Frequently, however, the superior point of view of the omniscient narrator is abandoned; figures in the novel then take over the task of reporting and relate their own experiences in interpolated first-person narratives. Their perspective is limited, of course, and the presentation of events is colored by their individual personalities.

A different type of narrator was made famous by Cervantes. The adventures of Don Quijote, it will be remembered, had allegedly been written down by the historian Sid Hemet Benengeli, and the original manuscript, several notebooks in the Arabian language, was by chance discovered in Toledo. The fortunate finder commissioned its translation into Spanish and then functioned as the editor of the work. Occasionally he comments on the skill of the Arabian narrator or expresses his doubts as to the reliability of a man whose national characteristic is an inclination to pervert the truth, thus alerting the reader to possible discrepancies and inconsistencies in the novel. In the *Don Quijote*, too, the successive narration of events is interrupted by interpolated stories told by fictitious characters. Obviously all these spokesmen, including the Arabian historian and the Spanish editor, are invented to populate the fictitious world. Although they may occasionally echo Cervantes' philosophy, not a single one is identical with the author of the literary work.

Cervantean overtones are clearly evident and have been traced in the novels of Henry Fielding. Yet his method is different from that of the Spanish work in two essential aspects. In *Joseph Andrews* and *Tom Jones* Fielding does not present a fictitious manuscript and does not provide an editorial frame comparable to that of *Don Quijote*. Instead he creates a narrator who plays a dual role. First, he intermittently wears the mask of a theoretician who propagates a new genre, the comic epic in prose, provides rules for its perfection, and analyzes with ironic pretense the method and techniques of a literary work seemingly in the process of being written simultaneously with the

[3]Goethe, *Sämtliche Werke*, xxxvi, ed. Oskar Walzel (Stuttgart/Berlin, 1902), 151–152.

commentary. Second, he enacts the role of a historian who allegedly presents an authentic story of contemporary men, relates the apparently actual events of their lives, and reflects on their morals and manners as if they were real human beings and not invented characters.

Distinctly different from the *personae* created by Cervantes and Fielding is the narrator of Laurence Sterne's *Tristram Shandy*. He recalls the typical first-person narrator of the picaresque novel, who is as fictional as the events he relates. Tristram, however, is more self-conscious than, say, Lazarillo de Tormes; he is fully aware of himself as a writer and speaks freely of the complex task he faces while relating his life from a rather eccentric point of view and communicating his clearly subjective opinions.

Although attempts have been made to isolate the influence of these predecessors on Wieland's novels, such studies have not convincingly proven that he favored one method of narration to the exclusion of others. Wieland was not an imitator who felt compelled to copy prefigured narrators, but he creatively and occasionally with parodistic intention borrowed characteristics from others, thus equipping his own spokesmen with devices passed on by tradition, yet modernized to suit their essentially different intentions.[4]

Wieland's first novel, the *Don Sylvio*, has a structure similar to that of the *Don Quijote* and presents an equally complex cast of narrators and spokesmen. They are identified in a preface playfully labeled the *"Nachbericht des Herausgebers"* erroneously placed at the beginning of the novel by a rather unreliable, naturally fictitious, copyist, one of the mediators who could possibly be blamed for other inconsistencies.[5] The story of Don Sylvio was allegedly told by the Spaniard Don Ramiro von Z**, then translated into German by a friend of the editor, and finally placed in the editor's hands for publication. The editor, however, leaves it to the discretion of the reader whether to doubt the existence of a Spanish manuscript or to suspend his disbelief and share in the ironic pretence. The apparently playful remarks should not be taken too lightly; they have a more profound, serious meaning, for they encourage the reader to penetrate the mask of fictitious spokesmen and alert him to frequent changes in costume.

Recollecting previous experiences with the critics of his literary works, Wieland could easily foresee the disparate verdicts on his first

[4]See Peter Michelsen, *Laurence Sterne und der deutsche Roman des 18. Jahrhunderts*, Palaestra, Vol. 232 (Göttingen, 1962); Guy Stern, "Fielding, Wieland, and Goethe" (diss., Columbia, 1954); Stephan Tropsch, "Wielands Don Sylvio und Cervantes' Don Quijote," *Euphorion*, 4th Supplement (1899), pp. 32–61.

[5]For the following discussion of the novel I am using the first edition of 1764, which is reprinted in the *Werke*, I, ed. Fritz Martini and Hans Werner Seiffert (Munich, 1964); page references are given in parentheses.

novel, and the predictable diversity of critical approaches to *Don Sylvio* is prefigured in the preface to the work, presenting three evaluations of it from different points of view. The editor himself develops the perspective of a critic who, like Horace, expects of literature that it should entertain and delight. Since the story of the young nobleman has provided his entire household with pleasant hours and has even made his sullen pedantic copyist laugh, it certainly must deserve publication.

This benevolent view is not shared by the second, much sterner critic who came upon the manuscript in a devious manner while secretly searching through the editor's papers. He is a Jansenist and cannot possibly approve of this type of literature. The inclusion of his critical attitude points, of course, beyond the frame of the novel. Wieland certainly expected the well-informed reader to recall the moral bias of the Jansenists toward all entertaining literature and probably hoped that they would remember one of the most famous representatives of Port Royal, Blaise Pascal, whose disapproval of the comedy might equally well apply to the satirical novel:

> Tous les grands divertissements sont dangereux pour la vie chrétienne; mais entre tous ceux que le monde a inventés, il n'y en a point qui soit plus à craindre que la comédie.[6]

The fictitious Jansenist of the preface expresses the bias of his order and his own subjective opinions, but he also speaks for a larger group of contemporary critics. The rejection of a literature that offered pleasant diversion and the strict insistence on the usefulness of art echoes the attitude of the German and Swiss theologians who were zealously attempting to reform literature and the theater.

The verdict of the Jansenist, who considers *Don Sylvio* an impious and dangerous book serving the secret purpose of a treacherous attack on the religious doctrines of his society, is not shared by the third, seemingly less biased critic, also a man of the church, whom the editor had asked for an impartial judgment. In his evaluation of the manuscript the priest approves the author's aim to entertain, and he sanctions his intention to ridicule the folly of man, his prejudices and erroneous opinions, the excesses of his imagination and passion. If this can be achieved with good humor and gentle satire, no harm will be done; in fact the exposure of immature superstitions and the ignorant credulity of the common people would never be damaging to the church, but rather a service to religion.

In his portrayal of the two critics the editor does not remain neutral. Through the slanted characterization of both men, particularly

---

[6]*Pensées*, ed. Léon Brunschvicg, I (Paris, 1904), 23–24.

through the clever use of descriptive adjectives, he presents an over-riding view, the kind of "poetic perspective" earlier defined and recommended by Wieland himself as an excellent literary technique.[7] The editor's qualifying terms place both characters in a brighter light, but also expose his own bias. The Jansenist is called a Petrinist and a heretic and is described as stubborn and obstinate. The priest, in contrast, is said to be a highly respected ecclesiastic, a most learned, pious, and honorable man. Obviously, the partial portrayal is intended to influence the reader and induce him to accept the more favorable evaluation of the story. Yet a discerning critic will have cause to doubt the reliability of the priest's judgment, for he is not an unerring expert on literary matters. His fallibility is subtly intimated in an unobtrusive allusion. In his approval of the author's intention to expose superstition and gullibility, the ecclesiastic considers it par-ticularly justified to deride "dasjenige, das Juvenal veteres avias nenne" (13). However, Juvenal never used this formulation in a rele-vant connection; it was Persius who stated in his fifth satire:

Disce, sed ira cadat naso rugosaque sanna,
dum veteres avias tibi de pulmone revello.
(ll. 91–92)[8]

Wieland's learned reader will recall not only this passage but perhaps also the larger context. He may assume that the author of the novel expects him to remember the first lines of the fifth satire:

'VATIBUS hic mos est, centum sibi poscere voces,
centum ora et linguas optare in carmina centum.'
(ll. 1–2)[9]

Thus Wieland ironically and playfully reminds the reader of the tradi-tion which permits a poet to wish for a hundred tongues to sing his song or a hundred voices to tell his tale.

In the same manner the fictitious manuscript was critically ap-proached from various angles, the events of the story are seen from distinctly different points of view, and through an adroitly devised rhetorical strategy Wieland seeks to induce his readers to adopt flexi-

[7]For a more detailed discussion of "poetic perspective" see Chapter 7 of this study.
[8]*The Satires of A. Persius Flaccus*, ed. John Connington (Oxford, 1893), pp. 104–105: "Attend, then, but drop that angry wrinkled snarl from your nostrils, while I pull your old grandmother out of the heart of you."
[9]*Ibid.*, p. 87: "Persius: 'It is a standing rule with poets to put in a requisition for a hundred voices, to bespeak a hundred mouths and a hundred tongues for the purpose of a song.'"

ble attitudes which closely approximate the diverse perspectives presented throughout the novel.

At the time when Wieland was writing his first novel, he also wrote his *Comische Erzählungen*, the comic verse tales that were to appear a year later, in 1765. It is not at all surprising, then, that the two works have important traits in common: they are ironic in tone and satiric in intent; dialogues and dramatic scenes are part of their structural pattern; multiple perspectives complement the central narrative; and the primary spokesman of each is, at times, playfully elusive and intermittently changes his mask and costume. His tendencies (by design of the author, of course,) to alter his identity, covertly or overtly, recalls the practice of other satirists and appears to be in striking parallel to a dominant feature of formal verse satire, the best-known classical and modern examples of which served Wieland as models for his own prose and verse satires. The conspicuous similarity in the role and appearance of the typical satirist of formal verse satire with the satirist of the *Don Sylvio* invites a closer comparison, even though the analogy may be a bit speculative here.[10]

Invariably the speaker of formal verse satire is an assumed identity, a *persona*, who has several distinguishable voices. One is that of the rational man, the *vir bonus*, the tranquil citizen whose ideal is the Golden Mean; in the age of Enlightenment he usually is the *honnête homme*. The second voice is that of the *naif*, the *ingénu*, the simple heart, and its owner is customarily the "vehicle of ironies." The third voice is that of a "public defender," a man of indignation who, like Swift's *personae*, may well respond with "perfect rage and resentment" to the corruption of the wicked world and advocate violent methods to bring mankind to its senses.[11] All three and possibly other voices contribute to the pattern of formal verse satire, the two layers of its general plan, a thesis layer attacking some specific vice and folly, and an antithesis layer recommending its opposing virtue.

In Wieland's first novel two of the satiric voices, that of the *ingénu* and that of the *vir bonus*, are distinctly audible. Significantly, the voice of the "public defender" is almost entirely lacking, most certainly because Wieland favored the mild satire of Horace and the moderate attitude of Lucian over the violent indignation of Juvenal and does not present a passionate attack on vice but a gently derisive

---

[10]In a separate study of Wieland's satire, for which I hope to benefit from the findings of recent American studies on English satiric literature, I shall try to demonstrate more thoroughly the connections indicated here. For a particularly informative discussion of the satirist as *vir bonus* and *ingénu*, see Mary Claire Randolph, "The Structural Design of the Formal Verse Satire," *Philological Quarterly*, xxi (1942), 368–384.

[11]Alvin Kernan, *The Cankered Muse* (New Haven, 1959), p. 19.

exposure of foolishness. Although the subtlety of the artistic arrangement prohibits exclusive categorization, the identification of
the two voices is conditionally possible.[12] The role of the *ingénu* is
assigned to Don Ramiro, the fictive chronicler, who allegedly tells a
true story based on authentic information. His identity is intermittently confirmed by references to his background. The first two chapters, particularly, emphasize the Spanish setting and reveal his
familiarity with the social customs of the country. His nationality
is verified by occasional references to his countrymen, as for example
when he admits that he has no confidence in the tales "von den
Gesichten unsrer frommen Landsmännin, der Schwester Maria von
Agreda" (55). The Spaniard's promises to observe the "Pflichten der
historischen Treue" and to relate everything "wie die Geschichte
meldet" (173) are meant to underline the narrator's dependence on
empirical reality. His involvement in telling the story is affirmed,
parodistically to be sure, by the fictive editor of the manuscript, who
refers to the "wahrhafte Urheber dieser merkwürdigen und
kurzweiligen Geschichte" (104), identifies him as "der Spanische
Autor, der im Gefolge eines bekannten Ministers seiner Nation sich
etliche Jahre in D** aufgehalten" (107), and explains the beginning
of the seventh book as an appropriate apology from the Spanish
author for his departure from the straight path of direct narration (348).

As in formal verse satire, the *ingénu* of Wieland's novel is the
medium of ironies. He is a man of moderate knowledge who admits
the narrowness of his perspective; he professes to be only partially
informed, indicates his uncertainties by the occasional use of "ver-
mutlich," and confesses his subjective point of view by humble admission: "Dieses ist wenigstens nach unserer Meinung die wahr-
scheinlichste Erklärung, die man von dergleichen Visionen geben
kann" (57). The choice and arrangement of his words convey, by
artistic design of course, effective verbal irony. He suggests, for
example, a false image of Donna Mencia when he calls the narrow-
minded and not too virtuous spinster "großmütig" or "edel" and
"keusch." The use of learned, often inappropriate metaphors and
similes which lend the subject an air of undeserved dignity creates
in its comic disparity and dissimilarity a substantial irony of reference: Don Sylvio's music teacher, a barber, is identified as the

---

[12]In contrast to Friedrich Beißner, Jörg Schönert makes the necessary distinction
between author and narrator in an excellent discussion of satiric aspects in Wieland's
Don Sylvio; see his *Roman und Satire im 18. Jahrhundert* (Stuttgart, 1969), pp. 131–
145. Although he distinguishes multiple levels of narration and sees important connections with Wieland's verse narratives, he does not identify the separate voices of the
satirist.

"Amphion der Gegend" (20); Pedrillo, the servant of Don Sylvio, is referred to as the "getreue Achates" (135); and the Procurator of Xelva, the misshapen suitor of Donna Mencia, receives the epithet "der neue Adonis" (60) and is unduly enobled by the name of Aeneas (74). In characteristic fashion the *ingénu* also reflects upon his involvement in the art of literature and speaks of technical matters; he apologizes for the poor choice of expressions and confesses to limited abilities as he describes Mergelina, the grotesquely ugly creature Don Sylvio is supposed to marry: "Wir wollen einen Versuch wagen, ob wir die Einbildungskraft unsrer Leser in den Stand setzen können, sich einige Vorstellung von ihr zu machen" (62). The central section of this attempt is a masterpiece of negatively allusive description meant to convey the strange mixture of physical colors whose reproduction would even tax the abilities of a Van Dyck: "Sie hatte weder blonde Haare wie Ceres, noch braune wie Venus, noch goldfarbe wie die Schöne mit den goldnen Haaren, die ihrige waren feuerfarbig und dabei von Natur so geradlinicht und kurz, daß sie die Kunst und Geduld einer Cypassis zu Schanden gemacht hätten" (63-64). A most revealing section packed with ironies closes the eighth chapter of the first book. The narrator has reproduced a passionately enthusiastic monologue of his hero and concludes:

Also sagt er und schwur; ihn hörten die Nymphen im Haine,
Und die Feen, und - - -

He is utterly amazed at his creating verse and contemplates the sudden unintended change in style:

Je nun! wahrhaftig! das sind ja gar Hexameter? Was für ein ansteckendes Fieber der Enthusiasmus ist! die begeisterte Rede des Don Sylvio ergriff uns, ohne daß wir es gewahr wurden, und wenn uns Apollo nicht in Zeiten beim Ohr gezupft hätte, so könnten unsre armen Leser mit einem ganzen Wolkenbruch von Hexametern geängstigt worden sein, eh wir gemerkt hätten, daß es nicht recht richtig in unserm Kopfe sei. Wir wollen also hier einen Augenblick ruhen, und, ehe wir diese wahrhafte Erzählung fortsetzen, unserm Blute Zeit lassen, wieder in Prosa zu fließen (35).

Ironically naive are his surprise at the verse form of his statement, the effect Don Sylvio's "Schwärmerei" has on his creator, the allusion to the God of poets; characteristic is the overt consideration of the reader, ironic the exaggeration "Wolkenbruch," the admission of a foolish act, the assurance of the verity of the story, and the reference to the creative act to be postponed for a while.

Very different in tone is the voice of the *vir bonus*; his role is enacted by the fictive editor who freely interpolates theoretical sections so that even the structure of the tale reveals two separate narrative voices. For example, at the end of the fifth chapter, third book, the editor interrupts the narration and inserts an apology on behalf of the translator. The Spanish author had ridiculed the political system of small republics, a topic which seemed rather unpatriotic to the translator; he therefore refused to translate the questionable part of the manuscript and it was accordingly excluded from publication. Whereas here a part is omitted with the consent of the editor, another chapter, the eleventh of the same book, is—like so many of the theoretical sections—clearly the product of the editor. The tenth book ends with the assurance of the spokesman that he will return without further digression to the characters of the story:

> Und nunmehr kehren wir, ohne uns länger mit solchen Subtilitäten aufzuhalten, zu unsern beiden Schönen zurück, welche wir, wie man sich vielleicht noch erinnert, auf dem Rückwege nach Lirias verlassen haben (139).

The following chapter does not at all fulfill this promise, however; it is designated "Eines von den gelehrtesten Capitel in diesem Werke" and continues to present "Subtilitäten" which are to be understood as the digressive reflections of the editor.

The fictive editor using the mask and voice of the *vir bonus* is emancipated from the playfully imposed ignorance of the Spaniard. He is in temperament close to a well-educated mid-century German who shares, as Wieland did, the contemporary interest in particular topics of philosophy, psychology, and literature; he is an arbiter of morals and manners who frequently intrudes, sometimes conspicuously, sometimes unobtrusively. Occasionally he even plays the role of the omniscient story-teller whose knowledge has few limits and whose privilege to enter into the minds of the characters is not curtailed.

The two voices of the satirist are not, of course, perfectly distinguishable, the territories of their owners are not exactly defined, and the perspectives presented often converge. Yet a distinct difference in tone and intention permits the conclusive identification of the second voice. The amusing naivete of the *ingénu* designed to appeal to the interest and emotions of the audience is occasionally abandoned, and a serious note revealing the ethos and authority of a solemn judge of human frailties addresses the intellect of the reader. Sometimes it is merely a parenthetical remark that reaches beyond the realm of the *ingénu*. The narrated information about Donna Mencia's temporary intention of entering a convent is, for example, accompanied by a brief remark of general validity:

> Allein, ihre Klugheit ließ sie jedesmal bemerken, daß dieses Mittel, *wie alle diejenigen, so der Unmut einzugeben pflegt,* ihre Absicht nur sehr unvollkommen erreichen . . . würden (17; italics are mine).

Such parenthetical comparisons and reflective generalizations are often made, particularly when the thought or act of an individual represents a more broadly valid, typically human response to a significant but not unique situation.

A similar kind of intervention is the implied commentary of the editor that is disguised as an extended simile and serves a dual function. Thus the society of females founded by Donna Mencia is described as

> eine Art von Schwesterschaft . . . , die in der schönen Welt eben das war, was die Mönchs-Orden in der politischen sind, ein Staat im Staat, dessen Interesse ist, dem andern allen möglichen Abbruch zu tun, und die sich den Namen der Anti-Grazien erwarben, indem sie mit dem ganzen Reich der Liebe in einer eben so offenbaren und unversöhnlichen Fehde stunden, als die Maltheser-Ritter mit den Musulmannen (18).

Both similes testify, in ironic overstatement, to the animosity between these eccentric women and the rest of the world, but they also expose the overzealous efforts of religious orders to play an important political role and characterize the unbridgeable gap between "infidels" and religious men of the east.

Broadly inclusive in design and perspective is the "narrator's" concern with literature, which serves as a convenient, often trustworthy, yet sometimes unreliably employed frame of reference. He frequently alludes to figures, situations, and concepts from works of fiction and nonfiction and tends to define his vision of life in relation to literature. The artistic strategy is aimed at the creative reader who shares Wieland's intellectual milieu and accepts the implicit invitation to see contrasts or associations prefigured in literature. The techniques of his critical commentary range all the way from brief references and occasional digressions into poetics to lengthy criticism, specifically of contemporary European literature. Since the fictive Spanish author could not possibly be well enough informed to speak with authority on the diverse literary matters intermittently treated in the novel, one must suppose that the fictitious editor playfully assumes the role of literary expert as well.

Of the many favorite contemporary topics treated in the novel, the one of particular interest here is the editor's discussion of satire, contained in the first chapter of the fifth book. Disdainfully he rejects obtrusively moralizing literature, the "Menge schlechter und mittelmäßiger moralischer Bücher in allen Formaten, welche unter viel versprechenden Titeln die arme Welt mit den alltäglichen Beobachtungen, schiefen, zusammen gerafften und unverdauten Gedanken, frostigen Declamationen und frommen Wünschen ihrer langweiligen Verfasser bedrucken" (194). The criticism must be understood as an aspect of the contemporary controversy concerning the value of moralizing novels, particularly the works of Samuel Richardson. At the time of its publication *Pamela* had been enthusiastically received as the "first novel" meant to replace the stylized representation of "reality" and the idealizing portrayal of man, typical of the *Romances* of the past, by the formal realism of the epistolary novel that presented "a full and authentic report of human experience."[13] Soon, however, in part through the efforts of Henry Fielding, the allegedly inferior quality and unhealthy tendencies of the Richardsonian novel, the "culmination of the forces of bad writing and fraudulent morality,"[14] were attacked by Richardson's antagonists and the novel's influence, principally on female readers, was denounced as a distinct danger to their morality. The inclination of some readers to identify with Richardson's heroine and especially the questionable conduct resulting from their imitation of the apparently virtuous but actually hypocritical Pamela were often ridiculed.

The autobiographical sketch of Hyacinthe interpolated in the fifth book of the *Don Sylvio* is to be seen in this connection and should be interpreted as Wieland's satire of similarly hypocritical behavior.[15] There are, the editor believes, books far better and more effective than moralizing novels, and his detailed description of their characteristic features is equivalent to an emphatic recommendation of the comic novel:

> Bücher, in denen die Wahrheit mit Lachen gesagt, die der Dummheit, Schwärmerei und Schelmerei ihre betrügliche Masken abziehen, die Menschen mit ihren Leidenschaften und Torheiten, in ihrer wahren Gestalt und Proportion, weder vergrößert noch verkleinert abschildern, und von ihren Handlungen diesen Firniß wegwischen, womit Stolz, Selbstbetrug oder geheime Absichten sie zu verfälschen pflegen; Bücher, die mit desto besserm Erfolg unterrichten und bessern, da sie bloß zu belustigen scheinen, und die auch alsdann, wenn sie zu nichts gut wären, als beschäftigten Leuten in Erholungs-Stunden den Kopf auszustäuben, müßige Leute unschädlich zu beschäftigen, und überhaupt den guten Humor eines Volks zu unterhalten, immer noch tausendmal nützlicher wären als dieses längst ausgedroschne moralische Stroh (194).

---

[13]Ian Watt, *The Rise of the Novel* (Berkeley/Los Angeles, 1957), p. 32.

[14]Ronald Paulson, *Satire and the Novel in Eighteenth-Century England* (New Haven London, 1967), p. 100.

[15]For a more extensive treatment of this feature see Guy Stern, "Saint or Hypocrite? A Study of Wieland's 'Jacinte Episode,' " *The Germanic Review*, XXIX (1954), 96–101, and Lieselotte E. Kurth, *Die zweite Wirklichkeit—Studien zum Roman des achtzehnten Jahrhunderts*, University of North Carolina Studies in the Germanic Languages and Literatures, Vol. 62 (Chapel Hill, 1969), pp. 150–153.

Although it does not lack light overtones and is made in a context of tonal and referential irony,[16] the extensive digression into the poetics of the satiric novel is seriously meant; there is no inversion of judgment, no undue exaggeration of detail, nor any other dissimulation that would invalidate the theoretical value of the pronouncement. This unequivocal advocacy of satire, the definition of its subject and the circumscription of its function and purpose, echoing Fielding's celebrated formula of the comic epic in prose, are reiterated by the *personae* of many other works by Wieland and are ultimately confirmed in two dialogues that are primarily concerned with the portrayal of man, the *Unterredungen zwischen W** und dem Pfarrer zu**** (1775), of which one point of view unmistakably coincides with Wieland's own position.

A second field of particular concern to the editor is the realm of psychology, and here too his reflections and digressions reach far beyond the text and context of the Spanish story. Don Sylvio is an orphan; his education is guided by an eccentric old aunt who believes in the reality of pseudo-historical novels and urges her ward to model his conduct after the examples of fictive figures. Thus encouraged to see literature, even the most idealizing kind, as a genuine representation of empirical reality, the young hero indiscriminately applies the principle to the fairy tales which he secretly devours and considers a reliable portrayal of a "real" world. His mind combines the "true impressions" received from empirical reality and the "false inscriptions" mediated by literature, so that fact and fiction are imaginatively united into a new reality, the private world of the hero who is convinced of the verity of his own creation. The psychological reflections accompanying Don Sylvio's behavior clearly reveal the voice of the *vir bonus*, the man less interested in telling a particular story than in suggesting universally valid explications for typically human conduct.

Despite his idiosyncrasies Don Sylvio is not uniquely individual but is a representative of a larger segment of society, and the editor's commentary generalizes the insights gained from the observation of the individual case. The relative isolation of young country squires and the lack of demanding duties usually furthers their inclination to live in a partly imaginary world often modeled after literature. The monotony of relatively few objects that with boring repetition impress themselves on the senses leaves a void which the constantly active imagination most

---

[16]The narrator's list of individual satiric novels that might serve as models for contemporary writers contains several works, among them Fielding's *Tom Jones*, which conform to the demands that man be portrayed in his true form and proportions; yet the inclusion of Rabelais' *Gargantua* and *Pantagruel* is one of the more ironic references that accompany the generally valid theoretical remarks.

readily fills, thus combining the marvelous with the natural and the true with the false:

> Die Seele, welche nach einem blinden Instincte Schimären eben so regelmäßig bearbeitet als Wahrheiten, bauet sich nach und nach aus allem diesem ein Ganzes, und gewöhnt sich an, es für wahr zu halten, weil sie Licht und Zusammenhang darin findet, und weil ihre Phantasie mit den Schimären, die den größten Teil davon ausmachen, eben so bekannt ist als ihre Sinnen mit den würklichen Gegenständen, von denen sie ohne sonderliche Abwechslung immer umgeben sind (22).

The editor's analysis prefigures Wieland's later description of *Schwärmerei*, "eine Erhitzung der Seele von Gegenständen die entweder gar nicht in der Natur sind, oder wenigstens das nicht sind, wofür die berauschte Seele sie ansieht,"[17] a definition which is part of a more comprehensive context, the contemporary attempts to understand and describe the phenomena of enthusiasm and imagination.[18]

An equally general commentary is made when the editor tries to answer a question raised in the title of the sixth chapter: "Warum Don Sylvio nicht gemerkt, daß der Frosch keine Fee war?" (29). The hero's belief that a benevolent fairy has been transformed into a frog is perhaps best explained as a false conclusion resulting from his prejudiced misinterpretation of real events. The editor's assertion "Nichts ist unter den Menschen gewöhnlicher als diese Art von Trug=Schlüssen" (31) is supported by two brief parables offering different perspectives of the *tertium comparationis*. The first one, describing the misconception of an old conceited fop who does not realize that his precious gifts cause the joyfulness of his mistress but rather believes that the pleasure of his presence makes her eyes sparkle, presumably draws on empirical reality for the vindication of the thesis. The second example is of a more literary nature, probably conveyed through the travelogues or exotic tales of the time; it sketches the experience of an Indian who had hoped to be protected against illness by an amulet purchased from a witchdoctor. A sudden illness does not (as it should) rid him of his superstitions, but makes him fear that either his trust in the charm is not firm enough or the amount paid for it was not sufficiently large to insure its effectiveness. The elucidation of Don Sylvio's behavior through these examples and the possibility of their duplication, "Dergleichen Beispiele ließen sich ins Unendliche häufen" (32), marks the hero's tendencies as typically human frailties; the serious discussion of such matters induces the reader to share the superior standpoint of the editor and accept his views as generally valid precepts.

[17]*Der Teutsche Merkur*, November 1775, 4th quarter (Weimar, 1775), p. 152.
[18]Victor Lange, "Zur Gestalt des Schwärmers im deutschen Roman des 18. Jahrhunderts," *Festschrift für Richard Alewyn*, ed. Herbert Singer and Benno von Wiese (Cologne, 1967), pp. 151–164.

A revealing theoretical digression of particular significance here is contained in the seventh chapter of the fifth book and treats the topic of point of view. To begin with, the editor cites the Terentian *Tu si hic esses, aliter sentias* and recommends its more general consideration to counteract the contradictions, misconceptions, and dissension caused by the diversity and clash of human opinions and passions. Unfortunately, however, man has not yet become tolerant enough to take this stand but tends to consider his point of view as the only correct one and expects others, "in allen Sachen und zu allen Zeiten gerade so [zu] empfinden, denken, urteilen, glauben, lieben, hassen, tun und lassen . . . wie er" (215). To be sure, no one will openly demand such conformity yet tacitly insist on it, for

> indem wir alle Meinungen, Urteile oder Neigungen unserer Nebengeschöpfe für töricht, irrig und ausschweifend erklären, so bald sie mit den unsrigen in einigem Widerspruch stehen: was tun wir im Grunde anders, als daß wir ihnen unter der Hand zu verstehen geben, daß sie unrecht haben, ein paar Augen, ein Gehirn und ein Herz für sich haben zu wollen? (215).

If only man were willing to abandon his limiting point of view, at least try to share temporarily the perspective of an opponent, acknowledge his right to individuality, and grant him the privilege of differing from the unavoidably biased opinions of others:

> Gestehen sie einander ein, daß Ich gar wohl berechtigt ist, nicht Du zu sein; hernach setzen Sie sich jeder an des andern Platz; ich will verloren haben was sie wollen, wenn Sie nicht eben so dächten wie er, wenn sie er oder in seinen Umständen wären, und so hat der Streit ein Ende (217).

The tolerance expressed here is explicitly sanctioned by Wieland in a different, non-fictive context. The fragmentary essay in exoneration of Erasmus of Rotterdam recommends in similar terms the same charitable attitude toward the views and actions of other men and cautions against premature and therefore probably false judgments: "Das goldne *Tu si hic esses aliter sentias!* legt uns als Pflicht auf, uns so viel nur immer möglich an den Platz und in den ganzen Zusammenhang der Person hineinzudenken und hineinzufühlen, über die wir urtheilen wollen." Yet a complete identification with another being is hardly possible, and conclusive evaluations can perhaps never be reached: "Und da, bey aller Bemühung, die wir uns hiezu geben können, doch immer noch sehr viel daran fehlen muß, daß wir alles so klar sehen, so lebendig und gegenwärtig fühlen, wie diese Person: was ist billiger, als daß wir unserm Zwischenurtheil soviel an Gelindigkeit zulegen, als uns an Information zum Ausspruch eines vollkommen gerechten Endurtheils abgeht?"[19] Even if a final

[19]*Der Teutsche Merkur*, December 1776, 4th quarter (Weimar, 1776), p. 267.

judgment could be formed, tolerance would always be appropriate: "billige Nachsicht gegen die menschliche Gebrechlichkeit [ist] die erste Tugend eines gerechten Sittenrichters." It is this advocacy of tolerance and admission of the almost incontestable validity of many points of view that lead to the presentation of multiple perspectives in all of Wieland's works.

The *Don Sylvio* is no exception. The events of the story are not seen from the narrator's standpoint only; he frequently shifts point of view and moves into the mind of a character. At the beginning of the novel he presents a summary of past occurrences which is accompanied by Donna Mencia's interpretation of decisive events in her life. Her views of man and world are peculiarly biased, and the terms describing them are clearly her own mental formulations. It is she and not the narrator who sees her single state as the result of the "empfindliche Kränkungen von der Kaltsinnigkeit der Mannspersonen" (17), and it is she who considers others as undeserving of her affection. Yet despite the ungratefulness of the world, she has resisted the temptation to enter a convent and secretly commends herself for thus having shown a high degree of practical intelligence.

Through the use of appropriate expressions, such as "ihrem Urteil nach" and "in ihren Augen," the narrator repeatedly reminds his reader that he is observing the events from her point of view and is giving her biased appraisal of particular values.

Don Sylvio's development into a seemingly perfect gentleman is observed, in the second chapter, by various experts; the servants, the vicar, the schoolmaster, the barber, "und andere Personen von Distinction" reverently admire the "Wunder-Gaben des jungen Herrn" und "die weise Erziehungs-Kunst der gnädigen Frau" (21). Donna Mencia is greatly pleased by the avidity with which her pupil imitates the sublime models and has no doubt but that a young man of such noble inclinations and heroic ideas will play just as important a role in life as the hero of the *Grand Cyrus*. Don Sylvio cannot help but agree with her and is easily convinced of his capability of imitating the heroic figures in a most exemplary manner.

The characteristic narrative techniques perceptible as early as the first chapter are applied with meaningful variations throughout the novel. The central events leading to the final "Sieg der Natur über die Schwärmerei" and the inner experiences of the hero are likewise observed from multiple points of view and presented in an intricate pattern of perspectives. Whatever Don Sylvio experiences in the fanciful world of his own making is at first seen from his point of view; the events of his chimerical existence and his dreams are reported with pretended objectivity impressively conveying the intensity with which he seizes upon the events of his imagination. A beautiful princess is the object of his affection, but she is unattainable, for she is in the hands of evil powers with whom he is constantly struggling:

> Bald mußte er sich mit Drachen und fliegenden Katzen herum balgen, bald fand er alle Zugänge zu dem Palast, worin sie gefangen gehalten wurde, mit Distel-Köpfen besät, die sich in dem Augenblick, da er sie berührte, in eben so viele Riesen verwandelten, und ihm den Weg mit großen stählernen Kolben streitig machten (28).

During his wanderings through the woods he finds the miniature painting of a shepherdess and is convinced that she is the bewitched princess whom he must rescue. Direct description cannot possibly express the anguish of the young man; it seems necessary to focus more closely on his troubled mind, and his thoughts are therefore presented in *erlebte Rede*, that is as narrated deliberation: "Allein was sollte er nun anfangen? wo sollte er die schöne Schäferin suchen? Wen sollte er fragen?" (36). He continues his contemplations, dwells on strange thoughts, "wunderliche Gedanken," and finally discovers the explanation for the most unusual coincidences: "Vielleicht liebt sie mich, dachte er, . . . und sie hat eine Probe machen wollen, was ihre wahre Gestalt für einen Eindruck auf mein Herz machen werde?" (37).

When not much later he has the opportunity of relating his experiences to Pedrillo, his story is so vividly colored by his lively imagination that the narrator finds it necessary to expose the subjectivity of Don Sylvio's report and to establish the need of differentiating between fact and fiction: ". . . so werden wir bei der Erzählung unsers jungen Ritters einen Unterschied machen müssen zwischen demjenigen was ihm würklich begegnet war, und zwischen dem, was seine Einbildungs-Kraft hinzugetan hatte" (56). These two perspectives are intermittently presented, and they are elaborately supplemented by others as the hero is observed and discussed by major figures of the novel.

An unusually effective device that betrays the influence of Shakespeare, whose works Wieland was translating when he wrote *Don Sylvio*, and that simultaneously reveals his intuitive sense of the theatrical, are the dramatic scenes that occur occasionally in the first novel and more frequently in later works. The third book, for example, contains a characteristically graphic, virtually three-dimensional depiction that could easily be transferred onto the stage with only minor changes in substance and arrangement. When after his early tiring adventures Don Sylvio searches for a place to rest, Pedrillo also looks around, and as he finds a suitable retreat he describes it to his master, thus practically providing the sketch for a dramatic setting:

"... ich sehe dort einen schönen grünen Platz, der gegen das Feld hinaus offen ist, dort hinter den Oliven-Bäumen; mich deucht, das sollte kein unfeiner Platz sein."

The narrator affirms the scenic beauty of the landscape and completes Pedrillo's description:

... es zog sich ein hohes Gebüsche von gelben und weißen Rosen auf der einen Seite um ihn her, und machte eine Art von natürlicher Laube, und wo er offen war, hatte man eine Aussicht über die schönsten Wiesen, die von bunten Blumen funkelten, und von hundert schlängelnden Bächen durchschnitten waren, deren Rand zu beiden Seiten mit fruchtbaren Bäumen besetzt dem entzückten Auge das Gemälde eines Paradieses darstellte (126–127).

An experienced stage designer would have no difficulty in using these descriptions as a guide for the construction of background and scenery.[20]

While Don Sylvio is still sleeping in the open arbor, Pedrillo, who had selected a more secluded spot for his slumber, wakes up and is the unobserved witness to a charming scene: two beautiful women dressed as shepherdesses and accompanied by handsome young pages, who remain in the background, have entered the arbor. They are fascinated by the sight of the attractive young man asleep in the grass and begin to deliberate about his identity and the circumstances of his life. The romantic features of the situation do not escape Pedrillo who cannot help but be influenced by the enchanted mood of the arcadian setting, and in contrast to his previous doubts in Don Sylvio's stories he is now ready to believe that his master's seemingly fantastic stories may well be true, for the beauty and splendor he is now observing seem to conform to Don Sylvio's description of the nymphs and fairies he has allegedly met in these woods.

As the young women watch the sleeping nobleman and conjecture about his identity, Pedrillo "enters" the scene and attempts to explain the situation of his master. His interpretation of the events is not at all as skeptical as it was formerly, but is instead a combination of the realistic perspective of the narrator with Don Sylvio's imaginative views. The mixture of fact and fiction does not, of course, clarify matters, but compounds the uncertainties of the observers. The dramatic quality of the scene is sustained by an interchange of information between Pedrillo, Donna Felicia, and Laura. Don Sylvio does not participate in the discussion but remains asleep throughout the con-

[20]The story of Don Sylvio was indeed dramatized; see Günther Bobrik, "Wielands Don Sylvio und Oberon auf der deutschen Singspielbühne (diss., Munich, 1909).

versation. The two women depart before he awakens and slowly disappear in the distance.

After a chapter of identification and explanation, "Wer die Dame gewesen, welche Pedrillo für eine Fee angesehen," and a chapter of reflections, "Eines von den gelehrtesten Capitel in diesem Werke," another dramatic scene containing an extensive, six-page dialogue between Donna Felicia and Laura is presented without a single word of intrusion by the narrator. The dialogue contains amusing contradictions. Donna Felicia and Laura converse about the external appearance of Don Sylvio; in fact they seriously quarrel about his physical qualities. They cannot agree, for example, whether he is more or less handsome than Don Alexis, whether his hair is blond or chestnut-brown, whether his mouth is too feminine or pleasantly masculine, whether his stature is nobly heroic or exquisitely delicate. Although they both describe the very same young man whom they observed not too long ago, their individual descriptions of Don Sylvio are distinctly different and reveal the subjectivity of their perception and recollection. This dialogue, like so many others in Wieland's works, is part of a larger pattern. The image of every one of his fictive figures is a complex mosaic to which each character, including of course the narrator and his spokesmen, among them the satirist as *ingénu* and *vir bonus*, and the hero himself through contemplation and reflection, in monologue and dialogue, contributes genuine fragments or, at other times, adds deceptively sparkling segments that are tinctured by an inventive imagination. The method could readily be called "the perspective portrayal of man." It is perhaps most efficiently applied and brought to perfection in the characterization of the protagonist of Wieland's second novel, *Geschichte des Agathon*, whose portrait exhibits the brush strokes of the many who participate in creating the intricate and colorful image of the hero.

Frequently, as the thoughts of fictitious figures are delineated or their dialogues are reproduced, the "linguistic perspectivism" that characterizes Wieland's model, the *Don Quijote* of Cervantes, is perceptible in *Don Sylvio*; and in a manner similar to that of the Spanish novel the German work reflects a "relativistic attitude" that "tinges" the linguistic details in the novel.[21] In contrast to the *Quijote*, however, there is no "para-etymological play" with the names of the hero and his companion. Yet a dual linguistic perspective is developed whenever Don Sylvio and Pedrillo converse about the alleged adventures of the young knight. Pedrillo's mispronunciation of names

[21]See Leo Spitzer, "Linguistic Perspectivism in the *Don Quijote*," *Linguistics and Literary History—Essays in Stylistics* (2d ed.; New York, 1962), pp. 41–85.

recalls a relevant motif in the *Quijote*. Like Sancho he cannot, for instance, correctly remember the name given to one of the more significant figures invented by the hero. To his uncultured mind the name of the good fairy "Radiante" appears as "Radicante" and at other times as "Rademante." Since Pedrillo has hardly any difficulty recalling the correct names of actual people, his alteration of invented names underlines the tenuousness of Don Sylvio's second reality. The reliability of other literary realms, myth and legend for example, is indirectly questioned through a similar confusion of names. A Homeric hero and a fifteenth-century Pope are fused into one personality and are fixed in Pedrillo's mind as the "Trojan Prince Aeneas Sylvios"; and the love of Zephyrus and Flora becomes in his imagination "die Liebe des Florus und der Zephira."

Don Sylvio's intolerance for the linguistic ignorance of his servant and Pedrillo's indifference toward poetic nomenclature must be understood symbolically. The hero's insistence on accuracy even in the smallest details parallels a historian's emphasis on authentic particulars. Since the fairytale world is real to him, the variation of a name would be a perversion of the truth; and if he were to permit nuances in minor matters, he could not possibly insist on his unique interpretation of significant events portrayed in the literary models. His emphasis on the unalterableness of detail is meant to lend credence to his views and to strengthen his belief in the reality of his semi-fictitious world. Pedrillo, in contrast, views his master's phantasies with suspicion and openly doubts that Don Sylvio's literary frame of reference has any empirically real qualities; he subconsciously stresses the fictionality of the invented realm by his liberal alteration of individual aspects. Since the names of fictitious figures were perhaps even arbitrarily invented by a poet who could well have chosen any one of the versions Pedrillo himself uses, to him it does not seem vitally important to use no other but that particular name.

The conflict of ideas becomes even more pronounced in the frequent conversations between master and servant. Following the principles of dialogue literature they are inserted into the novel in order to show the different perspectives under which the same events must appear to two persons of such different backgrounds and convictions. Whenever Don Sylvio tells of his adventures with fairies and sorcerers, enchanted birds and bewitched frogs, Pedrillo is ready to question the logic of the young knight's report and to point out the fallacious reasoning of his argument, as for example in the lengthy "Unterredung beim Frühstück" (108 ff). To consider their different attitudes as representative of idealism and realism would, however, be a misleading oversimplification. Pedrillo's role in Don Sylvio's life is to assert a sense of reality, to be sure, but the young knight performs a similar function for Pedrillo. For the servant also confuses fact and fiction, only his frame of reference is not fairytales but the "Gespenster-Historien" his grandmother used to tell. When in the dark of the night an oaktree appears to him as a monstrous giant, it is Don Sylvio who exposes the phantasy and ironically scolds the Quixotry of Pedrillo's behavior: "Weißt du wohl, Pedrillo, . . . daß ich deiner blödsinnigen Einfälle müde bin? Ich glaube zum Henker, du willst einen Don Quischotte aus mir machen, und mich bereden, Windmühlen für Riesen anzusehen? da siehe, wie viel ich mir aus deinen Riesen mache!" (87). With these words he draws his sword and cuts off a heavy branch to convince Pedrillo of his foolishness. Pedrillo, like Sancho, is a transposition of the hero in a different key. The parallelism is intended, for Wieland believed that both excessive enthusiasm and superstition are human foibles; depending on the disposition of the victim they result in markedly different conduct, "die Schwärmerei macht glänzende, kühne und unternehmende Geister, der Aberglaube zahme, geduldige, förmliche Thiere." It has always been necessary and invariably beneficial, "notwendig und heilsam," to make fun of the main springs of these passions; the best means of counteracting their excesses are "Scherz und Ironie . . . nebst dem ordentlichen Gebrauch der fünf Sinnen,"[22] and it was with this intention that the history of Don Sylvio has been written.

On an even broader scale perspectivism informs the structure of Wieland's novel as a whole. Two extensive narratives are inserted. The "Geschichte der Hyacinthe," related by herself and her lover, obviously from biased points of view, is one; the other, of a different sort, is the "Geschichte des Prinzen Biribinker", a fairytale as fantastic as those that served Don Sylvio as models for his mode of living. Don Gabriel is the main narrator of the interpolated fairytale, yet occasionally he assigns the task of relating major events to the fictitious figures of his tale, thus presenting several complementary and corrective perspectives which reveal the bias of every one of the narrators. Both interpolated stories clearly exemplify the major theme of the novel: the subjectivity of individual points of view and the resulting relativity of judgment. The multiple perspectives presented in the tales ultimately help guide Don Sylvio in his search for intrinsic values, and the complex process of his development confirms the author's conviction that the comparative approach to the greater questions of life leads to a more comprehensive grasp of the truth.

[22] J. G. Gruber, *Christph. Martin Wieland* (Leipzig/Altenburg, 1815), I, 189.

7 ‖ Aurora und Cephalus

The shorter works of Wieland contemporaneous with his first novel demonstrate his continuous consideration of multiple points of view, and they are invariably structured according to the principles of perspectivism. The *Comische Erzählungen* published in 1765 are similar in form and techniques to the verse narratives that appeared in 1752, but they are strikingly different in tone and intent and reaffirm the celebrated "metamorphosis" of the poet from a sternly demanding idealist into a charitable humanist who views the ludicrous with discerning irony and a compassionate tolerance.[1] The first edition of the collection contains the tales *Das Urtheil des Paris*, *Endymion*, *Juno und Ganymed*, and *Aurora und Cephalus*; they are unusual adaptations of Greek myths, satirically meant and designed to strike a double blow. At the time when Greek antiquity exerted its "tyranny" over Germany,[2] Wieland dared to expose the imperfec-

---

[1]For a brief discussion of this topic, see pp. 90–93 of this study.

[2]E. M. Butler treats this phenomenon in her well-known study *The Tyranny of Greece over Germany* (Cambridge, England, 1935). Her investigation is admittedly one-sided; she is, for example, not at all concerned with the rebellion against this "tyranny" and intentionally omits voices like that of Wieland, who receives only casual mention. For a more detailed analysis of Wieland's relation to Greek culture see William H. Clark's dissertation "Christoph Martin Wieland and the Legacy of Greece" (Columbia, 1954). Two further articles by Clark treat Wieland's relationship to Winckelmann: "Wieland and Winckelmann: Saul and the Prophet," *Modern Language Quarterly*, 17 (1956), 1–16; and "Wieland *contra* Winckelmann?" *Germanic Review*, 34 (1959), 4–13. Broader aspects are treated more comprehensively by Henry C. Hatfield, *Aesthetic Paganism in German Literature from Winckelmann to the Death of Goethe* (Cambridge, Mass., 1964). See particularly his Chapter III, "Antiquity and Reason: Wieland," pp. 33–44.

tions of legendary heroes and to dethrone the gods of Greece, portraying them in all their inadequacies customarily concealed. Thus humanized they became representative of man, a function which Wieland explicitly confirmed when in a letter to Salomon Geßner he stated "daß die komischen Erzählungen als wahre und satyrische Gemähde der herrschenden Sitten der großen Welt ... zu betrachten ... seyen."[3]

The literary method applied in the fashioning of these tales constitutes one of Wieland's favorite approaches; it is the creative reworking of traditional materials and the poetic mode of using literary artifacts for the purpose of symbolic extension; these techniques affirm his conviction that the artistic adaptation of subject matter previously presented in the writings of others is an act of genuine poetic invention: "Die Bearbeitung des Stoffes ist die wahre Erfindung." Since the manner of adaptation may testify more significantly to the abilities of a poet than the mere selection of particular subject matter, it was considered the duty of the literary critic to evaluate artistic accomplishments in the same way as an art critic would judge the work of a painter. Yet there were stern dissenters among the younger generation who advocated an almost exclusive originality and readily accused those who employed the adaptive method of brazen plagiarism, so that it became necessary to defend the artistic principles that were applied by the traditionalists. An appropriate comment calling the example of discerning art critics to the attention of literary critics was formulated by Johann Georg Jacobi and was published in Wieland's periodical *Der Teutsche Merkur*:

> Warum durchwandern wir nicht eine Bibliothek von Dichter=Werken eben so, wie Kenner ein Cabinett von Gemählden zu betrachten pflegen? Diese fragen nicht, ob der Mahler eine *santa famiglia*, oder Schlachten, oder eine badende Leda, oder Kinderköpfe gemahlt habe; sondern sie verweilen bey jedem Stück eines grossen Meisters, und vergnügen sich an dem mannichfaltigen Reichthum der Kunst. In jeder Gattung verehren sie die Meisterhand.[4]

A preliminary reading of Wieland's comic verse tales shows that they share various common characteristics, and the closer analysis of one of the tales may be sufficient to identify correlative features of particular importance to this study. *Aurora und Cephalus* seems the most suitable example because it is the last and by scholarly consent the best of the first four *Comische Erzählungen*.[5] The title of the col-

[3]*Auswahl denkwürdiger Briefe*, ed. Ludwig Wieland (Vienna, 1815), I, 52.
[4]*Der Teutsche Merkur*, October 1773, 4th quarter (Weimar, 1773), p. 10.
[5]Cf. Hans Sittenberger, "Untersuchungen über Wielands Komische Erzählungen," *Vierteljahrschrift für Litteraturgeschichte*, V (1892), 221; and

lection adequately informs the reader that he may not expect another serious treatment of mythological matter: no tragic tales, but gaily entertaining stories designed to excite mirth or ridicule, pieces whose tone admittedly approaches the burlesque.[6] The title of the last narrative indicates Wieland's emphasis in the adaptation of the legendary adventures of Cephalus. His version combines several motifs which are often separately and differently treated by historians and poets.

A brief summary of major events in the mythical tale may help to recall the story and identify distinctive features that are of relevance here: Aurora, or Eos, the goddess of dawn, punished by Venus with a constant passion for handsome young men because of her affair with Mars, was known to abduct whomever she wanted to possess, among them Tithon, son of Laomedon. At her demand Zeus made him immortal, but since she forgot to request eternal youth and beauty for him he became a feeble and ugly old man. Deprived of Tithon's physical love Aurora looked elsewhere for the gratification of her desires and soon became infatuated with the handsome young hunter Cephalus whom she carried off into her realm. He was, however, happily married to Procris, refused to become involved in an illicit affair, and wished to return to his wife. Only reluctantly did Aurora permit him to leave, and as she did so she expressed her doubts in the loyalty of Procris, intending, of course, to arouse Cephalus' jealous suspicion and induce him to see his own faithfulness as a foolish sentiment.

The relationship between Cephalus and Aurora and the fate of Procris are integral parts of almost every adaptation of the myth, but they are treated with striking deviations by different authors. Hesiod and Apollodor, for example, report the consummation of the union between Aurora and Cephalus and disclose the birth of a son. The conjugal fidelity of Procris is explicitly denied by Apollodor who tells of her affair with Pteleonte, whose generous present, a golden crown, made her accede to his wishes and caused the temporary separation from Cephalus who caught the lovers in their act of adultery.[7]

Friedrich Sengle, *Wieland*, p. 175. Modern scholarly opinion about the comic tales is divided. Michel treats the narratives with approbation (pp. 342-353), but Sengle does not think too highly of these "notorious" tales (with the exception of *Aurora und Cephalus*), *Wieland*, pp. 172-176, and "Von Wielands Epenfragmenten zum 'Oberon'," *Festschrift Paul Kluckhohn und Hermann Schneider* (Tübingen, 1948), pp. 266-285. Derek Maurice van Abbé, *Christoph Martin Wieland* (London, 1961), is rather selective in his treatment of Wieland's works; his third chapter, "The Rococo Virtuoso: *Komische Erzählungen*," contains more discussion of background than of the tales themselves. Other scholars merely touch upon the comic tales or briefly discuss specific aspects (with particular interest in their "Rococo features") in studies of a more general nature.

[6]*Ausgewählte Briefe*, II (Zurich, 1815), 249.

[7]These details and their sources were well known to the eighteenth-century reader through Benjamin Hederich's *Gründliches Lexicon Mythologicum* (Leipzig, 1724); for Aurora see cols. 405-408; for Procris, cols. 1669-1670.

Perhaps the best-known adaptation of the ancient myth, a uniquely idealizing version, was presented by Ovid in the seventh book of the *Metamorphoses*. It is not Ovid who tells the tale, but Cephalus, who in an interpolated story relates the events of his life with Procris. As is to be expected he offers a subjectively biased account in which he compassionately effects the exoneration of his wife and vindicates his own relationship with Aurora. He tells of his steadfast resistance to the seductive attempts of the beautiful goddess, her resignation, and the final warning:

> 'siste tuas, ingrate, querellas;
> Procrin habe!' dixit, 'quod si mea provida mens est,
> non habuisse voles.'[8]

Cephalus is not able to conquer the doubts cast upon his wife's fidelity. Disguised as a visiting stranger he tries to win her affection with precious gifts and attempts to seduce her with passionate declarations of love and desire. Although she asserts her loyal devotion to her husband, the stranger forces her at least to waver:

> . . . cum census dare me pro nocte loquendo
> muneraque augendo tandem dubitare coegi.[9]

Angered by her apparent inconstancy, he reveals his identity and accuses her of despicable unfaithfulness.

Continuing his narrative, Cephalus tells of her flight, his remorse, their reunion, and finally of the events that led to her death. It is this tragic aspect that has most often captured the imagination of poets and artists. The seventeenth and eighteenth centuries saw numerous adaptations of the story in almost every genre, in pastoral plays and operas, in tragedies and even in comedies.[10] The circumstantial depiction of Procris' accidental death, which was actually caused by her needless fear that Cephalus might have been unfaithful, is invariably intended as a deterring example of destructive jealousy, a function which was undoubtedly stimulated by Ovid's earlier version of the myth contained in the *Ars Amatoria*, where the episode was designed

---

[8]Ovid, *Metamorphoses*, ed. Frank Justus Miller (London/New York, 1929), pp. 392–393: "Cease your complaints, ungrateful boy; keep your Procris: but, if my mind can forsee at all, you will come to wish that you had never had her."

[9]*Ibid.*, pp. 394–395: ". . . and at last, by adding to my promised gifts, I forced her to hesitate."

[10]A complete analytical and comparative study of the different versions is still a desideratum. Elisabeth Frenzel, *Stoffe der Weltliteratur* (Stuttgart, 1962), has no entry "Aurora und Cephalus," and the references given under "Kephalus und Prokris" are seriously incomplete; Wieland's adaptation, for example, is entirely omitted. Charlotte Craig's study *Christoph Martin Wieland as the Originator of the Modern Travesty in German Literature*, University of North Carolina Studies in the Germanic Languages and Literatures (Chapel Hill, 1970), contains only a brief treatment (pp. 69-70) of *Aurora und Cephalus* which does not go beyond a casual mention of some of the sources.

to illustrate the distressing consequences of unfounded suspicion; it may also reflect the later moralizing treatment by Boccaccio as it is presented in the popular cyclopaedic compilations *De genealogiis deorum gentilium* and *De claris mulieribus*.

A well-known seventeenth-century narrative refashioning the events is interpolated in La Fontaine's poem *Les filles de Minée* (1685), in which a daughter of Minyas relates the story of Cephalus' adventures, of his abduction, his unwavering loyalty to his wife, and her untimely death. La Fontaine, as later Wieland, introduced uniquely modern overtones: beautiful goddesses married to old men are not bound by "our" laws and are permitted to abduct the man they wish to possess. Yet the victim is allowed to resist; he may even resort to the argumentation of the *précieuses* and try to convince the seductress that friendship is more noble than physical love:

> Il eut beau lui parler de la foi conjugale:
> Les jeunes déités qui n'ont qu'un vieil époux
> Ne se soumettent point à ces lois comme nous:
> La déesse enleva ce héros si fidèle.
> De modérer ces feux il pria l'Immortelle:
> Elle le fit, l'amour devint simple amitié.[11]

Wieland's contemporaries were acquainted with Ovid's tales, with some of the later versions, and probably with the factual accounts contained in the *Gründliches Lexicon Mythologicum* of Benjamin Hederich who offered a summary of all classical sources including those that report the adulterous affairs between Aurora and Cephalus, and Procris and Pteleonte. The poetic adaptations in German literature are strikingly diverse in form, emphasis, and tone. Klopstock, for example, used the mythological configuration as a symbolic extension in his *Elegie* of 1751, identified by the poet as a "tibullisches Lied"; Aurora is here the prototype of the gentle, affectionate, and tantalizing temptress, and Cephalus is the example of the yearning sentimental lover who desires to be united with the young goddess. A few years earlier, Johann Elias Schlegel had adapted the Cephalus and Procris episode in a cantata that depicts the fatal hour and the death of Procris in rather sentimental fashion; as might be expected, he excluded the events involving Aurora and Pteleonte. And later in the century Karl Wilhelm Ramler reworked the mythological materials for his "Melodrama" *Cephalus und Prokris*, which was published in 1778 in the *Theater Journal für Deutschland*. A unique feature of Ramler's work is the extensive use of monologues in which Procris and Cephalus recount and interpret the crucial events that

---

[11]J. de La Fontaine, *Oeuvres*, ed. M. Henri Regnier, XVI (Paris, 1890), 188-189.

lead to her tragic death. The artistic method is reminiscent of the process of "self-dissection" as it was advocated by Shaftesbury, and it may well reflect the stimulating effect of Wieland's frequent use and his emphatic recommendation of a device that seemed singularly suited for the presentation of intrinsically subjective views.

Wieland's own tale is markedly different in form and content as well as in tone and intention from these melodramatic versions. His treatment of theme and configuration is ironic and recalls the satiric adaptation of the ancient story by Alexandre Hardy, and the frivolity of his depiction resembles the spirit of the burlesque that permeates Calderon's reworking of the myth. The double purpose of Wieland's adaptation is characteristic, that is, the intention of placing a legendary event in a new and unusual light and his determination to do so in artistic fashion. One particularly distinguishing feature, common to the entire collection and shared with the earlier works, is the appeal to a creative reader who must be prepared to investigate the perspectives that are disclosed through meaningful allusions which indicate significant interactions between the text of the tale and the context of the reference. The first edition of Wieland's *Comische Erzählungen* carries the motto

Ex noto fictum Carmen sequar, ut sibi quivis
Speret idem—[12]

and, as is the case with every one of Wieland's fragmentary citations, it should be viewed in its original setting because the source conveys far-reaching implications that surpass the limited meaning of the lines that are quoted. The lines are taken from the *Epistula ad Pisones* of Horace, more exactly, from that section of the *Ars Poetica* that treats the function and form of Satyr plays. These connections are indeed revealing. The evocation of Horace reaffirms Wieland's allegiance to the "beloved" Roman whom next to Cicero he had admired most ardently from his early youth.[13] Although his first attempt at satire had been inspired by Juvenal and must have displayed in the typical fashion of the model personal invective and subjective animosities,[14]

---

[12]The work was published in 1765 by Orell, Geßner & Cie in Zurich, although the place of publication is not given in the first edition of the *Comische Erzählungen*. Line references in parentheses are to this edition. For a translation of the motto see p. 143 of this study.

[13]For a detailed and instructive treatment of Wieland's knowledge of Horace see Wolfgang Monecke, *Wieland und Horaz* (Cologne/Graz, 1964).

[14]Wieland refers to this early satire in a letter to Bodmer written in March 1752: "Im 12ten Jahr übte ich mich sehr in lateinischen versen, und weil ich in meinen Kindischen Gedanken zu stolz war, kleine Versuche zu machen, so schrieb ich ein Gedicht von 600 Versen in *genere Anacreontis* von der *Echo* und ein grosses Gedicht in *distichis* von den *pygmeen*, welches eine Satyre auf meines Rectors Frau war, und

Wieland would only infrequently play the role of a Juvenalean satirist who with fierce indignation attacks the destructive forces of evil and the atrocities of the wicked. He preferred a milder brand of satire; the various references to the writings of Horace in his personal letters show where his sympathies lay, and the characteristic features of his own kind of satire expressing his outlook and attitude toward life are unmistakably Horatian. Both poets focus on fools and foolery and expose in a light and carefree tone the errant behavior of men, or gods, whose deviant acts sometimes bring their own punishment. The reader will not find it difficult to identify to some extent with the one guilty of folly, but he does remain aloof enough to contemplate vital ethical questions which may ultimately lead to the recognition of a practicable code of conduct.

The major topic of the *Comische Erzählungen* is one Wieland has in common with Horace; it is sexual indulgence, and both satirists show that the real cause of sexual difficulties resides not in man's sexual instincts but rather in his inability to subject them to rational inspection and control. They show this with ironic good humor, and in contrast to Juvenal they do not denounce, unfairly ridicule, or triumph rhetorically over vice, for their irony is constructive and humane. When Wieland was attacked for his apparently frivolous treatment of the essentially epicurean problem, he could easily have defended himself with the proverbial citation from Horace: *ridentem dicere verum*, for what indeed "is to prevent one from telling truth as he laughs."[15] The initial reference to Horace is of further significance, more limited in scope, yet of equal importance. The section surrounding the quoted lines is concerned with the form and function of the Satyr play. To be sure, the *Comische Erzählungen* do not belong to the genre, but they do share salient features with the *novitas* of the Greek drama, and together with the first novel they constitute in the development of Wieland's work a comic interlude in which jest and seriousness are wedded.

Of even greater consequence than the larger section are the lines that immediately follow the fragmentary quotation, because they ex-

---

wobey ich den Vers des Juvenal zum Grunde legte

    et levis erecta consurgit ad oscula planta."

Line and context indicate which mode of portrayal Wieland selected:

    So high they build her head, such tiers on tiers,
    With wary hands, they pile, that she appears,
    Andromache, before: —and what behind?
    A dwarf, a creature of a different kind. —

It was, then, as early as this that the depiction of a figure considered from different points of view attracted Wieland and inspired his satirical portrayal of the wife of rector Johann Jacob Doll; see *Briefwechsel*, i, 49; ii, 89.

    [15]Horace, *Satires* i, i, 24.

press rather personal views which Wieland certainly shared; they indicate the stylistic intention of the poet, reveal the ease with which the language was fashioned as a deceptive illusion, and they betray a slightly conceited doubt in the ability of others to achieve such mastery of the language:

> ex noto fictum carmen sequar, ut sibi quivis
> speret idem, sudet multum frustraque laboret
> ausus idem: tantum series iuncturaque pollet,
> tantum de medio sumptis accedit honoris.[16]

Wieland's translation of these lines conveys a distinct sense of identification, and the section becomes even more meaningful when viewed as a description of his own design and intention:

> Aus lauter j e d e r m a n n b e k a n n t e n Wörtern
> wollt' ich mir eine n e u e S p r a c h e bilden, so,
> daß jeder dächt', er könnt' es auch, und doch,
> wenn ers versucht' und viel geschwitzt und lange
> sich dran zermartert hätte, doch zuletzt
> es bleiben lassen müßte!—Lieben Freunde,
> s o v i e l kommt auf die Kunst des Mischens an!
> So viel kann dem Gemeinsten bloß die Stellung
> und die Verbindung, Glanz und Würde geben![17]

The care with which Wieland forged his "new language" reflects his constant, intense concern for the individual word and for appropriate linguistic combinations. Even as a young man of seventeen he suggested effective stylistic principles and defined what he called the *Poetische Perspective*, in which the *Beywort*, the epitheton, was of extraordinary importance. These theories and their formulation intentionally manifest the valuable stimulus he received from contemporary poetics, among them Gottsched's *Versuch einer Critischen Dichtkunst* and Breitinger's *Critische Dichtkunst*, each of which presents an extensive treatment of the epitheton.[18] The first volume

---

[16]Horace, *De Arte Poetica*, 240-243: "My aim shall be poetry, so moulded from the familiar that anybody may hope for the same success, may sweat much and yet toil in vain when attempting the same: such is the power of order and connexion, such the beauty that may crown the commonplace." Ed. H. Rushton Fairclough (Cambridge/London, 1956).

[17]Wieland, *Gesammelte Schriften* (Akademieausgabe), trans., Vol. IV, ed. Paul Stachel (Berlin, 1913), pp. 361-362.

[18]Both works are mentioned in the letter to Sophie Gutermann (February or March 1751) in which Wieland discusses his thoughts on poetry; his formulation indicates that he is well acquainted with these poetics: "Ohnerachtet die Dichtkunst des berühmten Hrn. Gottsched, deren Lesung Mein Theurester Schaz ohnezweifel mit der unvergleichlichen *Breitinger*ischen verbinden wird, sehr schöne Anweisungen zur Dichtkunst giebt So weis ich doch daß es Ihnen, Mein Allerliebstes Herz, weder übel noch unangenehm vorkommen wird, wenn ich Ihnen einige meiner *Gedanken* über die Poesie mittheilen werde." *Briefwechsel*, I, 14.

of Breitinger's work contains a favorable evaluation of Albrecht von Haller's *Die Alpen* that is particularly pertinent here because it emphasizes visual effects and employs optical terms that foreshadow Wieland's own criticism of Haller: "Der Poet hat in diesem Gemählde alle Kunst der Optick und Perspectiv geschickt angewendet, auch dieselbe mit unterschiedlichen lehrreichen Betrachtungen unterstüzet."[19]

The second volume of Breitinger's *Dichtkunst* incorporates a comprehensive treatment "Von den Bey=Wörtern" which Wieland undoubtedly read with studious attention. The epitheta (Breitinger states) are comparable to light and color in painting and must therefore be selected with the same great care a good painter will exercise in the combination of these values. "Beywörter . . . sind die poetischen Farben, die den poetischen Schildereyen und Erzehlungen einen reitzenden Glantz mittheilen, und sie über die matte und historische Erzehlung und Beschreibung weit weit erheben" (249). Epitheta commonly function to circumscribe, limit, and distinguish thoughts expressed in human speech, and they designate an essential characteristic (*eine wesentliche Eigenschaft*) or an incidental quality (*eine zufällige Beschaffenheit*) of an object or a person. They perform a significant service for the literary artist, and the force of poetic representation will be intensified by the dexterous use of suitable adjectives. Their function in literature is essentially threefold: first, "sie dienen die Sachen zu mahlen und sie so lebhaft vorzustellen, als ob wir sie mit eigenen Augen anschaueten." Second, they serve "den Sachen einen wahren Schein der Grösse zu geben"; and third, they are designed "denselben ein gantz wunderbares Ansehen mitzutheilen" (263). The poet must be prudent in his choice of adjectives for it is the purpose of judicious selectivity to strengthen the verisimilitude of depiction and portrayal; he should achieve the highest degree of probability so that the artistically created "copy" causes the same impression and has the identical effect on the imagination of the reader as the actual model, the *Urbild*, would have.

In his theory of the epitheton Breitinger reiterates several times the concepts of impression (*Eindruck*) and imagination (*Phantasie* and *Einbildungskraft*) and indicates the vital role they perform in poetry. He therefore expects the poet to select his words and formulations with great care to awaken these faculties and stimulate the reader's active participation in the recreation of a work of art. It is, then, fortunate that in his appeal to the senses the poet is less limited than the painter, for through the felicitous choice of adjectives he can activate all of man's senses: "die Poesie ist eine Mahlerinn nicht

---

[19]*Critische Dichtkunst* (Zurich, 1740), I, 26. Later page references in parentheses are to this edition, Vol. II.

alleine für das Gesicht, sondern für alle Sinnen" (265). And if the poet is as ingenious as Virgil he will even achieve "daß die Phantasie des Lesers sich mehr vorstellet, als er sagt" (270). In the final section of his treatise Breitinger assigns a very distinct quality to the epithet: "Ich betrachte die poetischen Beywörter als kleine Beschreibungen, fast auf die Weise, wie die Metaphoren nichts anders als abgekürzte Gleichnisse sind" (285). These "miniature descriptions" adorn and enliven the poetic narrative; they take the place of more elaborate descriptions "indem sie eine Sache wie im Vorbeygange mit einem einzigen aber lebhaften Pinsel=Zuge nach der absonderlichsten Eigenschaft in einem hellen Licht vor Augen stellen," and they contribute significantly to the progression of the story.

Wieland in his own "Betrachtungen über die Dichtkunst," contained in a personal letter to Sophie Gutermann, affirms the importance of the epitheton; he attests to its vital function in poetry and agrees with the Swiss critic that among the linguistic means at the disposal of the poet, *Beywörter* are of primary significance and of greatest "efficacy" (*die ersten und geschiktesten*). More concise than Breitinger, he summarizes their essential purpose briefly: "Ein Beywort Soll uns allemal eine *nöthige, merkwürdige,* und in der *Situation* wo es stehet, *unentberliche* Eigenschaft eines Dinges anzeigen."[20] He also confirms the validity of the analogy between color and light in painting and epitheta in poetry. The *Beywort* is the poet's means of creating an approximation of perspective in his brand of art:

> Insonderheit mus das Beywort, die Sache, wobey es stehet, in ein helles Licht sezzen, und in einem schönen Verhältnis mit den übrigen, mit denen es verknüpft ist, vorstellen, welches mann die Poetische Perspective heissen könnte.[21]

Wieland's attentive reading of Horace's *Ars Poetica*, particularly his interest in the possibilities of moulding a new language from the familiar, his thorough study of Gottsched's and Breitinger's *Dichtkunst*, specifically his concern with the epitheton, and no doubt his intimate acquaintance with classic and modern poetry, are all reflected in the conscientious care with which he constructed the verbal frame of his works, among them the *Comische Erzählungen.* A brief analysis of representative lines from *Aurora und Cephalus* should reveal how effectively Wieland employed the epitheton, and it may incidentally disclose the measure of success with which he used common language in poetic context.

Almost every one of the more than nine-hundred lines of the verse narrative contains at least one epithet, sometimes two, occasionally

---

[20]*Briefwechsel,* I, 14.
[21]*Ibid.,* I, 15.

even more, and all of the suitable grammatical forms are represented: adjectives preceding the noun or in post-position, participials, adverbs, and prepositional phrases, substantives in apposition, as qualifiers of genitive objects, and as hendiadys. Through the efficient manipulation of these technical devices he made the epitheta perform their primary functions: to convey sense impressions, to activate or guide the imagination of the reader, and to stimulate his intellect or emotions. To be sure, the verse form of the tale required the occasional use of *epitheta ornantia*; following tradition, Aurora and her horses receive the attribute "rosenfarben"; Tithon is repeatedly characterized as old and ugly, and Cephalus as young and handsome. Yet even these seemingly conventional epitheta fulfill a more meaningful function: they underline the central conflict of Aurora, who should remain loyal to her husband but is repulsed by his appearance and infirmities, and should not seek an affair with Cephalus but is sensuously attracted by his youth and beauty.

Wieland's more specific epitheta are chosen with deliberate precision and are intricately combined into patterned units that mirror the form of the tale. The structure of *Aurora und Cephalus* is essentially dramatic, and the five-act pattern of classical comedy would easily accommodate the events of the story: the abduction of Cephalus; the return of Cephalus and the first temptation of Procris; the second temptation of Procris and her flight; Cephalus' search for Procris and the discovery of her adultery; and Cephalus' attempt at suicide and his rescue by Aurora. Beyond this the tale is rich in dramatic features, particularly dialogue, and is made up of structural units, many of which possess the distinct qualities of dramatic scenes. The intended appeal of individual scenes to the senses, the emotions, or the intellect is substantially supported by the felicitous combination of appropriate epitheta. There is also a frequent change in perspective, and the events are seen and evaluated from the point of view of the main characters, particularly Cephalus and Aurora, and the vocabulary, specifically the epitheton, is designed to fit the personality of the speaker and to reflect his emotions.

Although Breitinger had advocated the poetic address to all five senses, hardly any German writer employed a balanced language that would activate all senses in equal measure. A later critic, Jean Paul Richter, recognized the preference of his contemporaries for visual vocabulary, and he discussed the phenomenon in the *Vorschule der Ästhetik*. Through the analysis of style he has discovered that "in Europa bloß der fünfte Sinn, das Auge, am Schreibepult zu gebrauchen ist . . . Für Gefühl und Geschmack haben wir wenig Einbildungskraft; für Geruch . . . noch weniger Sprache."[22] Even the

[22]*Werke*, ed. Norbert Miller, v (Munich, 1963), 278.

auditory sense is often only incidentally addressed, and visual images or optical metaphors must serve to stimulate the acoustic imagination. These general observations inferentially also apply to Wieland, for he was one of the poets whose style Jean Paul analyzed in preparation for his work.

There are indeed very few epitheta in *Aurora und Cephalus* that impress the sense of smell or that of taste. Several of these describe the activation of Cephalus' senses shortly after his abduction when he awakens from his trance:

> Doch Düfte von Ambrosia
> Die ihm, mit süsserm Schwall als von den Zimmet=Hügeln
> An Ceylans Strand entgegenwehn,
> Ermuntern ihn zulezt die Augen aufzuriegeln;
> (172-175)

There are only a few more, among them the adjective *süss*, which is, however, frequently used as metaphor: *süsse Lust* (116), *süsse Irrungen* (137), *süsse Trunkenheit* (266), *süsses Gift der Sünde* (455), all of which describe the "sweetness" of erotic experiences.

The sense of touch is equally neglected despite the importance of physical relationships; only an occasional reference to bodily contact activates the tactile sense, as for example when Aurora holds Tithon "Erwärmend . . . in ihren Armen," or when Phryne, the prototype of a seductress, tempts a young lover:

> Ein Druk von ihrer weichen Hand,
> Ein Schmaz der buhlerischen Zungen,
> Erwekt von seinem Götter=Stand
> Die schlummernden Erinnerungen.
> (125-128)

The scene of Cephalus' abduction transmits another tactile experience:

> Doch plözlich fühlt von einer fremden Macht
> Der Jüngling sich ergriffen, fortgezogen,
> Und schneller als ein Pfeil vom Bogen
> Durch Luft und Wolken weg, wer weiß wohin gebracht.
> (163-166)

Although the sense of hearing is similarly neglected—there are only occasional evocations through expressions like *ungestört* (3), *leise* (28), *taub* (49), *lärmendes Gewühle* (356), or *liederreiche Kehlen* (514)—one of the crucial scenes of the tale combines most effectively the vocabulary of sound with that of motion. In the twilight of dawn Aurora's sense of vision is still impaired; as she searches for Cephalus she listens attentively to the sounds of the forest, and her impressions are conveyed through "miniature descriptions" of aptly chosen epitheta:

> Mit welcher Lust verschlingt ihr lauschend Ohr
> Der raschen Stöber Laut, die ins Gehölze dringen!
> Sonst hörte sie der Lerchen frühes Chor
> Gern neben ihrem Wagen singen:
> Allein ihr däucht in diesem Augenblik
> Hylactors Jagd=Geheul die lieblichste Musik.
> Sie sieht die muntern Jäger ziehen,
> Das Hift=Horn tönt, der Wald erwacht,
> Die Hunde schlagen an, die scheuen Rehe fliehen;
>   (154–162)

The details emphasized here do betray the selective subjectivity of Aurora's attention. Her interest in the gentle sounds of nature has diminished and she eagerly listens to the noises of the hunt that announce man's destructive intervention in the peaceful life of the forest. The scene may well contain the justification for the impending abduction of Cephalus. If man is permitted to ravage the forest and violate the animals, a goddess must be allowed to use man in like manner and expect him to serve her.

An equally subjective accent is perceptible in Cephalus' account of his love for Procris. The vocabulary of his report is designed to characterize him, and in well-chosen words he reveals his emotions. From childhood on they seemed destined for each other and were inseparable until manly duties forced him to leave her. Yet his thoughts had always been with her:

> Allein das Bild der holden Schönen
> Schwebt mir, wohin ich gehe, nach;
> Ein banges wehmuthsvolles Sehnen
> Ertränkt mein Aug in stillen Thränen,
> Und hält in öder Nacht mich wach.
> Izt däucht der Tag mich nicht mehr helle,
> Die Luft nicht blau, der Frühling todt;
> Nichts reizt mich mehr, kein Abendroth,
> Kein Hayn, kein Schlummer an der Quelle.
>   (358–366)

Ironically, it is during an intimate hour with Aurora that this emotional confession of his passionate longing for Procris is made, and his memory recalls the cherished image of his beloved whom he had met again at a festival of the gods:

> Procris, weiß und frisch=umkränzet,
> Mit ofner Brust und freyem Haar,
> Die schönste in der bunten Schaar.
>   (369–371)

Yet Cephalus does not confine his admiration of female beauty to one woman. Previously he had yielded to the attraction of Aurora, and while searching for Procris he has a tempting encounter with a beautiful dryad whose appearance impresses his senses profoundly; the effect is again conveyed through perfectly suited "miniature descriptions":

> Es wallt ihr langes Haar, so schwarz wie Vogel=Beer,
> Um Schultern, die den Schnee beschämen,
> Und was ihr Kleid, gebläht vom losen West
> Und bis ans Knie geschürzt, dem Jüngling sehen läßt,
> Ist mehr, als nöthig ist, um Herzen von Asbest
> Die Unverbrennlichkeit zu nehmen.
>
> (774-779)

In the same manner in which Aurora had rationalized her attraction to Cephalus, who seemed to her the double of young Tithon, Cephalus explains his enchantment as the effect of sympathy, the harmony of souls which have met and loved in a previous life. The sensuousness of the dryad's image is characteristic of many a physical description in Wieland's tales; the unequivocally erotic epitheta, the suggestiveness of the metaphors, and the vividness of the portrayal may well have stimulated the concupiscence of playfully licentious readers and were considered a "corrupt influence" for which Wieland was severely criticized by the more prudish among his contemporaries.

The examples cited here disclose that the language and imagery of the tale appeal most to the sense of sight, and they manifest the predominance of visual perception of the story's characters. Like Aurora, other female figures are easily impressed or repulsed by the external appearances of men, and it is essentially their sense of vision that induces them to reject or accept a suitor. This reaction becomes obvious in the portrayal of Cephalus when he appears as the disguised tempter of Procris. The ugly merchant is observed from the viewpoint of the women around Procris, and the artistic depiction reflects their detailed evaluation of the stranger conveyed in the "poetic perspective" of epitheta:

> Der Herr Amphibolis
> War, in der That, bey weitem kein Narciß,
> Und auch der jüngste nicht—ein See=Mann, stark von Knochen,
> Rasch wie sein Element, in Reden kurz und rund,
> Plump von Manier, und gar nicht ausgestochen,
> Großnasicht überdiß, und grösser noch von Mund.
>
> (549-554)

Contrary to Cephalus' expectation Procris is not at all impressed by his lavish presents, but is, rather, repulsed by his external appearance;

he must realize that it takes more than gold and jewels to win a woman. He therefore decides to appear again in a different disguise, this time as Seladon, anachronistically modeled after the handsome young lover of d'Urfé's novel *L'Astrée*.

It is at this moment that Wieland ironically exposes the intricate contrivance of his language and parodies the painterly qualities in the poetic portrayal of his figures; the narrator intrudes and calls on an eighteenth-century artist to create a painting of Seladon:

> Herr Heger, mahlen Sie zu dieser Phyllis Füssen
> Uns einen hübschen Knaben hin,
>
> (607–608)

and he supplies the visible details that could easily be reproduced on canvas:

> Ein rund Gesicht, wie einer Schäferin,
> Hellbraunes Haar, ein glattes Kinn,
> Ein schwarzes Aug, und einen Mund zum Küssen;
> Schlank von Gestalt, geschmeidig, zierlich,
> In allen Wendungen so reizend als natürlich,
> Wie Zephir leicht, und schmeichelhaft und dreist,
> Wie ein *Abbé*—kurz, schön als wie gegossen.
>
> (609–615)

This handsome young fellow could successfully have seduced Procris if Cephalus had not revealed his identity too early and driven his wife into angry flight. Yet her "sympathetic vibrations" had been awakened and when she met the real Seladon he had no difficulties winning her love.

Wieland's narrative contains yet another parodistic section which reveals the playfulness with which he imitated epic style, particularly the language of Homer. While Procris is loyally waiting for Cephalus to return to her, she embroiders a veil, *ein Schleier-Tuch*, for Minerva. Homer would of course not have been content with the mere mention of the fact:

> Homer erzählte gleich mit grossem Wörter=Pracht
> Was sie darauf gestikt.
>
> (506–507)

Although the narrator implies that an extensive description of this object is superfluous, he nevertheless inserts twenty-four lines which summarize with relative conciseness what Homer would have depicted. He begins with a rather static assemblage of details:

> Sonne, Mond and Sterne,
> Den Pol, der Götter Siz, und in der Ferne
> Den Erebus, ja gar die alte Nacht;

Das feste Land, ringsum verschlossen
Vom grauen Ocean, und Luft und Berg und Thal,
Und eine schöne Flur, von Sonnen=Schein umflossen . . .
(507–512)

In mid-section the narrator changes to a more dynamic representation and through the frequent use of *wie* announces action:

Dann wie im Herbst durch falbe Trauben=Gärten
Der Wein=Gott zieht, und mit zerstreutem Haar
Die Mänas, und mit taumelnden Gebehrden
Der Satyrn ungezähmte Schaar,
Die tanzend um den Wagen schweben,
Und wie sie den Silen, der fiel,
Lautlachend auf den Esel heben,
Und halbverstekt im Laub der Reben
Der Liebes=Götter loses Spiel . . .
(519–527)

All this and twenty times as much Procris would have embroidered on the veil if she had been a Homeric figure:

Das würde sie der gute alte Mann,
Der gar zu gerne mahlt, recht zierlich stiken lassen.
(531–532)

Whereas a very gifted poet may be pardoned for the extensive description of an art object at the moment of its inclusion in an epic work, an inferior writer should not even attempt it, for "was man ihm verzeyht, steht andern selten an" (533).

Despite the ironic overtones the judgment implied in these lines can be seen as a modest participation in a contemporary controversy. The description of Procris' embroidery is unmistakably modeled after Homer's depiction of the shield of Achilles, the "famous picture" which had been analyzed and debated by many scholars and critics who like Lessing in the *Laokoon* discussed the relationship between painting and poetry. The works of earlier critics, among them Scaliger, Perrault, La Motte, and above all Pope, whose translation of Homer was accompanied by "Observations on the shield of Achilles," were well known to Wieland, partly through Breitinger, who in his *Critische Dichtkunst* defended the artistry of Homer's representation against the criticism of contemporaries, and un-equivocally approved of the poetic depiction of artistic objects:

Also beschreibet der Poet, wenn er von einem Gemählde redet, nicht
nur *id quod pingitur*, sondern auch *quod intelligitur*; und dieses machet
seine Beschreibung und die Kunst des Mahlers zugleich recht wunderbar
(I, 304).

Wieland's imitation of Homer foreshadows rather wittily Lessing's serious evaluation of the creation of Achilles' shield as he develops it in the *Laokoon* of 1766. Like the shield, the veil is not described as finished or complete, but as an art object that is being made. The structural pattern is similar to the form of the corresponding section in *The Iliad*: a relatively static depiction, in fact the mere mention, of universal bodies precedes the dynamic description of human pursuits. Whereas the shield depicts primarily masculine activities, Procris' veil reveals her feminine interests as she embroiders charming nature scenes and sensuous games of love. The interpolation of this section into *Aurora und Cephalus* was no doubt facetiously meant to demonstrate the narrator's epic talent, and its brevity should be interpreted as the symbol of modesty assumed by a poet who in ironic dissimulation implicitly admits that he cannot possibly compete with the greatest poet of antiquity.

Wieland's initial evocation of Horace and the implied announcement of his intention to use commonly known words in the formation of a new language may also be understood as an indirect reply to Lessing who in the *Briefe die neueste Litteratur betreffend* had reviewed Wieland's *Sammlung einiger Prosaischen Schriften* of 1758 and had severely criticized the style and language of the young poet then living in Switzerland. The fourteenth letter contains a particularly disparaging judgment, accusing him of neglecting his knowledge of good German and of adulterating his mother tongue. Wieland, Lessing felt,

> verlernt seine Sprache in der Schweitz. Nicht blos das Genie derselben, und den ihr eigenthümlichen Schwung; er muß sogar eine beträchliche Anzahl von Worten vergessen haben. Denn alle Augenblicke läßt er seinen Leser über ein französisches Wort stolpern, der sich kaum besinnen kann, ob er einen itzigen Schriftsteller, oder einen aus dem galanten Zeitalter Christian Weisens liest.[23]

Moreover, Lessing claimed, specific sections of his works contain words that are not commonly known, and they do not clearly convey the author's perhaps exceptional ideas with which the reader would certainly want to become acquainted: "Sie haben eine Menge Wörter, die man hier nicht versteht, die aber viele Leser zu verstehen wünschten, weil sie wirklich etwas besonders auszudrucken scheinen." Infelicitously chosen words are not as numerous as one might infer from these remarks; Lessing himself admits that despite the unfortunate inclusion of strange and foreign expressions the *Schriften* are indeed very good reading, and he predicts that the tone of satire and

[23]*Sämtliche Schriften*, ed. Lachmann-Muncker, VIII (Stuttgart, 1892), 31-33.

the humor of various parts will pleasantly entertain and amuse the reader.

Wieland never ignored his critics; although he was often angered by unfair censure, he seriously considered constructive comments and frequently accepted reasonable suggestions for the improvement of his works, so that the new and always altered editions reflect his independent development as well as the unsolicited but nevertheless effective advice of his critics. Lessing's remarks may have stimulated him to guard against the use of unfamiliar and foreign words and to strive instead for a language constructed of commonly known expressions and terms. The comic tales of 1765 do indeed reflect this artistic intention as it is announced in the motto borrowed from Horace. There is only occasionally an unnecessary foreign phrase (one in *Aurora und Cephalus*), all of them eliminated in later editions of the collection, and there is scarcely an unusual word that is not easily understandable. The lines previously cited and discussed may sufficiently have revealed how effectively Wieland did employ the diction of common life and how efficiently the style of the tales supports the poetic function of his work.

As do Wieland's other works, the *Comische Erzählungen* share a characteristic feature, a wealth of allusiveness—especially to the classics, to the Bible, to commonplaces and contemporary writings— with a considerable body of eighteenth-century literature which is "constituted not only by its own verbal texture but also by the rich interplay between the author's text and the full context it allusively arouses, for these allusive resonances are not peripheral but functional to the meaning of the artistic product."[24] Quite often obtrusively overt or subtly hidden allusions are meant to bring into focus what may be called "perspectives in depth"; these become visible only to the creative reader who is well acquainted with the frame of reference and is willing to follow the intimative suggestions of the author. Explicit notes to clarify every one of the connections might well have been considered an insult to the well-educated contemporary reader. In fact, poets felt justified in presupposing a rather extensive knowledge of mythology, history, and literature, and Wieland stated this expectation in no uncertain terms:

> Ein Dichter ist berechtiget, bey seinen Lesern einige Kenntniss der Mythologie und Geschichte, und einige Belesenheit in Romanen, Schauspielen und andern Werken der Einbildungskraft und des Witzes vorauszusetzen; und es würde daher unnöthig seyn, zu allen solchen Nahmen Anmer-

---

[24]Earl R. Wasserman, "The Limits of Allusion in the Rape of the Lock," *JEGP*, 65 (1966), 444.

kungen zu machen, die einem jeden bekannt sind, der nur den kleinsten Grad von Belesenheit hat.[25]

Soon, however, Wieland became aware of the decline in learning that gradually disinherited younger generations from his referential system, and he made, reluctantly, liberal concessions when he added specific notes in the later editions of his works so that the deprived reader might recognize crucial changes and departures from source or model and, perhaps more important, not overlook essential connections invoked by pregnant allusions.

It is, of course, possible to ignore the resources outside a work, to read it merely "superficially," and still comprehend its essential meaning. Yet the reader who considers allusions an implicit invitation to penetrate below the surface will see relationships and can make comparisons that add a substantial perspective to the interpretation of a work. The examination of particularly intriguing allusions, their origins and associations should afford an instructive view of the depth perspectives thus exposed, and a detailed knowledge of the context may well increase the appreciation of Wieland's lively jests, his "muntere Scherze," as one of his perceptive reviewers called them.[26]

Several allusions from *Aurora und Cephalus* may serve as representative examples and as paradigms for the significant interaction between Wieland's text and the context it recalls.[27] The title of the tale becomes at once more expressive if the mythological relationships and the literary adaptations of relevant motifs are remembered. It indicates that the author does not intend to present another tragic tale in which Procris and Cephalus figure prominently, nor another tale in which Aurora and Tithon act out the unfortunate events of their marriage. The title announces a departure from conventional configurations and permits the assumption that the central event of the story is the abduction of Cephalus and his illicit affair which Aurora, an expectation which is immediately confirmed by the motto of the narrative: "—quod faceret quaelibet, illa facit." Although, following common practice, it is most certainly meant to foreshadow the events and to establish the atmosphere, the motto has apparently remained unidentified.[28] Wieland, who elsewhere acknowledges his sources, may pur-

[25]*Sämmtliche Werke*, IV (Leipzig, 1794), 24.
[26]See *Neue Bibliothek der schönen Wissenschaften und der freyen Künste*, I, No. 1 (Leipzig, 1765), 305.
[27]Annotated editions clarify a large number of the allusions, but they by no means identify all of them or explain their significance sufficiently. It is not my intention here to solve all referential riddles in *Aurora und Cephalus*; I shall for the moment only analyze a few of the characteristic and more important examples.
[28]The edition of the *Werke*, Vol. IV, ed. Martini-Seiffert, for example, does not identify the motto; the translation is given as "Was die eine gern tun möchte, tut die andere" (p. 852).

posely have omitted an accurate reference because the verse is not a
literal quotation but the adaptation of a line from Ovid. The *Ars Amatoria* contains a phrase which must have been the model. The eleventh
section of the second book is concerned with fidelity between husband
and wife. It tells of the marriage between Menelaus and Helena, of
the unwise departure of Menelaus, who left his wife when Paris was
their guest, and of the elopement of the two lovers. Menelaus, it is
argued, must assume part of the responsibility for the affair and its
disastrous consequences:

> Qui stupor hic, Menelaë, fuit? tu solus abibas,
>   Isdem sub tectis hospes et uxor erant?[29]

Paris, the adulterer, should be forgiven for he only did what any
other man in his place would have done:

> Quod tu, quod faceret quilibet, ille facit.[30]

It is this phrase that has been adapted as the motto for *Aurora und
Cephalus*; interpreted in its proper context it seems to plead extenuating circumstances for condonable adultery, particularly if the intended purpose of the *Ars Amatoria* is considered as background.
The mood thus invoked is apparently one of frivolity; these overtones,
some rather crude formulations, and several scenes were censured as
being utterly immoral by the reviewers of the *Comische Erzählungen*.
Yet Wieland felt that the verse narratives did not lack morality and
could easily be defended if they were considered from an appropriate
point of view: "Ich bin überzeugt," he wrote, "daß die komischen
Erzählungen sich aus einem moralischen Gesichtspunkte rechtfertigen
lassen."[31] Nevertheless, he heeded the advice of his reviewers and
through propitious changes in later editions, in part suggested by his
critics, toned down formulations and descriptions that could be interpreted as immoral or excessively licentious. Among the casualties was
the Ovidean motto of *Aurora und Cephalus*.

In the second edition the tale is introduced by another motto, an
equally enigmatic Latin quotation: "—Nihil est audacius illis Deprensis
—." Although neither Wieland nor his editors have identified the
motto it is possible to establish the source for this line: it is borrowed
from Juvenal and comes from the sixth satire in which he depicts the
rapid decline of morals in antiquity and expresses an almost savage
indictment of women. As soon as the connection is made and the context of the line is taken into consideration the mood initially invoked

---

[29]"Was that no stupidity, Menelaus? You went on a journey and left wife and friend
behind under the same roof" (trans. mine).
[30]"He only did, what you yourself would do, what anyone would do" (trans. mine).
[31]*Auswahl denkwürdiger Briefe*, I, 51.

by the allusion to Ovid changes considerably. The verses surrounding the formulation selected as the motto expose the adulterous inclinations of women and accuse them of using the most devious means to deceive their husbands. Even the eloquent Quintilian, who is asked to defend them, cannot find words to vindicate their behavior. One woman, allegedly representative of many, is therefore asked to speak in her own defense, and with insolent arrogance she addresses her husband:

> Olim convenerat, inquit,
> Ut faceres tu, quod velles, nec non ego possem
> Indulgere mihi: clames licet et mare coelo
> Confundas, homo sum.[32]

Her attitude, the satirist feels, is typical:

> Nihil est audacius illis
> Deprensis: iram atque animos a crimine sumunt.

The contrast with the first motto is striking. Whereas the verse from Ovid expressed an amused and tolerant understanding of the erotic games of Aurora with Cephalus and Procris with Seladon, the second motto introduces a severely moralizing tone and implies an unjustifiably harsh judgment of Aurora and Procris, whose infidelity is not at all as repulsive as that of Juvenal's figures. Wieland may have realized the inappropriateness of the implied moral verdict evoked by the reference to Juvenal, for in later editions he abandoned the verse and published the tale without a motto.

The many allusions contained in the verse narrative itself perform various functions; well-known writers and philosophers who have analyzed the nature of man are cited as authorities, and their theories confirm the verisimilitude of character portrayal in *Aurora und Cephalus*. Works of art are mentioned because they portray idealized, representative figures, and the artistically perfect images are excellently suited to complement the literary portrayal. Overt allusions to mythological and literary figures serve a similar purpose; they function as implied or explicit comparisons through which Wieland's figures are tacitly endowed with distinctive and characteristic features that may not be overlooked in the interpretation of the tale. These allusions are sometimes qualified by unmistakable references to uniquely literary episodes so that they amplify the depiction of particular scenes in Wieland's tale and explain the behavior of his figures.

---

[32]*Juvenal and Persius*, ed. and trans. G. G. Ramsay (Cambridge/London, 1950), pp. 104–107: "'We agreed long ago,' says the lady, 'that you were to go your way, and I mine. You may confound sea and sky with your bellowing, I am a human being after all.'" And the next two lines read: "There's no effrontery like that of a woman caught in the act; her very guilt inspires her with wrath and insolence."

Among the authorities who were consulted is Cicero. The first reference to his judicious views is made when Cephalus instead of kissing Aurora's hand inadvertently kisses another part of her body:

Indem er noch im Küssen ist,
Verirrt sein Mund —da seht mir doch die Musen!
Die kleinen Spröden schämen sich
Und halten plözlich ein — doch ich bekenn' es, ich,
(Und Cicero an Pätum spricht für mich:)
Verirrt — wie leicht verirrt man sich!
Verirrt sein Mund auf ihren Busen.

(234-240)

The unwillingness of the muses to speak of what might possibly be considered obscene motivates the narrator to use Cicero against their prudishness, and the inserted allusion is meant to recall an epistle to Paetus written in July of the year 45 b.c. The letter is of considerably greater importance than the brief remark may indicate, for Cicero discusses in meticulous detail the relevant topic of obscenity and its relation to language. Of central significance is the question whether it is advisable to substitute a seemingly inoffensive euphemism for the accurate yet perhaps indelicate word. Paetus had apparently done so and was criticized for it; Cicero explains his objections:

Ergo in re non est, multo minus in verbis. Si enim, quod verbo significatur, id turpe non est, verbum, quod significat, turpe esse non potest. *Anum* appellas alieno nomine; cur non suo potius? Si turpe est, ne alieno quidem; si non est, suo potius.[33]

The narrator of Wieland's tale obviously decided to disregard the coyness of his muses; he was not going to be artfully euphemistic but would follow Cicero's advice and call the object of Cephalus' attention by its accurate and proper name.

During this particular episode the affectionate young man is undoubtedly ready to transgress the limits of propriety, and to explain his behavior the narrator cites Cicero once more:

"Wer einmal, spricht Marc Tullius,
(Doch nicht im Buche von den Sitten)
Und wär's nur mit dem linken Fuß
Des Wohlstands Grenzen überschritten,
Dem rath ich, statt aus Blödigkeit

---

[33]Cicero, *The Letters To His Friends*, ed. W. Glynn Williams, II (London, 1928), 266-267: "For if what is indicated by the word is not indecent, the word indicating it cannot be indecent. When you speak of the *anus* you call it by a name that is not its own; why not rather call it by its own? If it is indecent, do not use even the substituted name; if not, you had better call it by its own."

Auf halbem Wege stehn zu bleiben,
Vielmehr die Unbescheidenheit,
So weit sie gehen kann, zu treiben."
(245-252)

The source of this recommendation is Cicero's epistle to the historian Lucceius whom he asked to eulogize his actions with warmth, and whom he encouraged not to be overly modest: "Sed tamen, qui semel verecundiae finis transierit, eum bene et naviter oportet esse impudentem."[34] A comparison of the two versions immediately reveals that the narrator of the verse tale presents an inaccurate translation clearly exaggerating the advisability of unrestrained transgression and applies it to an entirely different situation. Although the ironic intent of source and adaptation is explicit enough, a serious note of encouragement to go beyond the limits of modesty is perceptible in both formulations; yet whereas Cicero merely expresses reserved permissiveness, the German narrator delivers a provocative challenge. The comparison with the source exposes the corruption of the adaptation which is the more devious because of the deceptive assertion of authenticity.

An even more appropriate connection with the situation of the verse tale becomes obvious when the content of the sentence immediately following Cicero's request is considered. There he alludes to a relevant literary topic that was of considerable interest to eighteenth-century writers, particularly to Wieland and Goethe. It is the story of Hercules at the crossroads, allegedly told by Prodicus and related in Xenophon's *Memorabilia*. Young Hercules at the age at which he has to decide upon his future withdraws to a quiet place and contemplates the direction he is going to take. At this moment two women approach him, one tall, slender, pure, modest, sober, and dressed in white; the other plump, soft, her face made up, and dressed in such a fashion that

---

[34]*Ibid.*, I (London, 1927), 368-369: "But anyhow, if a man has once transgressed the bounds of modesty, the best he can do is to be shameless out and out." Wieland's own translation reads: "Aber wer einmahl über die Grenzen der Schamhaftigkeit gegangen ist, thut am besten, wenn er recht überschwänglich unverschämt ist." *Cicero's Sämmtliche Briefe*, II (Zurich, 1808), 228.

The later editions of *Aurora und Cephalus* tone down the boldness of the statement and add a note of caution; the line given here in italics is added:

"Wer einmahl—lehrt uns Markus Tullius,
Doch nicht im Buche von den Sitten—
Des Wolhlstands Grenzen überschritten,
(*Wofür man zwar sich möglichst hüten muss*)
Dem rath' ich, statt aus Blödigkeit
Auf halbem Wege stehn zu bleiben,
Vielmehr die Unbescheidenheit
So weit sie gehen kann, zu treiben."

Sämmtliche Werke, x (Leipzig, 1795), 208-209.

all her charms are revealed. The one represents virtue, the other is called happiness by her friends and is "nicknamed" vice by those who hate her. Both women plead the advantages of their own way of life. Although vice does so more eloquently than virtue and promises a life of leisure and enjoyment, Hercules choses the hard road that leads to virtue.

Cephalus, like Hercules, is at the crossroads and has to decide whether to succumb to vice or remain a faithful and virtuous husband. Unlike the heroic son of Zeus he gives in to temptation and becomes the lover of Aurora. His transgression is perhaps pardonable, for the voluptuous beauty of his temptress held too great a promise to be rejected. The first time Cephalus saw her she was lying on a day bed and presented such a splendorous picture that even Jupiter would have desired her. The allurement of her position cannot easily be described, but the allusion to a perfect portrayal in art should evoke a suitable image:

> Und diese Fee in einer Lage
> Wie Titian der Liebes=Göttin giebt.
> (185-186)

The relatively indefinite reference permits the reader to let his taste be his guide and recall from among Titian's several paintings of Venus reclining the one that pleases him most. To complete the image of Aurora he will perhaps immediately think of the two most suitable representations, the Venus of Urbino and Venus with Amor. Both show Venus reposing on a day bed, her nude body turned toward the viewer. The Venus of Urbino smiles enigmatically at the viewer; her face is oval, her body young and slender and seeming to palpitate with vitality. She is not alone; two servants are with her in the room and stand near a window that offers only a limited view of the exterior. The Venus with Amor seems equally contemplative, yet she does not look at the viewer but at Cupid. Her body is strong and supple, its curves are more voluptuous, and she seems momentarily relaxed. With the exception of Amor she is alone in a room that seems to adjoin an open terrace with an expansive view of the surrounding countryside. Personal preference may decide which of the two figures the reader will identify with Aurora. Yet the contemplation of either painting will take him one step farther than Cephalus, who after all is looking at a woman still partly dressed.

Among the many implied or overt comparisons of Wieland's figures with other literary characters is one which may particularly have delighted the informed reader. When Cephalus tells fervently of his love for Procris, Aurora interrupts him and sarcastically interjects:

Der Herr . . .
Hat, wahrlich! aus der Purpur=Flasche
Bescheid gethan, er liebt ja ungemein!
(407–409)

The allusion is amusingly anachronistic, for the purple flask is an object in one of the tales of Marmontel, "Les quatre Flacons." Alcidonis, its young hero, is protected by the fairy Galante who teaches him to understand women and be prepared for erotic involvement. There are, she tells him, three kinds of love, "la passion, le goût & la fantaisie,"[35] and the art of being happy depends on placing the nuances properly. She gives him four flacons. The contents of three will stimulate and intensify the emotions; if he drinks of the purple flask he will become an impetuously ardent lover. The fourth potion will return him to his natural state. When the woman he desires implores him to tell her that he loves her passionately and he only answers "I think so," she is not at all satisfied, and Alcidonis realizes that this is the time to drink from the purple flask. He goes into a corner, empties it to the last drop, and returns:

> Il reparoît, les yeux enflammés, le coeur palpitant, la voix éteinte. Plus de fadeur, plus de galanterie: son langage étoit rapide, entrecoupé, plein de substance & de chaleur. Les mots ne pouvoient suffire aux sentimens. Des accens inarticulés suppléoient aux paroles; un geste véhément, une action impétueuse en redoubloient l'énergie.[36]

Aurora's allusion to this episode should stimulate the creative reader to transfer Marmontel's description of the changed young man to Cephalus. Under the influence of the potion from the purple bottle he would act exactly like Alcidonis, and the ardent amour of his French counterpart prefigures the passionate infatuation of Cephalus. The well-informed reader will perceive the "depth perspective" revealed by the allusion and be thus able to add a characteristic feature to the image of Cephalus.

Allusions of this type also function to suggest negative possibilities. When, for example, Procris is tempted by her wealthy visitor she could have accepted his gifts and rewarded him with her love. Yet she did not do so and thus implicitly contradicted a theory of La Fontaine, who held that the key to the cash box is the key to a woman's heart. The narrator of Wieland's tale triumphantly denies the validity of such a reprehensible opinion:

Hans La Fontain! Nun sagt mir noch einmal,
Der Cassen=Schlüssel sey der Schlüssel zu den Herzen!
(577–578)

---

[35]*Contes Moraux* (Paris, 1779), I, 108–142, specifically, p. 116.
[36]*Ibid.*, p. 120.

The allusion is meant to recall La Fontaine's tale *La Coupe en-enchantée*, a complex texture of interrelated motifs which presents negative possibilities in multiple perspectives and parallels in several of the circumstantial details the episode of Cephalus' jealousy and the attempted seduction of his wife. The subtitle of *The Magic Cup*, "Nouvelle tirée de l'Arioste," refers La Fontaine's reader to the *Orlando Furioso*, which in turn borrowed the motif of the enchanted cup from Arthurian legend.

La Fontaine's story is introduced by universally valid reflections upon jealousy which characterize Rinaldo's host, the first-person narrator of the relevant episode in the *Orlando Furioso*, La Fontaine's protagonist Damon and, of course, Wieland's Cephalus:

> Les maux les plus cruels ne sont que des chansons
> Près de ceux qu'aux maris cause la jalousie.
> Figurez-vous un fou chez qui tous le soupçons
>   Sont bien venus, quoi qu'on lui die.
> Il n'a pas un moment de repos en sa vie.
> Si l'oreille lui tinte, ô dieux! tout est perdu.
> Ses songes sont toujours que l'on fait cocu.[37]

The literary configurations have significant aspects in common: the men are married to beautiful women but they do not trust their wives, and goaded by other women they decide to put their wives' fidelity to the test. The Mantuan of the *Orlando Furioso* is transformed by the sorceress Melissa into a handsome young man who strongly resembles the former lover of his wife. Unrecognized, he courts her and finally succeeds in winning her favors with a precious gift. When he discloses his true identity she leaves him in anger, returns to her former lover, and sends word that her husband should give up all hope of ever seeing her again. The Mantuan soon comprehends the foolishness of his action; yet he has one consolation, though a rather questionable one: whenever he places Morgana's magic cup, which had revealed Guenevere's secret to King Arthur, in the hands of a visitor, almost every one of the drinkers spills some wine, an infallible sign that he too is a cuckold whose unfaithful wife betrays his trust. Rinald is the only one who does not spill any wine on himself, and this is not because his wife was unwaveringly faithful but simply because he refuses to touch the magic cup and decides to believe unquestioningly in her loyalty. Damon of La Fontaine's tale has an experience similar to that of the Mantuan. The Enchantress Neira encourages him to test the fidelity of his wife; he assumes the identity of Erastus, a young man who is a constant visitor at his house, and tries to seduce her with charm and implora-

[37]*Contes et Nouvelles*, ed. Georges Couton (Paris, 1961), p. 172.

tions. She remains steadfast; only when he offers her a large sum of money does she sacrifice her chastity, and this proves, La Fontaine believes, the power of money: "L'argent sut donc fléchir ce coeur inexorable."[38] As is usual in Wieland's adaptations, the differences between his tale and the sources are more functional than the similarities. When Cephalus tries to seduce Procris with precious gifts, she is not like her predecessors swayed by these material things. In contrast to them she is motivated by true affection; it is the similarity between Cephalus and Seladon that entices her, and it is actually the power of sympathy that wins the victory of Seladon over Procris. Thus Wieland most emphatically contradicts La Fontaine's dubious assertion.

These are only a few of the many allusions contained in Wieland's verse tales, and it does indeed, as one of the eighteenth-century reviewers stated, increase the enjoyment of reading if the connections are recognized and interpreted and if the overtones are fully understood. The contemporary audience must greatly have appreciated the game of hide-and-seek suggested by all of Wieland's works; the allusions were a compliment to the intelligence of his readers, and some of them were challenging puzzles which provided stimulating entertainment at a time when it was still fashionable to gather for an evening of reading or get together for the discussion of literature.

The *Comische Erzählungen*, written simultaneously with *Don Sylvio* and sharing its spirit of satire, exhibit a perspective that is conspicuously different from that of the previous, more idealistic works, and as early as the time of their publication Wieland felt the need to justify the existence of these seemingly frivolous tales. The first edition is preceded by a page-long quotation from the younger Plinius, who in a letter to Titius Aristo defended his light verse against contemporary criticism:

> Quibus ego, ut augeam meam culpam, ita respondeo: facio non numquam versiculos severos parum, facio; nam et comoedias audio et specto mimos et lyricos lego et Sotadicos intellego; aliquando praeterea rideo iocor ludo, utque omnia innoxiae remissionis genera breviter amplectar, homo sum.[39]

Although Wieland did not translate the passage literally—he omitted the reference to Sotadic verse and wrote instead "ich lese die Satyren-Schreiber, selbst die allerfreiesten, und brauche keinen

---

[38]*Ibid.*, 180.

[39]Pliny, *Letters and Panegyricus*, ed. Betty Radice (Cambridge/London, 1969), pp. 328-329: "My answer to these critics will probably aggravate the offence. I admit that I do often write verse which is far from serious, for I also listen to comedy, watch farces, read lyric poetry, and appreciate Sotadic verse; there are besides times when I laugh, make jokes, and enjoy my fun, in fact I can sum up all these innocent relaxations in a word 'I am human.'"

Ausleger dazu"—the essence of Pliny's explanation is reiterated through the central statement "Ich bin ein Mensch" and underlines Wieland's personal confession of his "return to earth." The notable change in Wieland's public attitude, particularly toward questions of love and marriage, was readily recognized by the reviewer whose evaluation of the *Comische Erzählungen* was published in the *Neue Bibliothek der schönen Wissenschaften und der freyen Künste*. Since the tales appeared anonymously he can only guess who the author might be, but he does so correctly and remarks appropriately: ". . . es muß einem Leser seltsam vorkommen, daß wenn der Verfasser derjenige wirklich ist, den man uns genannt hat, er überall seiner sonst so angenehmen Liebesgrille der platonischen Liebe spottet."[40] Wieland had indeed and very obviously renounced the idealistic, poetically expressed belief in the prevalent existence of Platonic love among men, and the narrator's allusion to Helvetius in *Aurora und Cephalus* (68) must be understood as the evocation of an anti-Platonic, yet perhaps equally valid view of an authority who has no faith in the reality of metaphysical love but holds that most affection is actually stimulated by physical desire.[41]

Pliny's epistle expresses further sentiments which Wieland unquestionably shared, though he does not cite the pertinent section. The reader who accepts the exact reference at the end of Wieland's long quotation as an invitation to consult the letter in its entirety will realize that the second half is perhaps equally as important as the first; it is there that Pliny asserts his attentive regard for the critical opinions of others and indicates his willingness to adopt their suggestions for changes and omissions provided, of course, that they lead to the improvement of his works. Wieland too was much concerned about private reactions and public responses to his writings. The

[40]The review appeared in Vol. I, Part 1 (Leipzig, 1765), 300-314; see specifically p. 307. A second review, whose author was Thomas Abbt, appeared in the *Allgemeine deutsche Bibliothek*, I, 2 (Berlin/Stettin, 1765), 215-227. Praise and blame are expressed by Abbt in equal measure, and several of the unfair features of his criticism were discussed by Wieland in his personal correspondence. The textual changes of the *Comische Erzählungen* have been treated by Carl Scharf, "The Textual History of Wieland's Comische Erzählungen" (diss., Johns Hopkins, 1934); and by Aage Kabell, "Textgeschichtliche Beiträge zu Wielands Komischen Erzählungen Mit besonderer Rücksicht auf ein Handexemplar des Dichters in der Königlichen Bibliothek zu Kopenhagen," *Orbis Litterarum*, 4 (1946), 124-156. Scharf's dissertation is of a purely technical nature, and Kabell's investigation is limited in scope, as indicated in the subtitle of his article; he obviously did not consult Scharf's contribution (he does not refer to it) so there is considerable duplication.

[41]Claude Adrien Helvetius, *De L'Esprit*, 4th Discourse, Chapter x; the annotated German edition of 1760, *Discurs über den Geist des Menschen*, ed. and trans. Johann Christoph Gottsched, affirms this view: "Wenn man sich z. E. einbildet, man liebe nur die Seele eines Frauenzimmers: so hat man gewiß nur ihren Körper zur Absicht; und um dieser Absicht willen, und um seiner Bedürfniß,, besonders seiner Neugierde, ein Genüge zu thun, ist man zu allem fähig" (562).

Comische Erzählungen had apparently been discussed among the friends of Count Stadion at the castle of Warthausen, "Wieland's Parnaß," where he was a frequent guest and aimed to please his audience, for "gefiel er hier, so hoffte er den Besten zu gefallen."[42] Since these conversations are not recorded, the concise details and the actual extent of their influence on Wieland's verse narratives are not ascertainable.

More easily traceable is the effect of published reviews. A precise comparison of specific criticisms with the changes he made in later editions discloses the meticulous care with which Wieland read the reviews of his works. Understandably, he did not agree with every one of the objections raised by his critics and occasionally he even questioned rather angrily the soundness of their judgment, but he accepted advice whenever the change would constitute a marked improvement of his writings. One incident may suffice as example. As Cephalus awakens after his abduction and perceives the splendor of his surroundings, even the narrator marvels at the scene:

> Stellt, wenn ihr könnt, auf Säulen von Rubinen
> Euch einen Saal von Perlen=Mutter vor;
> In diesen Saal ein Bette mit Gardinen,
> *En pavillon*, von rosenfarbem Flor,
> Und reich gestikt; auf diesem Ruhebette
> Was Jupiter sich selbst gewünschet hätte,
> Die schönste Fee . . .
>
> (177–183)

The reviewer writing for the *Neue Bibliothek* was not overly impressed by this description and felt that a different setting might have been more effective: "Wir hätten uns noch lieber sie in dieser Stellung, in einer romantischen Gegend, als in einem Saal von Rubinen vorgestellt."[43] Wieland, it seems, did not mind this judgment and, with an ironic touch, even acknowledged the suggestion when for the second edition of the *Comische Erzählungen* he made the requested change:

> Der Perlenmutter-Saal mit Säulen von Rubinen,
> Den unsre Göttin sich zum Schauplaz auserkohr,
> Hat einem Kenner nicht romantisch genug geschienen.
> So stellt euch dann umwölbet mit Schasminen,
> Auf weichem Moos ein Blumen-Bette vor,
> Mit reichem Sammt bedeckt; auf diesem Blumen-Bette,

---

[42] J. G. Gruber, *Christph. Martin Wieland* (Leipzig/Altenberg, 1815), I, 179.
[43] *Neue Bibliothek*, I, 1, 308.

Was Jupiter sich selbst gewünschet hätte,
Die schönste Fee . . .

(167–174)

This kind of response to criticism (even if facetious) was characteristic of Wieland. It was not primarily a wish to please his reviewers but rather the sincere desire to correct his writings that stimulated many of the changes he made. The reasons behind the assiduous revisions of every one of his works for each new edition were intuitively recognized by Goethe, who identified Wieland's untiring efforts to bring his literary products to perfection in his address *Zu brüderlichem Andenken Wielands:*

> Diese sorgfältige Bearbeitung seiner Schriften entsprang aus einer frohen Überzeugung, welche zu Ende seines schweizerischen Aufenthaltes in ihm mag hervorgetreten sein, als die Ungeduld des Hervorbringens sich in etwas legte, und der Wunsch, ein Vollendetes dem Gemeinwesen darzubringen, entschiedener und deutlicher rege ward.[44]

The characteristic features of the *Comische Erzählungen*, that is, the imaginative adaptation of traditional materials, the insertion of meaningful allusions revealing important "depth perspectives," and the judicious selection of epitheta supporting the meticulous construction of "poetic perspectives," recall some of the seminal artistic elements of the earliest writings, and at the same time foreshadow corresponding, gradually perfected aspects of successive works, particularly the verse tales, among them the internationally acclaimed *Oberon* of 1780. These artistic qualities were well received by Wieland's contemporaries. Many writers, it will be remembered, shared his view that adaptation is true invention, and it is no coincidence that the literature of the time is rich in poetic variations on traditional themes, includes diverse combinations of favorite motifs, and presents well-known figures from legend and literature in a new light.

The excellence of Wieland's style was soon acknowledged by many. Lessing, for one, recognized the progress he had made in the fashioning of his poetic language and included him among the superior poets from whom he extracted linguistic examples in preparation for a new German dictionary. He frequently consulted Wieland's writings, particularly the *Geschichte des Agathon* and the verse tale *Der neue Amadis*, and he credited him with the felicitous coinage of new words, a gift which he called a "glückliche Wörterfabrik."[45]

---

[44]*Werke*, xxxvi (Weimar, 1893), 319.
[45]*Sämtliche Schriften*, ed. Lachmann-Muncker, xvi (Leipzig, 1902), 81. Wieland's contribution to the development of the German language was considerable, and Goethe was not exaggerating when he said that the German upper class owes its style to Wieland: "Wielanden . . . verdankt das ganze obere Deutschland seinen Stil. Es hat

Similarly propitious views were expressed by other critics, among them Georg Christoph Lichtenberg, who compared Wieland favorably with Shakespeare and praised his unique talent for finding among a thousand phrases the most appropriate to express a specific feeling or a particular sentiment:

> Wieland ist ein großer Schriftsteller, er hat verwegene Blicke in eine Seele getan, in die seinige oder eines anderen, mitten in dem Genuß seiner Empfindungen greift er nach Worten und trifft, wie durch einen Trieb, unter Tausenden von Ausdrücken oft den, der augenblicklich Gedanken wieder zu Empfindungen macht. Dieses hat er mit dem Shakespeare gemein.[46]

The allusive method prominently applied in all of Wieland's works met, as might be expected, with delighted approval, and the distinct advantage of the creative approach to his writings was readily recognized. The reviewer who published a comprehensive evaluation of the verse tales in the *Neue Bibliothek der schönen Wissenschaften und der freyen Künste* explicitly mentioned the strategic importance of interpolated citations and recognized the disclosive value of allusions: "Ovid, Lafontaine, Rost, und a.m. werfen ein paar Zeilen ein, und geben damit dem Leser weit mehr zu verstehen, als ein weitläuftiger Commentar darüber."[47] He also praised Wieland's vivid descriptions, his gay witticisms, the charming portrayals and even the mischievously satiric representations; he particularly commended the author's widely ranging literary knowledge and its ironic reflection in his tales: "Seine Belesenheit weiß der Dichter auf eine solch drollige Art anzubringen, daß sie diejenigen, die mit den Anspielungen bekannt sind, nicht ohne Lachen lesen werden." It is not difficult to agree with the reviewer; a thorough acquaintance with literature, even if it is not equivalent to the poet's extensive and profound knowledge, will indeed contribute considerably to the enjoyment of reading the *Comische Erzählungen*, and beyond that enhance the diversified experience derived from all of Wieland's other writings.

---

viel von ihm gelernt, und die Fähigkeit, sich gehörig auszudrücken, ist nicht das geringste" (conversation with Eckermann of January 18th, 1825). A comprehensive study of Wieland's linguistic influence is still needed. Eric Blackall in *The Emergence of German as a Literary Language 1700-1775* (Cambridge, England, 1959), because of the limits of the period selected for his study, discusses primarily the apparently sentimental and anacreontic language of the earlier works and briefly analyzes some aspects of irony in connection with the *Comische Erzählungen*. A recent study by Kyösti Itkonen, *Die Shakespeare-Übersetzung Wielands* (Jyväskylä, 1971), reviews the limited number of previous contributions and emphasizes the need for a thorough and extensive investigation. His own work is intended as a "Beitrag zu einem künftigen Wieland-Wörterbuch" (9).

[46]*Gesammelte Werke*, ed. Wilhelm Grenzmann (Baden-Baden, 1950), I, 326.

[47]*Neue Bibliothek*, I, 1, 303.

Continuing and Concluding Observations

The designation of Wieland's writings published between 1751 and 1765 as "early works" may appear unusual, especially if one remembers the customary grouping which considers the dialogue between Lysias and Eubulus of 1760 as the last of the *Jugendschriften*.[1] It seemed justified, however, to include for discussion here the first novel of 1764 and the comic tales of 1765, for both are transitional works which in significant aspects of form and content parallel specific features of older works and at the same time foreshadow comparable qualities in the later writings. The inclusion of these two works appeared particularly advisable since it was my intention to indicate most of the first important uses of the diverse point-of-view techniques that went into the making of the later works, and I hope to have shown that *Don Sylvio* and the *Comische Erzählungen* introduce, early and newly, such features. It would easily be possible to multiply the instances of perspectivism in the early works, but since the outstandingly consequential features have by now been identified the citation of further examples does not seem necessary. Yet it remains to be shown—even if only selectively and cursorily—that Wieland perfected the perspective method most imaginatively in his later works and used with extraordinary skill the various point-of-view techniques that were introduced so remarkably early in his youthful writings.

The novels that appeared from 1766 on present an almost bewildering variety of subjective perspectives that have puzzled those among

---

[1] See Bernard Seuffert, *Prolegomena zu einer Wieland-Ausgabe*, Part 1 (Berlin, 1904), p. 57.

the interpreters who felt the need to identify in each novel at least one
of the fictive spokesmen or invented figures with the author of the
work.[2] The occasionally spurious identifications are of course misleading, for they do not take into consideration the intention of Wieland,
who was much more concerned with presenting a well-balanced combination of diverse perspectives than with offering images and ideas
of absolute validity.

Wieland's second novel, the *Geschichte des Agathon* (1766), compares in its narrative techniques with earlier works in that it has several spokesmen, among them a fictive editor, clearly a man of the
eighteenth century, and a fictive historian, allegedly a member of an
ancient Greek society, both of whom indulge in reflections or commentaries and, at times, get entangled in amusingly anachronistic contradictions. The portrayal of Agathon was not planned as an idealistic
presentation of a perfect character, but was meant to create the image
of a real man, "das Bild eines wirklichen Mannes," which would not
unduly emphasize his virtues and completely obliterate his human
frailties. On the contrary, the editor announces, every aspect of the
hero's personality is to be depicted, and he will be viewed in many

---

[2]Even Wolfram Buddecke, who contributed an excellent study, *C. M. Wielands
Entwicklungsbegriff und die Geschichte des Agathon* (Göttingen, 1966), and who is
fully aware of the importance of perspectivism in Wieland's writings, at times
analyzes the opinions of fictive figures or *personae* as if they were Wieland's very
own views. When he, for example, states (p. 42) that Wieland was rather uncertain
about extent, effect, and nature of circumstances, of "Umstände," in the life of man,
he supports his argument by a questionable combination of evidence: a statement
excerpted from Wieland's personal correspondence (of 1782); a rephrased formulation
of a remark by Jupiter in a *Göttergespräch* of 1791; a thought expressed by the ironic
narrator of *Agathon* (1767); and a statement made by the first-person dialogist of the
*Unterredungen zwischen W** und dem Pfarrer zu*** (of 1775). Buddecke does not
consider the fictionality of at least one, probably two, perhaps even three of these
statements; omitting their exact dates he also does not bear in mind that they span a
period of twenty-five years and thus might well reflect (if indeed they were one man's
opinions) a gradual change of views. There are other, similar instances where Buddecke
discusses the opinions of fictive figures as if they were unequivocally Wieland's
views, so that he ultimately discovers more contradictions, "Widersprüche" (p. 49),
than Wieland's writings actually contain. A perhaps more serious confusion of author
and spokesmen is evident in an article by Alfred E. Ratz, "C. M. Wieland: Toleranz,
Kompromiß und Inkonsequenz—Eine kritische Betrachtung," *Deutsche Vierteljahrsschrift*, Vol. 42 (1968). The author indiscriminately identifies Wieland himself
with his literary figures. Even the opinions of distinctly different speakers are interpreted as Wieland's views, despite the fact that these figures are obviously characterized as representing opposite sides, particularly in literary dialogues. To mention
only a few, "Wieland" and "er" stand for Dschengis and Danischmend of *Der Goldne
Spiegel*; for Walder and at the same time for his adversary Diethelm, both participants
in the *Gespräch über einige neueste Weltbegebenheiten*. Even Ottobert, an interlocutor of the *Gespräch unter vier Augen*, who is unmistakably marked as an ardent
royalist ("ein ganz entschiedner Royalist") and thus a member of a group with which
Wieland did not sympathize, is included among those who allegedly express Wieland's
own thoughts (493–514). For a more recent discussion of social and political aspects in
Wieland's writings, see Bernd Weyergraf, *Der skeptische Bürger* (Stuttgart, 1972).

different lights. The main aim of the characterization is concisely stated in an appropriate remark which alerts the readers of Agathon's "history" to a variety of illuminations: "Seine Hauptabsicht war, sie mit einem Karakter, welcher genau gekannt zu werden würdig wäre, in einem mannigfaltigen Lichte und von allen seinen Seiten bekannt zu machen."[3] This intention is realized through the unusually skillful manipulation of the multiple points of view from which Agathon is observed. Every one of the spokesmen and figures of the novel, including of course Agathon himself, subjectively and sometimes even rather unreliably contributes to the creation of an uncommonly complex image of the hero. What emerges is neither a perfect figure, as customarily presented in the romances of the past, nor a truly mixed character, as is for example Fielding's Tom Jones. Agathon compares more readily to those figures of tragedy whose fate is influenced by the effects of a "ruling passion" or by the consequences of *hamartia*. Yet Agathon's imperfection is certainly not the equivalent of a tragic flaw; it must be seen as a "comic flaw," of which, incidentally, he is never completely cured. Like *Don Sylvio*, the *Geschichte des Agathon* contains the "history" of a *Schwärmer*; it thus presents a supplementary perspective of a personality that was much discussed in eighteenth-century letters and frequently depicted, especially by Wieland, whose diverse portrayals are meant to acquaint the reader with the chimeric ideas and unusually eccentric behaviour of typical enthusiasts.[4]

The *Schwärmer* is not the only figure that appears again and again in the works of Wieland; there are others that come onto the scene in more than one work, each time, of course, in a different context and alliance. There are, for example, representative women in Greek costume, among them Aspasia who makes casual appearances in several works, as in *Agathon*, and figures prominently in others, for instance the verse narrative *Aspasia—Eine griechische Erzählung*; the dialogue *Der olympische Weiberrath, Ein Göttergespräch*; and (to mention only one more work) the *Ehrenrettung dreier berühmter Frauen des Alterthums*. The fictive spokesmen who portray Aspasia and the fictitious figures with whom she associates observe and characterize her from their personal points of view and thus contribute significantly to the creation of a realistically complex image of Pericles' famous mistress. Such interconnections clearly reveal a characteristic phenomenon: perspectivism does not only inform the individual work but serves as a remarkably effective method of unifying important elements of the entire world of Wieland's fiction.

[3] *Werke* (Akademieausgabe), VI (Berlin, 1937), 3-4.
[4] For a stimulating study of the type see Victor Lange's article "Zur Gestalt des Schwärmers im deutschen Roman des 18. Jahrhunderts," in *Festschrift für Richard Alewyn*.

The next of Wieland's novels, *Sokrates Mainomenos oder die Dialogen des Diogenes von Sinope* (1770)[5] presents a severely limited, eccentrically subjective perspective; characters and events are seen almost exclusively from the point of view of Diogenes, the first-person narrator. His intrinsic bias and capricious selectivity is pointedly announced in the first sentence of the novel when he reveals his intention to write down "meine Begebenheiten, meine Beobachtungen, meine Empfindungen, meine Meinungen, meine Träumereien, meine Torheiten,—euere Torheiten, und—die Weisheit, die ich vielleicht aus beiden gelernt habe."[6] The title of the novel is slightly misleading, for it is not a collection of formal dialogues, but is, as Wieland states in the preface of a later edition, "meistens aus zufälligen Träumereien, Selbstgesprächen, Anekdoten, dialogisirten Erzählungen und Aufsätzen . . . zusammengesetzt" which all reflect the idiosyncrasies, the mood and values of the narrator; the work therefore received in its new edition the more appropriate title *Nachlass des Diogenes von Sinope*.[7] Despite the subjectivity of his views, or perhaps even because of it, Diogenes, the benevolent and optimistic humanist, can properly claim a place among those who inhabit the spacious world of Wieland's fiction, a colorful mosaic to which every one of the novels contributes unique but essential fragments.

Although the settings of many tales are foreign lands and the cultural context is occasionally even exotic, the universality of central themes is undeniable. A topic of general validity closely related to that of perspectivism is, for example, treated in a Mexican story contained in the *Beyträge zur Geheimen Geschichte des menschlichen Verstandes und Herzens* of 1770.[8] The tale constitutes a satirical treatment of the complex phenomenon of relativism; it presents, among other events, the first meeting of two young lovers. On one of his excursions into strange territory, Koxkox, a lonely and inexperienced boy of eighteen, discovers a beautiful girl asleep under a rosebush. He is so entranced by this unfamiliar sight that he cannot tell whether he is awake or dreaming. At precisely this point the narrator faces the problem of having to describe Kikequetzal, the pretty maiden, in such a manner that his readers are convinced of her extraordinary physical qualities. He tries to facilitate his task by observing her from multifarious points of view and seeing her as others might. A Mexican artist, for example, would perceive in her the Platonic idea of perfect beauty.

[5]The first edition of 1770 is reprinted in *Werke*, II, ed. Fritz Martini and Reinhard Döhl (Munich, 1966).
[6]*Ibid.*, p. 19.
[7]The third edition received this title and was published in Leipzig in 1795 as Vol. XIII of the *Sämmtliche Werke*.
[8]The work appeared anonymously in 1770 in Leipzig; the first section, "Erstes Buch," contains the story of Koxkox and Kikequetzal.

In his depiction he would no doubt emphasize her slender curved figure and the raven-black hair, her small forehead, large eyes, and above all the pouting lips, the pudgy nose, and her jonquil-yellow complexion.

Yet beauty, like truth, is only relative. A Chinese observer would never consider Kikequetzal the embodiment of perfect beauty; he might well mock her overly large eyes, the small forehead, and her distended nostrils. A Hottentot's idea of beauty, on the other hand, might again conform to that of the Mexican; yet heavier legs and shorter hair would certainly make her more perfect in his eyes. To these contrasting evaluations the Western European narrator adds his own views. Pretending to be unconcerned with physical aspects but vitally concerned with questions of literary aesthetics, he would prefer a heroine with a more beautiful, more musical name. Parodying the poetic names formerly current in literature, he suggests calling the maiden perhaps Zilia or Alzire, Adelaide or Cidalise.

A second aspect of the episode, the behavior of the male observer at this sudden encounter with a sparsely clad sleeping beauty, is also considered from diverging points of view. The narrator is convinced that a hundred different men would react in a hundred different ways to this particular situation. A painter would use the girl as a model for a piece of art; a traveler would describe her carefully in his journal; a poet would sit opposite her and write a madrigal; a hedonist would immediately provide a pleasant surprise for her; a stoic would prove to himself that he does not feel any desire for the woman, for wise men do not succumb to physical attractions; a missionary would at once try to convert her, and St. Hilary would walk past Kikequetzal without even looking at her. The reaction of each observer and the standpoint from which he views the object of his contemplation is obviously influenced by subjective factors: his education and profession, his philosophy and intellectual attitude, his mood and inclinations at the moment of the unexpected encounter.

This playfully satiric and ironic representation clearly carries serious overtones. It reveals the subjectivity of experience and points inferentially to the possibility of an equally subjective depiction of the episode by the individual observers. Any one of the participants in this particular experience may choose to relate the event. His account will, of course, be colored by a unique combination of subjective factors, and every version of the story will be unlike the others, clearly reflecting the personality of the narrator.

Most intricate in its combination of points of view is another novel, *Der Goldne Spiegel, oder die Könige von Scheschian*, of 1772.[9] In con-

[9]The first edition appeared in four parts in Leipzig; the revised edition was published as Vols. VI and VII of the *Sämmtliche Werke* (Leipzig, 1795). For a discussion of political thought in this novel see James A. McNeely, "Historical Relativism in

trast to the *Nachlass des Diogenes von Sinope*, in which the events were intimately related by one speaker, it presents an even more broadly polyphonic chorus of narrative voices than *Don Sylvio* or *Agathon*, and its framework is even more complex than that of the first novels. The "true history" of Scheschian is the object of nightly readings and discussions at the court of Schach-Gebal, and these are allegedly transmitted in an old manuscript. Three interpreters translated it into Sinesian, Latin, and German, and an eighteenth-century editor adapted the "document" for the contemporary reader. The narrative situation recalls the pattern of the *Arabian Nights*: a Sultan wants to be entertained; he does not, however, want to hear fairytales or "satires," but a true account, and he is therefore told the "history" of the kings of Scheschian. The two main narrators are Nurmahal, Schach-Gebal's wife, who begins the readings with episodes of an intimate nature, and Danischmend, who depicts the public domain and acquaints Schach-Gebal with political theories and government practices of the Scheschian rulers. Some members of the Scheschian court are permitted to relate their own experiences or to describe their civil projects, and they do so in interpolated first-person narratives.

Neither Danischmend nor Nurmahal dares to be completely frank for fear that they might offend the master of their fate; the philosopher therefore withholds the more liberal of his thoughts, and the Sultana is at times slightly dishonest, or, on other occasions, pretends to be not well enough informed to give an accurate account. Her intended or unwitting errors do not go unnoticed, and they are emended in a manner that is rather unusual for a work of fiction. For example, when she describes Scheschian as a country which at the height of its greatest power and prosperity was only "almost as large" as Schach-Gebal's realm, the Sinesian translator corrects her statement and explains it as a diplomatic falsehood: "Die Wahrheit ist, daß es weit größer war; aber die schöne Tschirkassierin hatte zu viel Lebensart, um dem Sultan eine solche Unhöflichkeit zu sagen. Beynahe so groß ist alles, was man in dergleichen Fällen wagen darf."[10] There are altogether forty-nine such footnotes ranging from one-line annotations to full-page explications. Every one of the translators, in each case clearly identifying himself, adds several notes; then there are "Anmerkungen eines Ungenannten," and beyond that there are also unsigned notes which presumably are supplied by the German editor of the work. In their totality these notes of information constitute supplementary and corrective perspectives which are in part designed to

---

Wieland's Concept of the Ideal State," *Modern Language Quarterly*, 22 (1961), 269–282.

[10]*Werke* (Akademieausgabe), IX (Berlin, 1931), 25.

present views and opinions that differ from those offered in the manuscript.

Der Goldne Spiegel is abruptly terminated; a discussion concerning academies and scholars promised in the last conversation between Schach-Gebal and Danischmend does not take place, and the novel remains open-ended. The perspective of the fiction is, however, expanded beyond the frame of the novel. A later work, the *Geschichte des Weisen Danischmend und der drey Kalender*,[11] relates the unfortunate fate of the exiled Danischmend, who despite his discreet prudence had expressed opinions that offended the Sultan, and it tells the stories of the three calenders that provided three nights of entertainment for Schach-Gebal but were not reproduced in the first version of the novel. Like virtually every one of Wieland's works, *Der Goldne Spiegel* was revised for the definitive edition of his works which began to appear in 1794. In contrast to the first version of the novel, which elevated Scheschian to an ideal society and did not impair its utopian character, the later edition continues the history of Scheschian into the disastrous future which saw the decline and fall of the empire. The narrator is still Danischmend, and it is of course no coincidence that he relates fictive events which parallel in important aspects those developments that in reality led ultimately to the French revolution.[12]

The *Geschichte der Abderiten* (1774--) is the fourth of Wieland's novels that are identified as "histories." Yet its emphasis is different from that of the earlier works. *Don Sylvio*, it will be remembered, tells the story of an adolescent country squire whose human contacts are limited; *Agathon* portrays a young man who in the course of his travels establishes influential connections and associates with politically powerful men. *Der Goldne Spiegel* depicts, to be sure in oriental costume but nevertheless universal in meaning, the ruling class; and Danischmend, the main figure of its sequel, may be seen as a representative court philosopher who hopes to inspire a sovereign with ideal principles and noble intentions. In contrast to these works, the *Geschichte der Abderiten* does not center on the story of one man, nor does it relate the history of rulers; the characters of the novel are representative of a different group, of a fairly prosperous, more or less well-educated middle class whose individual members often act as foolishly as the inhabitants of Abdera, the proverbial home of dupes and bunglers. The work thus broadens in typical fashion the perspec-

---

[11]The first version, *Die Geschichte des Philosophen Danischmende*, appeared in the *Teutsche Merkur* of 1775 and was published in successive installments; the revised version appeared in Vol. viii of the *Sämmtliche Werke* (Leipzig, 1795), under the title here given in the text.

[12]See pp. 174–178 for Wieland's writings on the French revolution.

tive of Wieland's fictive world and helps to complete the composite image of man, who is again observed from very different points of view and is presented in colorfully variegated lighting. Like other works of Wieland, the novel is satiric in its design and uses antiquity as its backdrop. The Greek setting is, however, more pointedly fictional than it was in *Agathon* or *Sokrates Mainomenos*, for example; the satire is operative on several planes and is on one level directed against the ancient Greeks; as a consequence it provides an image that is entirely different from the glorified portrayal of the Greeks as it was propagated by Johann Joachim Winckelmann and his followers. Clearly and intentionally the novel constitutes a corrective perspective created by one who did not enthusiastically submit to the tyranny of Greece over Germany but—and this is another plane of the novel's satire—subjected the *Gräkomanie* of his contemporaries to ironic criticism.

Wieland's presentation of multiple points of view and his introduction of supplementary or corrective perspectives continued to be distinctive characteristics of his later novels, indeed of virtually every one of his contributions to literature. Among the many works that could be cited to exemplify the inventive refinement of the perspective method, the best suited are perhaps the writings concerned with the political events in France during the last decade of the eighteenth century. Among the well-known contemporary authors of belles-lettres who wrote on the French revolution, Wieland was undoubtedly the most prolific participant in the debate. From 1789 on he published numerous pieces concerned with the crucial incidents of this major historical event; his contributions to the discussion, many of which appeared in the *Teutsche Merkur*, range from brief notes, serious or ironic, to extensive articles and lengthy dialogues, and most of them are made in typically Wielandian fashion. One collection of relevant works, the *Aufsätze welche sich auf die Französische Revoluzion von 1789 beziehen, oder durch dieselbe veranlasst wurden*,[13] could most appropriately carry the subtitle "Multiple Perspectives on the French Revolution." As might be expected, Wieland only rarely entered the debate with purely political articles directly stating or immediately revealing his own views, but major contributions were made by fictive figures who firmly believe in the validity of their subjectively biased opinions and eagerly defend their ideas.

The first dialogue containing reflections on the events in France, "Eine Unterredung über die Rechtmäßigkeit des Gebrauchs, den die

---

[13]A selection of his writings concerning the French revolution was published under this title in *Sämmtliche Werke*, Vol. xxix (Leipzig, 1797). I am here quoting from the critical edition, *Werke* (Akademieausgabe), Vol. xv (Berlin, 1930).

Französische Nazion dermahlen von ihrer Aufklärung und Stärke macht" (295–315), reproduces a conversation between Adelstan, a royalist, and Walther, an advocate of the people. Both present their arguments with conviction and eloquence. Yet whereas Walther, significantly under the influence of political publications, expects the revolution to progress smoothly and successfully, Adelstan fears that the "sweet hopes" of the idealists will not be fulfilled, though, ready to compromise, he desires as ardently as Walther that this "infinitely important revolution" will come to a good end for the benefit of all Europe.

A second piece, the "Kosmopolitische Addresse an die Französische Nazionalversammlung" (316–335), is presented by Eleutherius Filoceltes, a clever rhetorician who debates point and counterpoint and raises provocative questions to which, in the final analysis, he does not offer any answers, for "Die Zeit allein kann auf diese Fragen die wahre Antwort geben."

The third important contribution to the political controversy are the "Unparteyische Betrachtungen" of 1790 (336–362); they are signed with the initial W. and clearly present Wieland's own views. Despite the announcement of neutrality in the title, these reflections are not impartial in the strict sense of the word. Wieland finds it quite natural that the point of view from which the events of the French revolution are observed has changed: "In allen diesen Rücksichten finde ich also nichts natürlicher, als daß der Gesichtspunct, aus welchem die französische Revolution anfangs beynahe in ganz Teutschland angesehen wurde, sich bey den Meisten nach und nach verrückt hat" (338). He admits that it seems virtually impossible to remain neutral between the two quarreling parties—"wovon die eine, auf Unkosten der andern, sich im Besitz von Rechten behaupten will, welche sie nie hätte haben sollen, und d i e s e, auf Unkosten j e n e r, Rechte wieder an sich zieht, welche sie nicht hätte verlieren sollen,—" (358). Although he does not remain completely neutral, he still feels that his rejection of blind prejudice is the equivalent of impartiality, particularly since his views lack the unfair bias of those who in their writings defend the attitude of the aristocracy with unreasonable indulgence and attack the acts of the lower classes with violent accusations. Such distorted views, he feels, particularly if they are published in respectable periodicals, are often uncritically accepted by the reading public and need to be corrected. A fair and rational man, Wieland implies, would realize which party deserves to be supported, for "hier sind die Parteyen, zwischen welchen ein U n p a r t e y i s c h e r zu wählen sich genöthigt sieht, u n g l e i c h g e n u g, um seinen Willen nicht lange im Zweifel zu lassen" (358). Since he is convinced that the revolution is a necessary and beneficial undertaking, "ein nothwendiges und heilsames Werk," perhaps even the only means of saving and restoring the French nation, and will in all probability provide greater happiness for its people, there can be no doubt as to who possessed his sympathies at the time this essay was written.

Other discussions of the political events are contained in a group of letters, actual and fictitious, in which diverse opinions, including Wieland's own views, are expressed; they were published in successive issues of the *Teutsche Merkur* and again reveal the author's predilection for the illumination of an issue from various, often sharply contrasting points of view. Even the gods and famous historical figures, departed long ago, are enlisted to shed from their superior vantage point in Elysium some light on the events in France, and they do so in several *Göttergespräche* that appeared in 1790 and 1793. The first carries the title *Der vierzehnte Julius*; the participants in the conversation speak about the impending celebration in Paris and raise the seemingly trite question of whether Jupiter Pluvius should not divert the heavy rains about to fall on Paris so that the festivals are not spoiled. The argument soon becomes political and more essential problems are discussed, specifically the possible reasons for the revolution and its justification. Two of the gods enthusiastically hail the triumph of reason over old prejudices and welcome the "Triumph der Bürgerfreyheit über monarchischen und aristokratischen Despotismus."[14] The French kings, however, are more restrained. Henry IV, for example, fully approves of a liberal constitution and the relative equality of all citizens, but he cannot sanction the actions that have been taken in modern France, because they reveal rashness, partiality, and ignoble passions, intrigues and secret plots, all of which ultimately lead to a condition of lawlessness utterly detrimental to the noble cause of the revolution. Numa Pompilius, the legendary prince of peace, must agree with Henry, and, perhaps recalling his lasting success with remedial legislation, believes that a moderately progressive change is always more beneficial than a radical revolution.

The great women of legend and history are also allowed to voice their views and they do so in a *Göttergespräch* entitled *Der olympische Weiberrath* (1790). Juno, who characterizes herself as the protectress of the monarchy, rejects the "democratic pestilence," as she describes the state of affairs in France. Semiramis, the legendary queen of Assyria, also believes that the monarchy is the most natural form of government, "die natürlichste, und eben darum die einfachste, leichteste und zweckmäßigste aller Regierungs-

---

[14]*Der neue Teutsche Merkur*, 3rd quarter, September 1790 (Weimar, 1790), p. 72.

formen," and she therefore defends it with conviction.[15] Aspasia cannot completely agree, for such views do not take into consideration "the great plan of nature" for the continuous development of mankind and its progress toward an enlightened society. Her reasoning echoes the argument of historical relativists who maintain that conditions vary from place to place and at different times so that a state prospers most when the governing body adapts to the individual needs of the moment. Livia, known for her political influence on Augustus, expands the discussion by presenting her thoughts on the personality of the perfect ruler. She believes that during the many decades of his reign Augustus proved that a state can indeed flourish under the extended rule of a single man. The ruler must, however, possess superior talents, abilities, and dedication. If he does not have these qualifications or lacks the dignity that should characterize the first man of the state, then he should abdicate or be dethroned.

Elisabeth of England proposes still another solution. She knows of unfailing means to achieve a proper balance between a ruler and his people. Her preliminary remarks are so extensive that Juno becomes impatient and inserting one of the many humorous notes to be found in these dialogues urges her to come to the point: "Du könntest mich beynahe so ungeduldig machen wie ehmals deine Liebhaber, Königin Beß! Deine Maaßregel, wenn ich bitten darf!"[16] Elisabeth proudly relates that one of the most superior nations of the world—her own, of course—has found the answer: the oppression by monarchic and aristocratic despotism has been eliminated by providing a liberal constitution for the nation, an agreement "worin die Rechte aller Classen der Staatsbürger klar und bestimmt ausgedruckt und durch gehörige Veranstaltungen gegen alle willkührliche Eingriffe verwahrt sind."[17] The women are easily convinced that England has indeed found the best means to govern her people and that her experience deserves to be conveyed to all rulers on earth, a task which they realize is not easily accomplished.

Another *Göttergespräch, Für und Wider*, appeared in 1793 and depicts Jupiter, Juno, and Minerva in a conversation which was held on the 21st of January, the day Louis XVI was executed. The events of the past two years have affirmed Juno's derogatory opinion of the French revolution, and she expresses her contempt in no uncertain terms. Jupiter, however, is more tolerant. To begin with, he will not lose his composure, for he has long enough observed the follies of man: "Wie kannst du erwarten, daß einer, der dem Lauf der Welt schon über fünftausend Jahre aus einem so hohen Standpunkte zusieht, sich durch etwas, das bey diesen Lilliputern da unten begegnen kann, aus der Fassung bringen lasse."[18] He knows that man's imperfection is one of the major causes of his dilemmas, and after a long discussion with his irate wife he finally admits "Was können wir von den Sterblichen fodern, wenn Götter selbst nicht weiser sind."[19]

These conversations are characteristic of Wieland's dialogues. Every one of the interlocutors has ample opportunity to express his views; no one is forcibly converted or sternly silenced; in fact, the conflict of opinions often remains essentially unresolved, for each of the participants is right if an issue is considered from his point of view and, as a consequence, the others tolerantly acknowledge the relative validity of his perspective. Whenever an agreement is reached, the consent is amiable and derives from the conviction that new insights require a more or less modest change in attitude and a partial subscription to the opinions of others.

Jupiter and Numa, who both figure prominently in the dialogues concerned with the French revolution, discuss in another *Göttergespräch* important historical events of quite a different nature, namely the dethronement of the gods and the destruction of the pagan temples in Rome during the reign of Theodosius. Perturbed by the fate of the gods among men they touch upon vital questions of religious truth and attract, as if by "a new kind of magnetism," a stranger who desires to join in the discussion. He identifies himself as one who possesses the talent of appearing wherever he wants to be; and when two men are searching for the truth he seldom fails to be present as the third participant; "Ich besitze die Gabe zu seyn wo ich will; und wo ihrer Zwey Wahrheit suchen, da ermangle ich selten, sichtbar oder unsichtbar der Dritte zu seyn." This formulation recalls a statement of Jesus as it was related by Matthew (18:20): "For where two or three are gathered together in my name, there I am in the midst of them." The stranger is indeed none other than Christ, whom Numa, rather disrespectfully, describes as "Ein sonderbarer Patron."[20]

---

[18]*Der neue Teutsche Merkur*, 1st quarter, February 1793 (Weimar, 1793), p. 185.

[19]*Ibid.*, p. 209. In an earlier *Göttergespräch*, also a conversation with Juno, Jupiter has expressed more optimistic views of man and his striving for independence; but the deplorable events of the revolution disillusioned him, and it is only his tolerance and understanding of human imperfection that prevent him from denouncing their actions as unsparingly as his wife. See *Der neue Teutsche Merkur*, 4th quarter, November 1790 (Weimar, 1790), pp. 270-283.

[20]*Neue Götter=Gespräche* (Leipzig, 1791), p. 134.

The conversation immediately focuses on the central topic of the dialogue, on the relationship between point of view and truth. Jupiter, speaking of "facts," maintains that their appearance necessarily depends on the standpoint of the observer and on the quality of his eyesight: "Wir sprachen bloß von Thatsachen; und diese erscheinen, wie du wissen wirst, einem jeden Zuschauer, nach seinem Standpunkte und nach Beschaffenheit seiner Augen, anders als den übrigen." The stranger does not explicitly deny Jupiter's opinion, yet he claims that only from one point of view can matters be observed correctly, and that is the center of the universe, "Der Mittelpunkt des Ganzen." Questioned by Jupiter, Christ affirms that he knows "das Ganze" and its center, which is nothing less than perfection, "Die Vollkommenheit, von welcher alles gleich weit entfernt ist, und der sich alles nähert."[21] Asked by Numa how matters appear to him when observed from this point of view of perfection, he first describes in much detail the incomplete and faulty qualities he does *not* perceive:

> Numa.
> Und wie erscheint dir jede Sache aus diesem Gesichtspunkte?
> Der Unbekannte.
> Nicht stückweise, nicht was sie in einzelnen Orten und Zeitpunkten ist, nicht wie sie sich gegen diese oder jene Dinge verhält, nicht was sie durch ihre Einsenkung in den Dunstkreis der menschlichen Meinungen und Leidenschaften verliert oder gewinnt, nicht wie sie durch Thorheit oder durch Verdorbenheit des Herzens vergiftet wird.[22]

The implications are easily deduced; man's vision is imperfect, and in contrast to Christ he perceives only fragments of the entire unit; place and time of observation influence his judgment; opinion and passion blind his view, folly and depravity contaminate the object of his attention.

Christ, however, believes that now—the time of the encounter is around 381 A.D.—a new era has begun, that night and darkness are over. Jupiter cannot possibly agree, because for almost an eternity he has observed man in his folly and does not expect him to change as profoundly as Christ would want. Yet he is willing to tolerate the optimism of the stranger who, after all, is still a very young man; his charming enthusiasm, "diese liebenswürdige Schwärmerei," is not only excusable but is, at his age, a truly honorable virtue, "ein wahres Verdienst." He therefore allows him to describe his plan to redeem humanity and lead it to universal happiness, "die allgemeine Glück-

---

[21]*Ibid.*, p. 135.
[22]*Ibid.*, p. 136.

seligkeit." When after his last enthusiastic words the stranger disappears, he leaves behind two puzzled pagans. Numa poses the skeptical question: "Was sagst du zu dieser Erscheinung, Jupiter?" and the god philosophically answers: "Frage mich in funfzehn hundert Jahren wieder."[23]

History affirmed, of course, the justification of Jupiter's doubts in the perfectability of man. After fourteen hundred years humanity did not live in perennial bliss, neither was man able to observe the universe from the central vantage point of perfection, and the nature of truth was still very much debated. It was to be expected that Wieland would participate in this most vital discussion, and in one of his essays, published in 1778 in the *Teutsche Merkur*, he had indeed raised the question "Was ist Wahrheit?" and attempted to provide a convincing answer.

The greatest folly of man, he believes, is the tendency to think of his own opinions as axioms or irrefutable truths and attempt to force others to subscribe to his subjective values. Truth is relative: "Die Wahrheit ist, wie alles Gute, etwas verhältnismäßiges."[24] And it does not reveal itself entirely to anyone: "Keinem offenbart sie sich ganz." Everyone perceives only fragments of it, glances at it perhaps from behind or sees merely the fringe of its garment, each from a different point of view and in another light. Everyone hears only a few sounds uttered by its divine voice, and no one hears the same. How, then, can man under these circumstances arrive at an approximation of absolute truth? Wieland suggests one possible solution: instead of arguing about the source of truth and trying to establish who has seen her in the most beautiful light, men should sit together in peace, reveal the fragmentary images they have seen to each other, combine their knowledge and thus get closer to a more complete vision of truth:

> Anstatt mit einander zu hadern, wo die Wahrheit sey? wer sie besitze? wer sie in ihrem schönsten Lichte gesehen? die meisten und deutlichsten Laute von ihr vernommen habe?—laßt uns im Frieden zusammengehen, oder, wenn wir des Gehens genug haben, unter den nächsten Schatten- gebenden Baum hinsitzen, und einander offenherzig und unbefangen erzählen, was jeder von ihr gesehen und gehört hat, oder glaubt gesehen und gehört zu haben; und ja nicht böse darüber werden,

[23]*Ibid.*, p. 151.
[24]*Der Teutsche Merkur*, 2nd quarter, April 1778 (Weimar, 1778), p. 9. The essay "Wahrheit" appeared as one of the "Fragmente von Beyträgen zum Gebrauch derer, die sie brauchen können," pp. 9–17; a second essay, entitled "Bescheidenheit," pp. 17–21, treats related questions.

CONTINUING AND CONCLUDING OBSERVATIONS

wenn sichs von ungefehr entdeckt, daß wir falsch gesehen oder gehört . . . haben.[25]

This is precisely the method Wieland employed in his own search for truth. Personally he was known as a man who would not insist on maintaining or defending, indeed not even on establishing a fixed point of view. His adaptability was recognized by his contemporaries and was in fact applauded by some. When Falk and Goethe, for example, conversed about Wieland's translation of the letters of Cicero, Goethe commented on the freshness and immediacy of the German rendition and expressed his belief that the flexibility of Wieland's vantage point and his habit of presenting alternate perspectives contributed importantly to the excellent quality of the translation:

> Das macht, es war Wieland in allen Stücken weniger um einen festen Standpunkt als um eine geistreiche Debatte zu tun. Zuweilen berichtigt er den Text in einer Note, würde es aber auch nicht übelnehmen, wenn jemand aufträte und wieder durch eine neue Note seine Note berichtigte.[26]

Wieland's supreme tolerance toward the opinions of others and his conviction that the combination of a variety of individual perspectives as well as the viewing of matters from multiple points of view will eventually reveal a segment of truth that is much more comprehensive than the portion any individual could ever perceive explains the diversity of precepts and positions contained in his works. Every one of the invented spokesmen and fictive characters contributes at least partially valid views, and many of these figures are eminently qualified to occupy a seat among those who, fairly and responsibly, are searching for truth.

The universal validity of Wieland's artistic method and its applicability to life itself was a century and a half later—perhaps without intent—confirmed by Ortega y Gasset, who in his discussion of the doctrine of the point of view employs formulations that are strikingly similar to Wieland's thoughts and language. Every life, Ortega maintains, "is a point of view directed upon the universe. Strictly speaking, what one life sees no other can." "Reality," he later continues, "happens to be, like a landscape, possessed of an infinite number of perspectives, all equally veracious and authentic. The sole false perspective is that which claims to be the only one there is."[27]

[25]*Ibid.*, p. 16.
[26]*Goethes Gespräche*, ed. Wolfgang Pfeiffer-Belli, I (Zurich, 1949), 670.
[27]*The Modern Theme*, trans. James Cleugh (New York, 1933), Chapter x, "The Doctrine of the Point of View," pp. 91–92.

Ortega's emphasis on the importance of the combinatory principles in man's search for truth is surprisingly close to Wieland's ideas as expressed in his essay on "Wahrheit." Ortega writes:

> Integral truth is only obtained by linking up what I see with what my neighbour sees, and so on successively. Each individual is an essential point of view in the chain. By setting everyone's fragmentary visions side-by-side it would be possible to achieve a complete panorama of absolute and universally valid truth.[28]

The inclusion of Ortega y Gasset here is not meant as a documentation of Wieland's influence on the Spanish philosopher; the common intellectual background of both writers may well account for the essential similarities in their views. The function of this brief reference to a well-known author of our century is intended as evidence of Wieland's modernity. More deliberately than any other writer of his generation he served as transmitter of traditional features, and at the same time he introduced thoughts and techniques that were exceptionally progressive. Timeless in significance are the artistic application of the philosophic principles of perspectivism to the literary treatment of appropriate themes, the relativity of all values, and the variability of man's judgments. The humane spirit of understanding and tolerance that permeates his works can certainly be seen as a constructive attitude of lasting importance.

[28]*Ibid.*, p. 95.

‖ Bibliographical Note

In this study I have made reference to a considerable number of critical works on Wieland, indicating their importance or defining particular points of disagreement. Full bibliographical information is given at the first appearance of a title, and all are included in the index.

The acknowledgement of these learned contributions does not, of course, do full justice to the dedicated efforts of previous scholarship. A detailed bibliography of all secondary literature that furthers an acquaintance with Wieland or enriches the understanding of his works would constitute a list of at least a few hundred titles. A large number of these are described and characterized in two informative surveys. The first one, "Wieland-Forschung," appeared in 1950 in the *Deutsche Vierteljahrsschrift* (xxiv, 269–280) and is by Fritz Martini. In his thorough analyses of the secondary literature he reveals the complex reasons for the sporadic interest in Wieland and for the unusually tardy progress of the critical edition of the *Gesammelte Schriften* which was launched at the turn of our century but is not yet complete.

A second survey, particularly useful to the nonspecialist, *Christoph Martin Wieland*, was prepared by Cornelius Sommer and published in the *Sammlung Metzler* (Stuttgart, 1971, 67 pp.).

These two *Forschungsberichte*, even if combined, do not yet constitute the equivalent of a thorough and reasonably complete Wieland-Bibliography; such a comprehensive bibliography, however, is now being prepared by Hansjörg Schelle.

‖ Index

THE JOHNS HOPKINS UNIVERSITY PRESS

This book was composed in Baskerville text and
display by Jones Composition Company from a design
by Edward Scott. It was printed on S. D. Warren's
60-lb. regular paper and bound in Holliston Roxite
cloth by The Maple Press.